TRAVEL LIGHT

TRAVEL LIGHT

Regular People Go on Adventures Too

Laura R. Holmes

Content Queens, LLC
Nunica, MI

Published by
Content Queens, LLC
Nunica, MI

Publisher's Cataloging-in-Publication Data
Holmes, Laura R.

Travel light : regular people go on adventures too / by Laura R. Holmes. – Nunica, MI : Content Queens, LLC, 2019.

p. ; cm.

ISBN13: 978-0-9846481-4-6

1. Holmes, Laura R.--Travel. 2. Voyages and travels.
3. Voyages around the world. 4. Vacations. I. Title.

G460.H65 2019
910.4--dc23   2019936953

Project coordination by Jenkins Group, Inc.
www.BookPublishing.com

Cover and interior design by Michelle Dewey
Cover Photo: Connemara National Park, Ireland

Printed in Korea

23 22 21 20 19 • 5 4 3 2 1

Traveling light means much more than cramming a ton of stuff in a carry-on for your next adventure.

Lighten up and find balance in life, work, and play.

Let the light of your soul shine out in the world; exceptional travelers are patient, humble, and kind, open to new people and experiences.

To be light is to be carefree, to have fun.

Travel light without the cell phone and burden of stress. It's OK to leave your work behind.

Lighthearted travelers laugh at unexpected happenings along the road. Sometimes when you stop looking for your destination, it finds you.

Be enlightened: try something new and let travel change you.

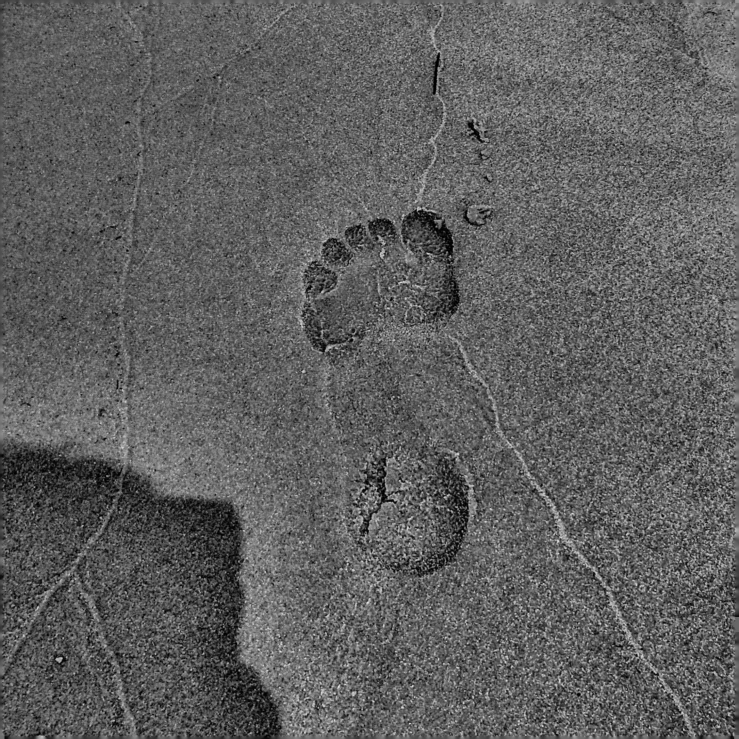

Contents

Introduction

I am giving you the green light to travel more and work less, to go on a quest to eradicate vacation deprivation. Overworked and overburdened people around the world, join me in a quest to achieve better balance in life-work-play. This memoir explores the lighter side of travel with doses of humor, adventure, and personal transformation. Exploration and vacations need not be exclusive to the wealthy. Regular people go on adventures too. Travel more and the experiences will make you laugh and provide increased levels of happiness in life.

Most of us DO NOT make vacation or travel a priority. Are you currently experiencing vacation deprivation? Working too much? Is your life or relationship stuck in a boring routine and you lack motivation to change? When is the last time you got away?

It's time to start planning, get off the couch, and go. Jet across an ocean or stay close by. It's not important to fly overseas if cash is an issue. Plan something even an hour away from home and that too can provide a vacation high. Turns out many of us need some urging or inspiration to take a vacation. We all deserve a break from our work schedules. We should go see the world or even a new place in our home state or country. We want to experience a holiday with family or dear friends. And we need a chance to open our minds beyond the familiar and the routine of our daily lives. Let travel change you, especially when you immerse yourself in a different culture. A new and unfamiliar place holds all sorts of customs and social nuances, leading you to a new, open-minded view of others and more defined sense of self.

How do you fit in the world?
Travel and find out!

You'll return with a better sense of who you are and how lucky you are. Discover an appreciation of the world's customs or religions. Different does not mean bad or wrong. Plus, you'll notice new things and experience the elusive lost-in-the-moment feeling. From that point on, you can break the routine of a relationship, your home life, daily habits, or unmotivated work. Travel teaches you to notice your surroundings even when you are home, in the car, or at the office. You'll learn to be mindful about things you see and do every day. For example, after a two-week excursion in Tanzania on a photo safari and Kilimanjaro climb, when I returned home, I marveled at the simple yet exotic porcelain flushing throne.

I'd love to give you a nudge and tell you a few tales about how travel has changed me. I hope the stories in this collection provide a catalyst to start you toward a new destination. Travel is always personal, and we'll arrive or walk away with very different memories and some uproariously funny stories to tell. It's time to plan that trip you've back-burnered for so long. I have discovered that vacation surprises have made me laugh and taught me many valuable lessons. Curiosity is a powerful emotion, and you'll find it will lift your heart and mind (even in the planning stages). Once you've opened your mind to the world, to travel, and to stretching your limits, you'll be incredibly happy to learn you can never go back.

Travel can become part of your soul if you can learn to absorb a moment rather than just look. When you travel, pay attention to the details and really listen to and engage the people you encounter. Travel is about connection, not just the place. The number and quantity of places visited have nothing to do with true travel pleasures. Plus, the world is an inherently beautiful place, and not to see as much of it as you can would be downright rude to the creator of the universe.

Let's be sure we are all clear on an important point. Most of us DO NOT make vacation or travel a priority. Statistics show that many of us are experiencing vacation deprivation, tipping the work-meter scale to stressed. The life-work-play equation works only when it's in balance.

Expedia* published a report in 2011: Americans earn fewer vacation days compared to other countries and leave two days unused annually on average. Does this sound like you?
The study shows we skip vacations for the following reasons:
- *Banking days for the future: 23%*
- *Coordinating family schedules: 23%*
- *Can't afford it: 19%*
- *Have to schedule too far out: 18%*

The best vacation-friendly countries understand how important morale is: France, Germany, Spain, Denmark, and Brazil. Conversely, the United States shares bad company with Canada, Mexico, Singapore, Japan, and South Korea. *The Atlantic** also found similar statistics. Americans don't use the paid vacation they have. More than 50% of working Americans had up to two weeks of unused vacation time at the close of 2011. No surprise either that Americans work longer hours than any other advanced country except Japan and South Korea. The long-hour work culture that permeates our economy—has this become the American dream? I think we need to work toward a new solution with new priorities. We need to make life-work-play balance a reality and make vacation a priority.

Studies also show that travel is good for your overall health and wellness. And, as I suspected, the anticipation leading up to a trip is almost as beneficial as the actual holiday. My travel buddies and I call this phenomenon "peaking." But don't take my word for it. Researchers from the Netherlands measured the effect that vacations have on overall happiness and how long it lasts. They studied happiness levels in 1,530 Dutch adults; 974 took a vacation during the 32-week study period. The study, published in *The Journal of Applied Research in Quality of Life,** showed that the largest boost in happiness comes from the simple act of planning a vacation. In the study, the effect of vacation anticipation boosted happiness for eight weeks. Eight weeks is a significant amount of time, and I am all about boosting happiness for myself and for others before, during, and after the trip. What keeps you from planning a getaway?

Looking for ideas on where to go and how to afford it? I'd love to give you the green light and send you packing. Read on, discover the power of travel in these stories, and discover it for yourself soon and often.

Remember: it doesn't matter how far you go; what matters is how far you'll let yourself go.

The Cast of Characters
PWDS (People Who Don't Suck)

I don't typically travel alone, so for some helpful background information, I've included descriptions of each of the travel companions in Travel Light *stories. Choose your travel companions carefully for their true character will be revealed on the road!*

X

Theresa

An engineering and innovative dentist by day, she works to live and lives to play. We traveled together to Africa in 2001 and climbed Mount Kilimanjaro and have been taking trips and adventures together ever since. She's single and is afflicted with a similar syndrome called SIDs—Severe Independence Disease. So we understand each other, and I am blessed to have such a great friend who loves to do the same things as I do. She is a trusted and worthy travel companion, and I credit her with introducing me to adventure travel.

Steve

I noticed his never-ending energy and infectious smile on the beach volleyball courts of Grand Haven. We became fast friends. Steve has an exuberance for life and travel; I admire his dedication to approaching life as if he were a kid. We share a passion for all things outdoors and have hiked through both mountains and jungles together. We agree that the best thing to do when you get back from a trip is to start planning another one. Computer guy and software developer by day, he splits his time between Grand Haven, Michigan, and his condo in Florida on Siesta Key.

Kim

Kim, who is Steve's better half, has a gentle, patient, and giving personality that is a must-have on any camping, skiing, or bike trip. She is resourceful and is never flustered by travel obstacles like weather, delays, sore muscles, or encounters with wild animals. I love her "Let's get muddy or snowy" attitude! We've shared many views and destinations together on skis and snowboards, on bikes, and on our own two feet and are planning many more. A massage therapist by day, she is also a mother of two boys, Alex and Zach, who seem to be following in her footsteps.

Jen

Jen is a longtime friend from many sandy beach volleyball days, though we have both branched out to other activities that do not involve our aging shoulders. She's earned the nickname Calamity Jen. Whenever I travel with Jen, it is almost a guarantee that something unexpected will happen. So I've learned to hang on tight while the ride is in progress. It might be a wang-tang on a ski trip, a jaunt down a spur trail, or a barrel roll down an Irish bog. Her busy schedule includes her son Gavin and Ironman husband Jim as well as surviving breast cancer and balancing a career.

Andrea

Kid sister to Theresa, Andrea brings her creative perspective to any trip, and she finds artistry in things I might not consider. She may prefer to shop over hiking up a mountain, but she'll find something or some detail that I would miss because I am moving too fast. Sharing a bottle of Tuscan wine under an olive tree in Italy is a moment neither of us will soon forget.

Ginger

When I first met Ginger, I was struck by her talkative and energetic personality. I found out a mutual friend had given her the nickname Guaranteed Fun, so traveling with Ginger seemed like a no-brainer. Always on the go, she travels for work and pleasure and is a skilled linguist and speaks both French and German. She would rather spa than hike in the rugged Pyrenees, but I credit her willingness to try. She brought balance and a great sense of humor to our activity choices in Spain.

Deb

Deb is a longtime friend and college teammate and classmate, and we've managed to stay in touch through a variety of athletic activities like soccer, skiing, and golf. Her infectious laugh is reason enough to travel with her, but, ultimately, we are both drawn to the mountains in winter to find the perfect ski run that will make our legs tremble. Math teacher, mom, wife, and now attorney, she keeps a very full schedule.

Randee

Her fortieth is what got us moving toward the Italy trip. She too believes in celebrating milestone birthdays. As Theresa's oldest friend and roommate from college at Michigan Tech, together the two of them can belt out pretty much any show tune or Babs song.

Jim

The other half of Calamity Jen, Jim has helped balance out the bro-to-ho ratio in my life and in travel. He's skilled on a bike and on the patio grill. Jim had his hands full rescuing Theresa, Jen, and me from Sedona bike mishaps. Find him in a tie by day and spandex at night.

Maureen

Our claim to sports fame was a second-place finish in the MPVA Holland Beach Volleyball Open Tournament in 1996. The tournament final was televised on PASS Sports. With our TV and volleyball careers winding down, we fit in time to catch up on the golf course. Mo's mantra: Life is about fun and just being happy to be here. She trades banker blue for shorts and sand on her days in Grand Rapids.

Josh

We met in June of 2014, so though a late arrival for this book's batch of trips, he has an important place in these stories and in my heart. See chapter 6! Lucky for me, he likes to do many of the same activities: hiking, biking, golf, and backpacking. When he is not coaching elite or travel soccer, we'll be out playing together.

Chapter One
The Year of 40, 2009

To celebrate a milestone birthday, take a trip every month of the year.

"*Deferring your happiness is not a good idea. Don't wait until you're retired to live your life; try something new and take the dream vacation.*"

To celebrate turning 40 (Sept. 4, 2009), I decided to take a trip every month in that year. One spring day in May with time to reflect, I felt a realization surfacing. Four months had passed, and I had been on four getaways. It was an official streak and imperative to keep the momentum going. As it sank in, I started a list for the remaining months. Why not commit to a new investment policy for the year and invest in having fun, instead of sinking it into a poorly performing Roth IRA or 401(k)? I mentioned the idea to a few close friends and they loved it. They agreed with my new investment policy and happily helped me work toward the goal.

I had plenty of excuses, but it was time for a personal reward. A milestone birthday, at any age, is the perfect catalyst to get you moving toward a new challenge. "WORK" is a crappy four-letter word that gets thrown around as an excuse for the inability to travel. There is a work-around. The more I traveled, the more efficient I became at work, in less time. With the carrot of travel, perpetually dangling in my reach, I focused, completed tasks, and signed new business with renewed motivation, which created more time for play. My business and soul were both rewarded by a new approach to work-travel balance.

With my milestone birthday as a catalyst, it was time to assess my life and look ahead. On the cusp of 40, I compiled a stat sheet (plus this would come in handy if I wanted to start online dating):

Relationship Status: Single, divorced, no kids (DNK)

Sign: Virgo
(I look at stars but honestly do not know what they mean)

Current Residence: A condo in Spring Lake on Michigan's west coast

Political Affiliation: The Cocktail Party, until the other two figure it out

Education: BA and MA

Income Level: Enough, but not enough not to worry

Religious Views: Progressive, because God is too big for one religion

Employer: BYOB (Be Your Own Boss). I co-own a small business called FineLine Creative

Community: Volunteer director at a local nonprofit, Michigan Irish Music Festival

Play: Retired semi-pro beach volleyball player

Now: biker, skier, hiker, golfer, and yogi

Friends: PWDS (People Who Don't Suck),
an adventurous group who are my support group in
travel and life

Family: Mom and Dad taught me to travel
at a young age

I became Aunt LaLa to two nieces and
three nephews

Two younger siblings, Ben and Charla
(bonus, we get along)

Bucket List: I am an aspiring author and plan
to publish a travel book

Daily Dose: Laughter and exercise

Life Goals: I want to become a philanthropist via my
publishing company

Travel stats:
    Africa: Tanzania
    Western Europe: France, Spain, Ireland, Italy,
    Switzerland
    Central America: Costa Rica
    South America: Peru
    North America: Mexico, Canada, Alaska, and
    almost all 50 states

Future plans: Travel more, work less, read more, write
more, and buy a smaller television

After reviewing my personal statistics, amassed in 40 years, I hoped a plan for the next 40 would rise to the surface. Thankfully, I was not upset at the prospect of turning 40—it was just another opportunity waiting around the bend on a trail; 50 would be the new 30. With that thought, I set off to notch a trip each month in my year of 40. It wasn't easy, but creative scheduling and long weekends worked for the in-state trips. I took Fridays off to turn a two-day weekend into a three-day and used holidays as buffers to create longer stints. Ironically, I worked pretty hard at planning and staging trips, balancing my travel agent duties with regular work.

My mantra in that year: 40 was the new 20. Pop culture circulates a theory that 40 is equally or more glamorous than being young and 20 years old. Agreed. I would NEVER trade my 30s and almost-40 self for being 20 again. My 20-year-old self did not have a clue! By age 30, you begin to understand. Then by 40, you've hopefully gained the knowledge, experience, and resources to actually pursue some of the dreams you've been thinking about all that time. I am fond of a phrase my friends get tired of hearing me say: "Life begins at 30!" Odd, that was the age of my divorce. So, as I contemplated turning 40, the realization was that I was just getting to the good stuff.

The prospect of turning 40 did make me take stock in what I had experienced so far in life (see previous life-stat sheet). In the few short months before my milestone birthday, I thought of where I wanted to go and where I had been. My pensiveness included both emotional and some physical markers from my past. When it came to geography, there were a few dots on the map. I lived in South Carolina in the early '90s pursuing higher education at Winthrop University. There was a year spent in western Maryland as part of marital duties, but I always found my way back home to Michigan. My significant emotional marker was a divorce in 1999; I really believed that the big D would not happen to me. *Wrong.* In the years after that, I reshaped my life, redefined my goals, and set off on a much different path. My new path turned out to be adventurous, rewarding, and fun. And it is possible to have a successful and meaningful life as a woman even if you are not married and do not have children. I took up the habit of adventure traveling, did more volunteering, started a new business, and became an entrepreneur. Upon turning 40, I understood, as an unattached woman, that I was not sick, just single.

look who's ready for cake...

Happy 40th Birthday
Laura

Blue January

My collection of trips to celebrate 40 began internationally in nearby Canada. Operating on the principal of HDL (high-deserve level) living, I started the year with the idea of balancing work-life-play. Nothing significant gets done during the week of Christmas and the New Year anyway. Everyone is busy conjuring up New Year's resolutions which I don't believe in. The timing makes a great opportunity to get away for at least a week; the trick is still fitting in holiday celebrations with family. The first month of the year, I rang in the New Year Canadian-style at Blue Mountain Ski Resort in Collingwood, Ontario. I crossed the border via Port Huron and drove the seven hours with my adventure friend Theresa for three days of double-planking. We were blessed with blue skies and Great Lakes powder and a nicely appointed slope-side condo, the Mosaic at Blue.

Funny—the New Year's Eve party was the lowlight compared to the groomed corduroy runs under the lights. Blue Mountain is a gem, tucked on the shores of the Georgian Bay. Both the bustling resort village and the blue groomers made me feel like I was in a miniature snow globe resembling a Colorado mountain resort. Except for the runs, which topped out at 800 vertical feet, Blue Mountain stacked up well. The trip was not about mountain statistics and extreme skiing anyway; it was about getting away and getting some fresh air. I was delighted to do some of my first night skiing. One of the best times to be on the mountain was about 4:30, after the afternoon groom. Depending on the time of day, I was able to ski both perfect corduroy and fluffy fresh powder. And when fingers turned cold and cheeks glowed pink, we'd ski down to a waiting bar in the village for hot chocolate and skier snacks. I squirmed my way to the bar and removed my snow-covered hat, goggles, and gloves for warm-up sessions.

Blue Mountain is a busy place, catering to Toronto-ites heading up north to get out of the city. We battled a few lines to take the high-speed chairs up, but the views at the top of the expansive Georgian Bay were worth the wait. And, bonus, Theresa and I discovered our new favorite snack, aptly named a Beaver Tail in Canada. These delicious fried pastries, copiously sprinkled with cinnamon sugar, could be purchased at a quaint little hut that you could ski right up to. I devoured my Beaver Tail and also savored the sticky, sugary residue that lined the corners of my mouth. We licked the cinnamon from our fingers and slid our gloves back on to head down more runs. We returned to the Beaver Tail hut no fewer than four times during our three-day trip.

February Ski Bunnies

The après-ski toasts would continue, my ski legs grew stronger, and the runs transitioned from feet to miles (sometimes well over a mile on a top-to-bottom run). As February arrived, I glommed on to a midmonth trip Theresa planned to visit friends in Aspen. Word spread and it turned into a girls' getaway for four. Andrea (T's sister) and Laura (the other Laura) joined for my second winter getaway. The four of us flew to Denver then drove into the ski mecca that is Aspen/Snowmass for four days of whirlwind action on the slopes. As is always the case, we all tried to chase Theresa down the rolling runs, arriving panting as she patiently waited for us at the bottom near the lift lines.

Snowmass elevation is an impressive 12,510 feet at its peak, which stretched the limits of my lungs and legs. Staying hydrated at elevation, especially when skiing, is important to ward off altitude sickness. Luckily again, my group was greeted with predominantly blue skies, great snow conditions, and festive après sessions and dinners. Our hosts provided the highlight for this trip, allowing us to bunk at a truly glorious mansion—an Italian villa–home, spanning no fewer than 11,000 square feet. It was much like having our own personal ski lodge. Having friends strategically placed around the globe and in many states provides great opportunities for cheap lodging and more frequent travel. My tip: just don't be afraid to ask.

A Heavenly March

I only had to fly home and work for a few weeks before jetting off yet again on the third ski trip of 2009 to South Lake Tahoe during the first weekend of March. A diverse group of five PWDS friends assembled for a stint at Heavenly Ski Resort, a resort so big it reaches into the two states of Nevada and California. My ski pals were Steve, Kim, Theresa, Deb, and Jen on my non-beach spring break vacation. It was on this trip that we used the phrase "bro-to-ho ratio," in which Steve, the only guy, had the dubious distinction of entertaining five girls.

The day before we arrived, the area near South Lake Tahoe received the biggest dump of powder it had seen that winter; Heavenly Resort received between 48" and 70" of new snow within 24 hours. As we learned, that is too much snow for any resort to handle. But our first day (the day after the dump), the Snowcats had been out, so we could choose uncut powder and trees or soft groomed runs basking in the sun.

On the mountain, the views of Lake Tahoe are nothing short of heavenly, with a deep aquamarine blue contrasting vividly against crisp white-covered mountains. Four days of skiing made my legs tremble, but I managed to survive the group's pace with hot tub visits, doses of ibuprofen, and heaping piles of pasta at evening meals to refuel. I escaped injury at least on this trip, unlike Kim and Jen. Kim was accidently bodychecked into an evergreen by Steve on an off-piste (and out-of-control) run through powder and trees. Jen developed a wang-tang on her shin, so dubbed by a toothless ski patroller during her stint on the slopes. Her ill-fitting boots rendered her unable to ski on the last day, which was brilliantly sunny yet again. We also fit in an eventful evening out to the casino district and danced for hours at Club Blu until our legs would carry us no farther. I blame Club Blu, the stripper pole, and a bachelorette party for my late arrival at noon to the gondola the next day. It was probably best to fly home on the fifth day, to let our legs and laugh muscles recover from overuse. (For more on this adventure, please see chapter 7.)

Irish in April

It would have been easy to decline the invitation to Kansas City, citing a three-month vacation spree. I should have said, "No, I have to work and be responsible." Thankfully, logic and HDL (high-deserve level) thinking returned in time for me to fit in my fourth trip of the year. I dutifully put in extra hours at work leading up to leaving yet again. I checked sales numbers, ran my reports, and submitted several quotes. I hoped I could manage my workload and escalating email in-box while mobile. April came into view, and it was time to hang up my ski and boot bag and trade it in for a different sort of adventure. My involvement with Michigan Irish Music Festival had secured my invitation to attend an Irish/Celtic festival planners convention and music showcase in Kansas City, Missouri. It was essentially a four-day April weekend. Tip: the long weekend is a great tactic to get away without taking a huge chunk of vacation days. Take Friday, Monday, or both and turn a weekend into a mini-trip.

My fellow board members and I took the short flight to KC, and we checked into the Radisson downtown, where the conference and seminars would be held. We met up with our festival friends for some culinary artistry called "barbecue" at our first dinner. Two of three days were packed with tips, tidbits, and sessions on how to market and run a successful music festival or event. The evenings were filled with Irish music, many bands eager to play our festivals, and never-ending rounds of Guinness on tap. Boulevard Beer and Pub played host to our group one night. The view from the roof deck looked out over an impressive span of metropolitan cow town.

My roommate Diane and I did not spend much time in the hotel room because the schedule barely allowed time for a pee break—it was simply a place to shower and collapse late after the music faded and bars had closed. During the daytime hours, I ran from one event to the next with my conference lanyard swinging from my neck. With many an Irish tune still churning in my head, I collected my notes and headed back to Michigan for a return to my day job to start saving for the next trip.

May Is Zoo Time

It was late May, and a pattern had emerged. I sat in my leather recliner as I sipped coffee and looked out my window at robins searching for the worms of spring. I thought about the first four months of the year and my trips so far. May would not find me out of Michigan but on my seventh-consecutive Zoo-de-Mack bike weekend. I smiled at the realization that May was the fifth adventure of my year of 40.

The thought turned my cheeks and face into a broad grin. A streak had officially begun, and I approached the year with a voracious commitment to go away each month on an adventure. I updated my list and added a few ideas for June and the coming summer months.

The Zoo weekend did not disappoint, and it proved to hold an astounding amount of adventures, laughs, and surprises. Our group totaled seven: two were rookies, including Theresa's kid sister Andrea. Returning ZDMers included me, Steve, Kim, Jen, and Theresa. If you are not sure what this oddly named bike festival is all about, it began with Motown roots. Two Detroiters, longing to escape the Motor City, planned a bike ride for 2,000 of their closest friends, bookending the ride with two parties in beautiful northern Michigan. The fun begins at Boyne Highlands Ski Resort at the Zoo Bar on Friday night. Then, on Saturday, if you successfully ride the 51 miles along Lake Michigan with beautiful views, you will end up in Mackinaw City. To celebrate riding this significant distance (and, by the way, IT IS NOT A RACE), your registration includes a ferry ride to magical Mackinaw Island, where endorphin- and alcohol-induced fun continues well into the night.

We added a bonus Friday on the way up north to Boyne Highlands, which meant I took a day off to extend my weekend. At my office (FineLine Creative), we call this flextime, which is an option for all our employees to set their own schedule: For example, most of us work longer days Monday through Thursday, setting us up for a shorter Friday or a day off altogether.

Our three-hour drive was punctuated by hunger, and we stumbled onto a jewel in K-Town (Kalkaska) called Gio's Italian Restaurant, where we dined in an environment fit for giants of a time long since passed. Gio's was, simply put, enormous, as was everything inside. The building itself was massive, the tables were huge, and the bathrooms and even the meatballos were oversized. I thought perhaps I had been transported to a version of Everything Is Huge Twilight Zone. My suspicions were confirmed when I entered the restroom and a 6-foot-7-inch woman strode past me to return to her table. This sent Jen and me into a laughing spasm during our potty break. When we returned to our huge table, we discovered that the big cocktail menu had Mike's Hard as a drink choice. We weren't interested in the lemonade anyway. In between fits of laughter, with our feet dangling above the floor due to the height of the oversized chairs, we all ordered various Italian delights paired with Gio's famous meatballos.

We had chosen not to dine in the main dining area because a dinner show (Broadway Review) was in progress, performed by local talent. Our food arrived, and as you will guess, it was tasty and the portions were large. Gio's did not disappoint. We collected our leftovers, paid the bill, and continued on our way toward Petoskey and Harbor Springs.

The morning dawned with clouds and a cold rain, just as the weather forecasters had predicted the night before. I felt lethargic but perked up after a cup of coffee and some eggs, then joined everyone in the tasks of pulling on padded-ass shorts, filling water bottles, and checking air in tires. The brisk air actually made me feel better, and by 11:30 we made it to the starting area. Every year, we always hope to start riding by 10:00, but somehow it never happens. After another early start fail, we took the traditional photo by the Boyne entrance sign, and our caravan pedaled up the first hill. My knuckles were numb within seconds. Andrea was the caboose of the group, and Theresa and I came next, nervously hoping she would keep up. Each of us had our own pace. Steve and Kim, on a tandem, set the fastest pace. They torched the hills, both up and down, with two sets of legs pedaling.

We did reconvene at the lunch break and halfway point at the Leggs Inn. We all shivered in the lobby by a small wood stove. Jen came close to losing her pinky toe to frostbite, and I sat on the floor in a numb daze, munching on my unsatisfying turkey sandwich with a slice of American cheese. Theresa worried about her sister. Steve and Kim seemed the best for the wear so far. Andrea eventually showed up at lunch, about 40 minutes after us, all smiles and content to ride at her own slower pace. We had been worrying for no reason. After a half-hour rest, we all set off to conquer the second half of the ride, with only one stop for a photo along the lake. The wind forced us to turn up the pace, riding with our heads down quickly to get the bone-chilling ride done.

This year was no exception. I looked up and was excited to see the Mackinaw Bridge in the distance, signaling the home stretch. With the cold ride behind us, we looked forward to hot showers on the island at the Cottage Inn. We made a final dash to the Arnold Ferry docks to store our bikes and grab our gear for Mackinaw Island. We jammed on the packed ferry, then ohhhed and ahhhed as the catamaran rode up and down some above-average swells on the lake crossing. The short ride deposited us on the island, and we all ran for the warmth of our B&Bs, jockeying for position to get in the shower.

As was previous years' tradition, we decided to meet at the Village Inn for dinner. After a festive meal and full stomachs, we all set off on our traditional bar-hopping escapades. We made rounds at the Pink Pony and quickly left for the Irish Pub, a perennial favorite. True to tradition, we snared a table near the band, and Theresa instantly made friends with a group of guys next to us. Another round ensued, and two more guys squeezed into our group, introducing themselves as Logan and Blain. Clearly, bar names. To counter, I introduced myself as Bri. Blain turned out to be Phil, who quickly attached himself to my hip and managed to stay close for the rest of the night. He put his arm around me as if we had been dating for months, and I never once had the urge to shrug it away. Logan found a seat on Jen's lap, and Theresa shared a shot with tablemate Jim, who had fallen in deep like with her.

We moved on to the Mustang for some dancing and realized that Logan and Phil were tagging along. We finished off our night after dancing for hours to a DJ. I had twirled and two-stepped with Phil (the Texan) on the dance floor; we intermittently shared a beverage plus a few smooches while catching our breath in between dances. Besides the Texas tidbit, I didn't know much more about him since we did very little talking. The island magic had

infected our crew, so last call came as a sad announcement. I had to say goodbye to my new boyfriend Phil—our relationship duration was about four hours.

We walked arm in arm down to the ferry docks so he could catch the last boat back to Mackinac City. After he and I shared several kisses goodbye, Jen pulled on my arm and suggested it was time to go. I realized she was fending off Phil's friend during my amorous escapades. She was the voice of reason in my cloudy head. I nodded in her direction. I turned my attention back to Phil. He pulled me close again, and my soft lips met his one last time. I had to let my sailor go. I waved goodbye, and then we walked away (stumbled, rather), giggling like middle-school girls.

June Multisport

At midyear the streak lived on. June's trip was a multisport adventure I described in a Facebook post: six people, six bikes, one suburban, two coolers, and 10 hours to West Virginia. My tripmates this time included my neighbors Dar and Sarah paired with Steve, Kim, and Theresa. Again, Steve was quite pleased with his bro-to-ho ratio. In the driving rain on a Wednesday morning, we loaded a white Suburban with all our gear, piling in with anticipation of hiking, biking, and rafting the next day. While driving, Theresa reminded us that the campground was planning a pizza party that night for our group arrival. The weather improved, and, eventually, the sun came out in force, and the humidity kept rising through Ohio into West Virginia.

A wide river gorge and green-topped mountains finally closed in around us on a windy road to Anstead, West Virginia, and NARR Campground and Resort. We were pleasantly surprised by the spacious cabin tent. Upon discovering six bunks, not four, Sarah and Dar promptly abandoned the idea of tent camping, especially with the threat of rain. The pizza

party exceeded expectations, and so did the rafting the next day. The New River was swollen with a deluge of rain, churning the white water to zesty for the expedition through the waves. I remember laughing at Dar before we started paddling because she kept repeating a phrase. Over and over she murmured, "My intention is to stay in the boat. My intention is to stay in the boat." There were varying levels of fear and anticipation among our group. On the other side of the spectrum, Steve, Theresa, Kim, and I all volunteered to sit up front. The river was fittingly wild. I almost managed to lose my brand-new waterproof camera on the first day of its use—thankfully, a small miracle occurred. It had washed out of my pocket and into the bottom of the raft, discovered by Kim. I was ecstatic when she held it up for me to verify it was mine. The camera, once found, was put to good use recording our adventures on water with our guide Jenna then after at NARR's High Country Café.

The June trip was not a one-hit wonder. We fit in a short hike to the Endless Wall overlooking the gorge and even got to climb down a 100-foot ladder to the base of the cliff, my first bout with vertigo on that trip. On days two and three, we logged big doses of mountain biking after getting great tips from our new friend at the Marathon Bike Shop in Fayetteville.

It rained on us for the first couple of miles, but we all thoroughly enjoyed the trail that turned into an awesome downhill, leaving us all ridiculously muddy. We rocketed down a multimile downhill while mud splatted in our eyes, making it difficult to see. Thankfully, a well-placed waterfall crossed the single-track trail, where we all stood under the spray for grime removal before continuing down to an old-fashioned coal mine area. The hundred-plus steps that had to be descended, then ascended later, wore us out. When we did climb back on bikes, legs were bordering on exhaustion with many miles back to the car.

After equal amounts of hiking and biking (there is a hiker in every biker), we trudged up a long, rocky hill that required us to walk/push our bikes. Hiking in my bike shoes increased the level of difficulty, causing my cleat to slip on a rock and sending me earthward with a thump. Blood trickled from my knee, and amid cursing and mumbling, I finally heard confirmation that we were almost back. I was tired and hungry, on the verge of bonking—so hungry that I ate part of a mint/chocolate protein bar that Kim conjured from her bike bag. I HATE mint and chocolate! But I gulped two bites down and hauled my aching ass down the last miles of trail. For the record, we overdid it on that day. Later, a shower made my aches and abrasions all better.

The final activity, my friends suggested, was saving the best for last: rock-climbing with Alyssa (a former student of Sarah's whom we randomly ran into at NARR the previous day). We drove along the river for a few miles and met up with her and her boyfriend. She set us up on an 80-foot pitch and belayed for each of us. All of my crazy monkey-like friends scrambled up the face without much trouble, and my fear of heights kept me from

going much past 30 feet up. Reluctantly, I had slipped on climbing shoes and started up the rock face. Alyssa was not keen on having me quit early and would not let me down until I had tried one more time to go up one more section of rock. I made it up about 30 feet and then pleaded to be let down. To celebrate the climbing success and to thank Alyssa, we all headed to Pies & Pints Restaurant for pizza. Then after one more restless night in our cabin tent, we packed up and headed back to Michigan on Sunday.

Golfing in July

I managed not one but two adventures in my own home state in July—adventures in golf, to be exact. When we played a course where every hole is flanked by water and the skies above also poured the same wet stuff, I found myself dodging not only raindrops but also thunder and lightning. Garland Resort in Lewiston (east of Grayling) was the site of my first soggy weekend swinging the sticks accompanied by two friends, Maureen and Theresa. The weekend became affectionately known as "Golf Vegas" for two reasons. First was the Vegas-style lounge act that played at the bar: Jeff & Sue— the Cult of 2. This husband-wife duo belted out covers of Stevie Nicks, Pat Benatar, and other '80s classics with videos playing on the big screen behind them. Second was the five-to-one

guy-to-girl ratio that we encountered while staying and playing two rounds of golf. A guy sauntered up to me on our first night and said, "Are you up at Garland to play?" It seemed like a stupid question at the time. Why else would I be hanging out at a golf resort? But, as I watched the local women turn into golf groupies and dirty dance with drunk golfers (still in their pressed shorts and collared shirts) until the wee hours, I began to understand the question. Scores at Garland were not just recorded on the card for some guests.

The moist (I hate that word, by the way.) golf adventures would continue later that month at Crystal Mountain Resort, which hosted the Women's Michigan PGA Pro Am tournament. We did not encounter any Las Vegas–style entertainment, but just as it rained buckets on us the first day, we managed buckets of fun later after the golf clubs were put away. My teammates included Jeff and Laura and Jimmy, and our pro was Jillian from Calgary, Canada. My team had flashes of brilliance and moments of anguish as well; we had several birdie putts miss by millimeters, one thrown club, several drives over 300 yards, and a natural eagle posted by Jimmy. I earned a coveted closest-to-the-pin award on the last hole. My accuracy—or luck— at that moment earned me a red Calloway golf shirt as a prize.

My team fell just short of making the podium, and our bitter rivals edged us by a tenth of a point to take third-place honors. Our rival team, Theresa, Jim, Christine, Michael, and their pro, gave us a ribbing when the awards were handed out on Sunday. Even in a losing effort, we conjured up some revenge fun on the last hole. On the fairway, we tossed a bag of marshmallows all over the landing area in hopes of confusing our rivals as they teed off behind us. We all cackled as we drove off in our carts and looked back at a smattering of white blobs all over the pristine green fairway.

A Surprise in August

Summer is exquisite in a Michigan August, leading me to stay around the Mitten again. There were many adventures to count in the month leading up to September, the month I would actually turn 40. As it turned out, we celebrated my fortieth in the form of a semi-surprise party on August 15 with 40+ close friends at Dockers Bar & Grill on Muskegon Lake. A consortium of friends had planned a surprise. Unfortunately, word had leaked around, leading several people to slip up in random conversations at the beach volleyball tournament I was playing in. I was tipped by comments like, "Hey, sorry I can't make your party later." I responded with a perplexed, "What party?" and then attempted to shrug it

off so they would not feel bad about blowing the surprise. My group of friends would have something brewing, especially since I had taken liberties planning birthday parties for many of them. Not to mention, that particular Saturday, everyone who called me was overly concerned about the time we should eat dinner. Normally, nobody cared, and being an hour late would be standard fare. Something was definitely up.

I played along when we carpooled to our dinner spot in Muskegon. I was the only person in the car who wasn't nervous. Surprise or not, walking out on the patio to the hoots of 40 people brought a wide smile that fixed on my cheeks for hours. There was cake, food, signature birthday blue martinis, and a custom T-shirt complete with a logo and tagline. I held it up to read: "*Good for another 40.*" Hours passed, and many spirited conversations and well wishes eventually tapered off. A smaller group made our way down to the Pere Marquette Beach on Lake Michigan. We took up a competitive game of strip-volleyball on the beach courts, which of course I won. The security guard asked us to move on before any serious nudity began. For the evening finale, we all stripped off our remaining clothes and skinny-dipped in Lake Michigan on a balmy night. Steve stole the show with his partially submerged handstand. Due to the bright full moon, the glow shone over the non-submerged parts. We all laughed at Steve's exposé and swam around in the warm water. I am not that talented in the water, so I kept below the surface. That party eventually had to end, but it did give way to more celebrations of life and love later in the month.

As busy August rolled on, my brother Ben got married on the next weekend. The setting was idyllic, with views of Little Traverse Bay from the patio at the Perry Hotel in downtown Petoskey. At the hotel I had rented a suite, which served as my room—but also it became pre-wedding headquarters, a changing area, and the general hub of activity. Ben and Sara's rehearsal featured

a luncheon at Harbor Point Golf Club, then a spirited nine holes of golf. We split into teams, and bets ensued, when I realized I was the only woman invited to the golf outing. Ben split us up into four foursomes, and I was lucky to be teamed up with an old friend, Scotty, who had flown in for Ben's wedding. We got a chance to reconnect in between golf swings and also chatted at length later at dinner and the next day after the wedding.

Sunday dawned bright and sunny. The outdoor wedding paired with the lake views would sway any romantic. My newly wedded brother was surrounded by photographers, family, and friends. I smiled back at him as he clinked my glass and flashed his signature grin. I also managed a dance with my two-year-old nephew, Luke (who was adorable in his khaki shorts, tailored shirt, and tie) and with the equally handsome Scotty. The celebration went on, into the night, and I finally begged off when Ben and Sara started assembling a group to make a late-night stop at the local casino. I was exhausted and in desperate need of some sleep. The day after the wedding, Scotty convinced me to take Monday off: "Stay one more day and play a round of golf with me." Initially, I fussed about missing work and almost made the grave mistake of returning to the office. He was persistent, which spawned an email to my

business partner about my change in plans. I made the right choice and stayed an extra day.

Socks in September
It was September 6 when I typed a post that my fortieth birthday was officially in the books. I smiled at the dawn of the day, thinking how lucky I was—about all sorts of things. There was no drama, and I was thankful for the lack thereof. Instead, the day turned out to be sufficiently normal. I went to work, found black balloons and crepe paper all over my office, then had lunch and cake with coworkers. Later, I was treated to an hour massage from Kim, followed by a dinner of grilled surf and turf with dear friends (Steve, Kim, and Theresa). We paired dinner with a very expensive bottle of wine I had smuggled in from a trip to Italy a few years back. It was a 2000 Brunello from Casonova de Neri in Tuscany. It had been lounging in my wine rack and was waiting for the right occasion to uncork its contents. My fortieth seemed a fitting occasion to share it with friends who appreciated a good bottle of Italian red. *"Cent ani!"* we all toasted together. (It's an Italian toast for "May you live to be 100.")

September continued on, and near the end of the month, a spontaneous weekend trip came to fruition. After some phone chats with Scotty, who lives in Boulder, Colorado, he and I decided I should fly out for a long weekend. Of course, he knew about the vacation streak and thought it was important to help me achieve my goal. It was great: the more people I told about my travel goals, the more people volunteered to help plan or tag along. The idea had gained a fair amount of impetus. I had never been to Colorado in the fall, so the prospect of seeing the foothills without a blanket of snow seemed exciting. Scotty was a great host, and it started with a pickup at Denver International Airport then eventually pizza for a late dinner on our first night.

Our next days were filled with hikes in the foothills under a beautiful autumn sun and evenings filled with gourmet food and good conversation. Downtown Boulder was fun to explore, with a myriad of shops infused with all things adventure and a great variety of brew pubs and ambiance-drenched restaurants and boutiques. Scott's friends and coworkers at SmartWool's Boulder office were excellent company and very generous. The trip became iconic because of the large bag of ski and hiking socks that they sent me home with. Scott had hooked me up, sending me home with freebies for family and friends

after a tour of their corporate headquarters in downtown Boulder. Most of my close friends refer to my September travels as the socks trip to Colorado.

October on the Lake

I didn't travel far in October, but it's been established that distance is not what creates the mental benefits of getting away. Doing something adventurous close to home can be weighted just the same, especially if it gets you out of a dull routine or makes you nervous. Sailing on Muskegon Lake on a brisk Saturday was well out of my comfort zone. As an earth sign (Virgo), I began to understand why water signs are so very different. I had stayed on a boat before, but it was a 46-foot yacht on a week-long trip to northern Michigan many years ago with an ex-boyfriend.

A 20-foot sailboat outing proved to be one of the most adventurous things I did all year, a mere 20 minutes by car from my condo. My unfamiliarity with a sailboat and all its mechanisms turned my adventure into part comedy. It was cold and windy, and I was with a group of friends and a skipper who mistakenly thought I had some level of experience. Honestly, I don't know the difference between port and starboard. I was clear on what the word "head" meant, at least. I just prayed I wouldn't have to use it. Skipper Ken taught me to steer, then I ducked and weaved around the sail as we traversed around the lake. It was cold, and my hands were numb, but I tried to be tough and not appear to be chilled to the bone. Had I dressed more appropriately, I would have thoroughly enjoyed cruising around the lake, wind whipping my hair while the boat tipped sideways picking up speed. My water experience is in the realm of paddling a kayak, not piloting a sailboat. I was happy for the invite but even happier when we returned to the dock and to the yacht club restaurant that served hot chocolate.

November/December in Siesta

The gray skies descended as winter in Michigan approached. The final two months of the year are tough, with a scarce glimpse of the sun. It was a perfect time to plan a jaunt to sunny Florida. My year of 40 ended in sunny Sarasota and Siesta Key after the Thanksgiving holiday and into early December. Steve and Kim hosted at their condo, along with Theresa. The four of us flew south to learn we had duplicated the car rental process at the airport. Both Theresa and Steve had rented a car. After lamenting the wasted money, we drove to the key, and I smiled at the palm trees and expanses of water, the intercoastal rivers, and then the gulf. We celebrated our arrival with tacos and margaritas

and settled in, thinking about the next day at the beach. I fell asleep with a warm ocean breeze blowing in the window.

Late morning, we set off for the beach after sleeping in, and we joined a group playing beach volleyball on Siesta Key beach. We fitted in some volleyball and flying disc throwing/catching and walking along the coast. I was coated with a fine layer of powdery white sand that the sun sealed on my bikinied body each day. The sun was consistent, fading my Michigan gray sky memories.

The highlight of this trip was a near-death experience caused by accidently pissing off an alligator. We drove to Myakka River State Park, where you can rent canoes or kayaks and paddle through a river that is filled with gators sunning themselves nearby. Steve and Kim explained that they had done this activity before, and they seemed nonchalant about any risks being near these sharp-toothed reptiles. Kim and I were canoemates, and Steve and Theresa shared the other. We paddled and also pushed our canoes through a shallow river flat area and on the return to the mouth of the lake.

Floating in our canoes, Steve and Theresa suggested we pose for a photo with the gators behind us in the frame. Kim and I coasted closer and slowly toward some gators sunning themselves on a muddy bank. As Steve was taking our photo, in deadly swift motion, two unnerved gators slid into the water, thrashed their tails directly under our canoe, and splashed Kim and me. Petrified, I drew in a short breath and shouted an expletive while holding my paddle to my chest. With eyes closed, I prayed intently I was still upright in the canoe and unharmed. I eventually opened my eyes. Steve managed to capture this exact moment on camera. I was completely happy to get out of the canoe and move on to another activity after that. I turned in my canoe and paddle, and we drove a short distance in the park to hike to a bird-watching area.

On the drive to the condo, I realized it was time to head back home. Thoughts came and went about our several days of multisport activities and trying to keep up with Steve's pace. Volleyball, biking, walking, canoeing, pissing off gators, and golfing had made this trip a true multisport vacation. Admiring tan lines in the mirror, I packed my bag and thought of home. It was time to shift gears into the holiday season and the wrap-up of the year of 40.

Since the year of 40 and successfully pairing travel with my business responsibilities (that "WORK" word), I've continued to make getting away a priority. It's rewarding and motivating, and the experiment produced results on several levels. I feel like a travel evangelist up at the pulpit, summoning people to vacation and to do it more often. It may be unrealistic for some to travel every month, but increasing your dosage is the underlying message. "Don't let three months go by without a simple getaway," I imagined exclaiming to friends and colleagues, holding a good trip guide in my hand. Vacation depression symptoms are easy to manage with a regimen of planning and a list of ideas of where to go next. In between planning Q2 business sales projections or my daily tasks for FineLine Creative, I carve out time to research travel deals online or scour magazines and books for

the next destination. As I discovered in research, even travel planning has the proven benefits of boosting happiness levels.

People soul-search and contemplate all sorts of notions or schemes on the verge of turning 30, 40, 50, or 60. When it comes to travel, do not wait until you are retired to do this. Climbing a mountain, for example, would be better tackled before arthritis sets in. Deferring your happiness is not a good idea. Instead, change your routine, create your own reward system, and catch a glimpse into our amazing planet and its people. It's not important where you go or how far you go but rather making the commitment to yourself. A camping trip an hour away can be just as rewarding as a trip to Paris or Belize. Create your own personal stat sheet, start a travel wish list, jot down some ideas, and go.

January
February
March
April
May
June
July
August
September
October
November
December

Travel is the only thing you
buy that makes you richer

Chapter Two
Paris Power Tour and the Mount Blanc Alps

France, Italy, Switzerland, 2005

Based on 2017 statistics, 42% of Americans have passports. Canadians come in at 66% and UK residents are on top at 76%.
Source: www.statista.com

Fitting in travel wasn't always easy for me either. I worked too much, I did not have flexibility in my schedule, and I worried about money and taking time away. Over time, I've learned some valuable lessons, and by my early thirties I began to realize time and experiences were so much more important than money, pleasing a boss, or climbing someone else's corporate ladder. I decided to make my own ladder and climb it to independence and increased adventure in life and travel.

I was sitting in my car in the front parking lot of the ad agency, nervous and sweaty. I dialed my cell phone and looked out the windows, scanning left and right. The line clicked, then connected. I took a deep breath when a voice came on at the law office.

A woman replied pleasantly to my request, *"Stand by, I will send you right through."*

My attorney came on the line. *"Hey, Laura, I heard you'd be calling."*

"Yes. I want to quit my job and start a new marketing company," I spoke the words quickly before changing my mind.

"Oh, man." Long pause. *"Your boss is going to go apeshit."*

"I know; that's why I'm calling you. What should I expect?" I babbled on, worried about my boss's reaction and how to combat a legal onslaught. *"You know him, his personality, his temper. It's keeping me up nights."*

"Don't worry," he said, *"You'll do great. Besides, you're smarter and better looking."*

I was assured for the moment by his casual air and admittedly laughed at his vote of confidence in my ability to succeed. I set up an appointment to form an S corp and quit my job three months later. It was 2003, and I was 34 years old, recently divorced, and with a meager savings account. It was a risk. A variety of catalysts led me to find the courage to quit and take the leap of faith. I became a believer in BYOB (being your own boss).

Starting a small business gave me the flexibility to travel more, and my income would be predicated on my own achievements and hard work. I began a journey to achieve better life-work-play balance. My hope is to inspire other women and men to create the change in their own lives, be it travel or other outlets.

The new business began in 2003, and my wanderlust continued uninterrupted in 2004 and beyond. Thankfully, the fledgling business provided enough income to buy groceries and periodic plane tickets. In June of 2005, I finally got to use my language classes from college.

I drove my friends and coworkers crazy leading up to the Paris trip while practicing phrases that might be useful traveling in France. Hallway conversation is much more cosmopolitan when you say *bonjour* instead of "hello," *au revoir* instead of "goodbye," and *bien sur* instead of "of course." Phrases turned into sentences, and I found pleasure reading a French-English dictionary in my spare time.

I got hooked on language back in high school. My instructor at Traverse City Public High School was a Frenchman, Monsieur Lampart. My entire class should credit him for teaching us real French, not an American textbook version. My senior year, I tested my brain by signing up for French class in second hour and Spanish class directly after. My two hours of fusion morphed into a fourth romance language called Spançais. The French studies continued, from '87 to '91 at Alma College. I'd decided to become an international business major with a minor in *le langue de l'amour*, before graduating in 1991. The business major didn't stick, but, luckily, the language did. I ended up with a political science degree and the all-important French minor. Then, for a long while, the language remained dormant in the depths of my brain. Pre-trip, to kick-start the re-learning process, I listened and repeated to an audio course behind the wheel during my daily business travels. Luckily, it all came flooding back. *Ahh … oui … magnifique … très bien … voila!*

With French verb conjugations rolling around in my mind, planning for the trip began. Since tackling some of the world's most famous hikes in Africa and Alaska, it seemed fitting to add the Alps to this list. After researching several options, the Mont Blanc Alps three-country circuit sealed the decision. The idea of getting a passport stamped in France, Switzerland, and Italy within five days added a certain *je ne sais quoi*. In the planning stages, my cohort Theresa suggested we spend a few days in Paris to see some of the world's most impressive cathedrals, monuments, and art museums. We decided to cover Paris on the front end of the trip and then book a guided hiking trip for the Alps adventure.

After some research, we booked a group trip, Le Tour de Mont Blanc, with a company called All-Mountain Travel, which provided a French-led guide. During the research, I discovered a $3,000 difference between the most expensive and the cheapest outfitter. The price difference was wrapped up in the lodging choices, so we chose rustic/casual vs. hotel/luxury. With the usual lead-up to any adventure trip, we reviewed the daily itinerary and equipment/packing lists with a blend of excitement and nervousness. The pre-trip happiness boost began in earnest. Several of the hiking days included six to eight hours of hiking paired with 4,000 feet of elevation gain. Weak thighs would not be an option if I wanted to enjoy the hiking portion of this trip.

Paris Power Tour

A power tour = a short span of time where two friends cram in too many epic sights. During the red-eye to Paris, I managed a couple hours of fitful sleep and awoke to an announcement putting us one hour away. In a groggy daze, I made it through customs and collected my over-packed luggage. Hefting our heavy duffels, we solidified fears of being labeled high-maintenance American tourists. I tried to shake off my sleepy head for the first opportunity to use my French to ask for directions to our city transfer area. *"Ou est le station … de transfert?"* I fumbled, vowing to get better. We met our driver at the transfer area, and he whisked us off toward Paris with every bit of flare as a NYC taxi driver. Parisian driving was devoid of rules, with zero lane discipline. We glimpsed some Parisian staples on our commute that included the Eiffel Tower, Arc de Triomphe, and Notre

Dame Cathedral. The history and architecture were stunning, rendering us helpless gawkers pressed to the window. On day 1, we would pack in almost eight hours of architecture, history, and art interpretation.

Our hotel, the Sully St. Germain (SSG for short), located in the Latin Quarter, was just two blocks from the famous university Le Sorbonne. The SSG was comfortable but very cozy (a nice way of saying tight quarters). We checked in with our host, got keys for a fifth-floor room, and encountered the tiniest elevator in Paris. It had been purposely stationed at the SSG to confirm over-packed status. The plaque displayed a three-person maximum, but in the case of two robust American girls and their over-stuffed bags, it meant one at a time. I scolded myself to pack less next time. Finally on the fifth floor, we laughed at the elevator adventure and pushed open the door to a compact room. To save room, we pushed the two twin beds tightly together so we had more space to move around and change.

I took a peek outside our window and called to Theresa, "Let's have a vat of coffee and lunch." Just across the street was a café, La Barnum. With a slight burst of energy, we walked across the street and sat outside. I smiled and ordered in French, *"Pour moi, une omelette du fromage avec un café au lait … aussi avec une bouteille d' Evian."* The bottled water was a mistake. Bottled water was not a good value anywhere in Paris, at €4. The café was sumptuous, and I savored every drop of the life-saving caffeine. Over breakfast, we made a brief sightseeing plan and became versed in a new tipping culture. The bills included *service compris,* which meant the tip is included. The coffee and food helped, but we both agreed we needed to freshen and change before venturing out. Time-change daze fading, it was late afternoon when we ventured out across the Seine River.

From our side of the city, we had unobstructed views of Notre Dame's spires. In hopes of God and Mary blessing our trip, we started the Paris Power Tour with a world-famous religious icon, the Notre Dame Cathedral, flanked by its two bell towers and signature flying buttresses with surrounding heavenly spires. Hundreds of others lined up for views while I searched for the marker on the stone in front of the cathedral, indicating Paris's center point. The marker, called the Rose Line, was made more famous because of the book *The Da Vinci Code.*

We took plenty of photos here and made a wish at Paris Point Zero to follow tradition. Theresa, with eyes looking up to the cathedral that celebrates the Virgin Mary, made the sign of the cross on that spot before signaling she was ready to move to our next stop.

In total opposition, we headed to the Pompidou Center, also known as the Museum of Modern Art. I agreed with architectural purists: the styling does not fit with the rest of the city's historical décor. The weird-looking circular ports and tubular walkways, paired with heavy amounts of steel and glass made for an interesting juxtaposition. The Pompidou's colorful splashes of paint seemed a rude interruption in an otherwise flowing conversation. The odd structure would give way to even more mind-bending sights on the inside. To find the entrance, we ventured through a busy courtyard, where musicians and street performers amused tourists from all over the world. At the ticket window, I used some passable French to purchase a *Carte de Musée* for three days. We rode up several levels and started roaming the expansive exhibit halls, where we found the art to be truly modern. In some cases, we had difficulty determining whether the artist was inspired or chemically altered.

Theresa motioned me toward a brow-scratching display. I looked up and observed testicular-like stalagmites, like you might see hanging from a cave, with color literally thrown on canvas. Modern art has a humorous side, and the most intriguing display was interactive; it included four young women who performed interpretive movements around protruding tall pieces of wood, bolted on the floor. Perplexed, we watched while one girl pinched her belly fat repeatedly, another sat and rocked herself on the floor, and the third, scantily clad, walked among the others mumbling undecipherable phrases. She wore a white tank top that was long enough to cover a portion of her derriere, but at first glance it appeared she was sans panties. *Mon Dieu*! Representative or symbolic, unable to determine its purpose other than shock value, we continued on to the fourth floor. We finished our tour with a section of graphic art, video displays, and other modern paintings. We had worked up an appetite in our attempts to decipher meaning in French modern art.

Theresa, the director of logistics, studied the Paris Metro map. She proved extremely efficient at this task the whole time in the city. My role was to look through our guidebook for suitable restaurants. The Paris Metro, like other big-city trains, has a labyrinth of underground tunnels that were uber efficient at getting us around without the hassle of a car. Off at the Bastille stop, we arrived in the midst of a busy roundabout. The Bastille monument stood proudly at its center, erected to commemorate French Independence Day, July of 1830. After the quick history lesson from the Bastille plaque, we walked down the Rue de Antonette

to the restaurant L'Impasse. We asked the hostess about a reservation at 7. By her reaction, that was entirely too early for dinner. So, instead of having a glass of wine, Theresa and I wandered around the area and stumbled onto Place de Vosgues while taking pictures of a beautiful stone archway. The restaurant was still empty at 7:30; we noted again our uncool dining timeframe. Analyzing my outfit, I felt underdressed for the occasion but forgot quickly, amused to be able to order more wine

and food in French. Our waiter was formal and attentive. I should mention some advice: take your time to order, to receive your food, and also to receive your bill. Thankfully, the pace is much slower than in American restaurants. François (not sure if that was his name) had a tendency to pass by our table and wink at me in between courses. He also surprised the hell out of me when he popped into the WC while I was washing up. Again a wink with a muttered apology. Dinner was a two-hour experience that included wine, a plat du jour, and dessert. I had a traditional carrot/mushroom salad to start, with duck breast glazed in a cherry sauce and crème brulée for dessert. Theresa ordered a very rare beef fillet preceded by smoked salmon drizzled in dilled olive oil. Dinner was skillfully prepared, attractive, and tasty. Francois had disappeared in the kitchen without a wink goodbye. We paid the bill without a tip and took our leave.

For sightseeing dessert, we took the Metro to the stop nearest the Eiffel Tower for a nighttime view of the world-famous landmark. It was almost midnight when I looked up at the impressive tower and all its lights. It was much more impressive lit than the muted steely gray appearance of the day. The lights flickered like subtle fireworks to my drooping eyes. Happy to see this sight from the ground, we did not

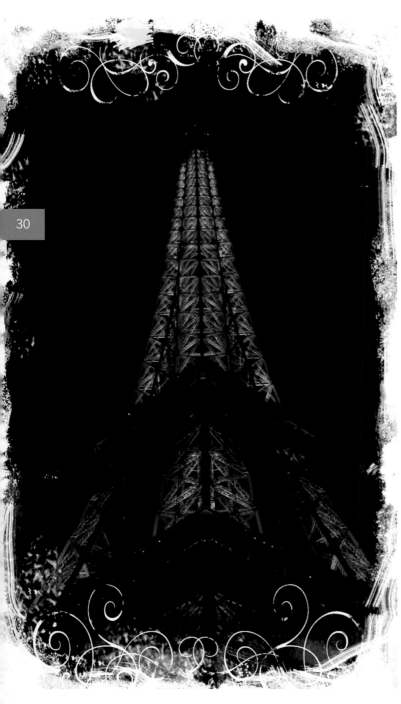

venture to the top, which kept away any possible vertigo flare-ups. We marveled at the tower, vying to get decent night photos from the vantage point of the Marine Museum steps. There was a solid crowd of people milling around while street vendors peddled mini-replicas of the tower. The lights flickered, the tower winked, and I blinked from exhaustion.

Museums and Club 79
In between epic landmarks and museum visits, our day was interrupted by an American teen throwing a fit over a hot dog order at a food cart. The reverie of Tuileries Gardens was broken as the boy made a scene, stomping his feet and demanding a dog. Ordering a hot dog in Paris is truly a grave culinary mistake. A croque monsieur or baguette sandwich would have been a much better choice. I glared at the crazy American family, considering what I might do if he were my child. Theresa and I hurried away from the scene to a quiet nook overlooking a small creek. I tore into my baguette and chips while staring at the huge downed logs covered in moss.

Our museum checklist included the Louvre. En route to the most well-known museum in the world, I felt goose bumps speckle my arms. It was worth the fee just to admire the exterior; the Louvre is housed in a restored palace that sprawls over several blocks, connected to the famous garden Les Tuileries. We entered through the striking glass pyramid that was added as the museum's main entrance in 1989, designed by American architect I.M. Pei. The purpose of the addition was to allow the sunlight to brighten the underground floors. Brightening the basement, functional or not, had caused much angst with Parisians because of the sharp contrast with the classical gothic design. The opposing opinion claimed it as a clever solution to provide the museum a spacious central entrance. Straddling the fence on the two opinions, I passed through with my ticket.

Once inside, we navigated the crowds to catch glimpses of iconic art: the Venus de Milo sculpture, the Wings of Victory, and the *Mona Lisa*. The *Mona Lisa* painting—her eyes really do follow you. We gazed at ultra famous artifacts at every turn and many Greco-Roman sculptures in the first hour of the visit. I attempted to read the explanation placards in French on the paintings and sculptures, trying to leverage some of the artists' original intent. Theresa had opted to rent an audio guide in English, which gave her lots of background and history on each item and section in the museum. It was overwhelming, so I was upset to note it took two hours to cover just one wing. We meandered toward an area that featured French and Italian painters. I sat on the benches, admired the art, and rested my feet from marching around on stone floors. My prolonged gazing was part curiosity and part laziness.

Religious themes dominated the subject matter. In close second was war/conflict, followed by an obsession with depicting nudes! Naked bodies were everywhere in the Louvre. In that setting, it was not obscene—merely art and artist expression. Nude women seemed the predominant choice for sculpture and paintings, but I do recall noting plenty of sculpted manly

parts as well. Art critics agree that the Louvre houses the most expansive art collection in the world and an exceptional amount of nudity without the R rating. Unable to see everything with our limited time in the city, we exited through the famous glass pyramid again. Four hours in the Louvre was not a proper allotment of time, but the power tour persisted.

Next stop was the Musée D'Orsay just across the river. We had to wait to cross the busy street while a political delegation and their motorcade passed. D'Orsay is famous for its collection of Impressionist works, mostly paintings. We were treated to more epic art including paintings by van Gogh, Renoir, Monet, Manet, Degas, and many more. An Impressionist painting is worth a study if you are not familiar with this style. Impressionist paintings look completely different up close compared with viewing them from 10 feet away. Up close, paint strokes look like blobs, and the strokes of color seem rough and unconsidered, but as you pull back, defined shapes and landscapes take form. Impressed with the style, we spent some important time hanging out with the Impressionists before moving on to a few sculptures by famous lovers Camille Claudelle and Auguste Rodin. I studied one sculpture that depicted the pair's tumultuous relationship. The medium was white marble, revealing two bodies

intertwined in an agonizing yet tender embrace. Theresa reminded me that our next stop was Rodin's own museum, so we didn't linger over their sculptures.

Museum number three (after a brutally long walk, lost on side streets) was the Rodin Museum and an accompanying sculpture garden. When Theresa bought our tickets, she was disappointed to learn that Camille Claudelle's works were on tour and had been shipped temporarily to Canada. We both were really looking forward to appreciating a woman's artistic vision. After a long sigh, Theresa and I toured inside and out and admired Rodin's *The Thinker*, *Hell's Gates*, *The Hand of God*, and *The Kiss*, among others. The best part of the museum was the outside galleries, especially on a sunny Parisian afternoon. Ready for a break we wandered into the main courtyard that held a pond with perfectly trimmed living green archways. We relaxed and stretched out on the grass. I rolled on to my stomach, put my chin in my hands, and looked up into the eyes of a man in the sculpture, isolated in the middle of the pond. The sculpture was Rodin's

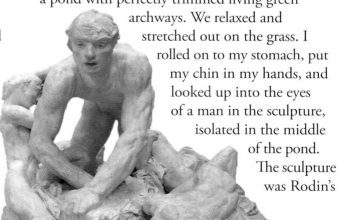

interpretation of a man who had died of hunger while his son clung to his side during his torment. The emotion was palpable, and I was drawn in to the man's expression. Rodin was very adept at making you feel the emotion of the characters he sculpted.

Museum day moved into late afternoon with more walking. Along our return, we spotted La Grand Épicerie (supermarket,) where we bought some pre-dinner snacks. This market was stocked with intriguing displays of fresh veggies, fruit, seafood, and, of course, cheeses. We decided on a traditional baguette, brie, and bananas. Back in our room, we spread the creamy brie on the crusty-edged baguette for a quintessential French snack.

Our jaunt around Paris continued at a quick pace. We were tired, but with so much still to see, we pushed on. Next stop was the famous Avenue des Le Champs-Élysées. The street was magnificent at night, bustling with traffic and lined with expensive boutiques. We walked down this famous street toward L'Arc de Triomphe and tried to capture night photos of this impressive monument. The bustle of people around the area was daunting, and the cafés were full of fashionable locals and tourists taking in the impressive night views.

On the walk back to our Metro stop, we spotted a neon Club 79 sign on a side street, a discotheque we had read about in the Pariscope guide. Theresa and I had discussed the idea of clubbing in the city of lights. *Isn't that what you do in Europe?* It might have been a good idea had we not been so tired from the lengthy promenade around the city. The sign should have been warning enough, but I talked Theresa into going in for one drink, only to learn there was a €15 cover charge.

A short visit proved to be accurate as we entered the main area, realizing the median age was just slightly under the club's namesake age. Scanning the room, we realized we were going to become the prey of aging salesmen in suits. I walked up the first flight of stairs to the second level in search of a cocktail and a view of the not-so-crowded dance floor. We found a small table and tried to ascertain whether we had a waiter or needed to go to the bar for our nightcap. During our discussion, a middle-aged gentleman approached in a suit, to whom Theresa turned to give him her order. By his trite remark and the scowl on his face, apparently we had taken his table. He seemed quite annoyed to return to his table only to be asked for drinks by two demanding American girls. *"Zut alors,"* he sighed. *"Je suis desolée,"* I returned with a half smile. I apologized in

English as well, then excused us from his table while suppressing a giggle. We agreed it was time to go. There would be no dancing tonight.

Back at the hotel, the same man who checked us in was behind the counter. At the SSG, the staff requested your key upon your departure and then again on your return. (If I were a hotelier, I wouldn't trust my guests either.) In my best French, I asked for our key. *"Bon soir, le clé pour la chambre cinquante-trois, s'il vous plaît."* Surprised, he looked up, smiled, and seemed ever so pleased to see us, then commented on my French and asked where I had learned. Blushing, I assured him I only spoke a little. He was especially friendly to us for the rest of our stay.

Montmartre, Sacre Coeur, and Alligator Shirts

One of our power tour days featured a much-needed sleep-in. We enjoyed a final *petit déjeuner* at the hotel and set off walking by late morning. First stop was a bustling department store, Le Samarataine. At a street-side vendor, we pounded some juice and water then headed to Le Carolle Boutique. This elegant store was lined with fashionable women's clothing. We walked around and admired the wares and their equally pretty price tags. We hit two other shops, and Theresa found *les chemises* for her and her sister. We headed out the door but set off the security alarm instead. One of the shirts in T's bag still had a security tag on it. We were exonerated after its removal and sent on our way.

Our plan for the day was to head north to the Montmartre district, then to see the famous cathedral Le Sacre Coeur (the Sacred Heart). We booked a guided tour in advance to give us the complete art history of the area. At the Metro stop Abess, which let us out directly next to a café, we met our guide Iris. She led us through Montmartre's history and winding streets. The highlights of the walking tour included van Gogh's residence and Le Bateau Lavoir, which had housed many art greats like Picasso, Toulouse-Lautrec, Renior, and others. We walked past tributes to many artists and by Lady Dalida (a comedian/singer). The neighborhood possessed a casual, artsy vibe dotted with quaint and friendly cafés.

The power tour paced on. Our afternoon exclamation mark was admiring Le Sacré-Coeur Basilica and gazing out at the incredible view of Paris. Montmartre and the basilica are in the northern part of Paris at a slight elevation, which gave a great vantage point to see the size and scope of the city. The view was the day's finest moment, sitting on the front steps and enjoying the sun. Despite the busy scene, I found a spot to sit and soak in the view while Theresa made a quick tour on the inside of the Sacred Heart. We lingered and rested while the afternoon faded. With a nod, we agreed to walk back down the hill to finish shopping. I had scoped out some painting reprints by Lautrec, and Theresa wanted to hit the Antonelle clothing boutique, which was back near the Bastille monument.

We had the boutique to ourselves, and I attempted to ask the clerk for sizes and muddled through conversions from European to US sizes. We tried on several tailored shirts with wide collars and unique patterns. Petite sizing is the norm, which is why we kept asking for the next (*le prochain*) size. Hopefully, the slender Parisian clerk did not judge her shapely American patrons, who clearly were solid size 8s. I held up the tiny shirts and began to understand what copious amounts of red wine, cigarettes, and cheese did for French women. In the end, I bought a tailored shirt for €48, secure in the knowledge that I would get compliments back home.

The wannabe fashionistas continued on. I had been incessantly bugging Theresa to be on the lookout for a Lacoste boutique in order to purchase a coveted alligator shirt. I had obsessively talked about needing a shirt from the country that birthed the brand. Exceptionally ill-timed, I picked our last day to complete the mission. Theresa still ribs me about my lapse in judgment. She informed me, "I am sitting down and ordering a beer at the Irish Pub while you find your beloved shirt." In hindsight, a cold beer would have been a better choice than power walking to the Lacoste store, only to be mystified by the inflated prices. My clothing fetish ended in utter failure when I refused to buy a T-shirt priced at more than €50. "*Merde*!" Cursing in French, I walked out empty-handed. I made it back to the pub, and Theresa looked mystified. Palms up, she lifted her arms, "Where is your shopping bag?"

"I couldn't do it," I said, explaining how expensive the prices were. She was befuddled that I had forced her to walk well out of our way to find my beloved store … where I bought NOTHING. I slumped into a chair beside her and ordered a beer. We had seen enough of Paris and the City of Lights. The sights, the history, and the museums were a lot more important than a stupid alligator shirt. I began to see the absurdity in my quest. We melted into our pub chairs for another half hour before heading back to the Sorbonne neighborhood for one last meal.

We settled on a Franco-Armenian restaurant called Le Vartan. It proved to be one of our tastiest meals in the city. After being seated, we struggled through the French menu of Franco-Armenian dishes and ordered some starters, then promptly found the English menu posted on the wall directly behind our table. We laughed, then ordered dinner that included a Russian salad, chicken in a spicy sauce, and a lamb/veal mix for dinner. We did not linger after dinner but headed back to the SSG to repack for the train to Chamonix in the morning. As we repacked, we both chortled at the amount of clothes we had brought. Dress pants, a skirt, and several nice shirts for some phantom fancy dinner. My feet and legs were achy, so I sat on my bed and tried to organize all my crap without standing up. There were no clubs, just sleeping in preparation for an early wake-up call.

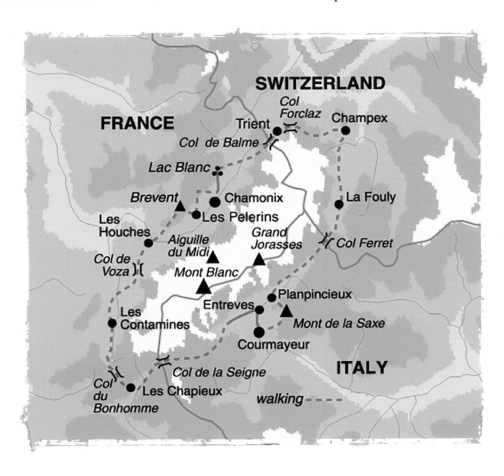

The Mont Blanc Alps: Three Countries, Five Days
Le Train à *Chamonix*

The trip moved from city lights to the snow-capped Alps. We hauled our overstuffed duffels to bus station 63, which would take us to the train station. We milled about, waiting for the bus, until we thought to look at the schedule posted on the sign. A chart clearly showed the next arrival in 30 minutes. Spurred into action with the news, Theresa, the quicker thinker (She was in charge of logistics, after all.), hailed a cab to the station. Le Gare de Lyon was an overwhelming maze where we scanned all the displays for our departure. We located our gate only with assistance from the ticket booth. The last task was to heft our bags onto the train before enjoying a relaxing four-hour ride. Too embarrassed to ask for help, it took both of us (with a mighty heave) to hoist them up the steps to a baggage section. In our seats finally, we had several hours to watch the French countryside fly by.

My obsession with train travel began that day. Train love is all about legroom and spontaneous get-up-ability, not at all like being confined in the car or on a plane. It's also equally perfect for scenery gawking or napping. The destination was a small town just over the eastern edge of France,

called Martigny, Switzerland. From there, we would take another train into the Alps. I dozed and split waking time admiring manicured fields and wine country zip by more than 100 miles per hour. We passed mustard country via Dijon and crossed the Swiss border at Lausanne. The scenery became progressively more mountainous as we rolled into our stop exactly on time.

The Paris bustle faded away as we disembarked and stood near the tracks, looking around for lunch. Martigny's quaint downtown held a few shops and, thankfully, a pizza pub. We had two hours to kill before the Mont Blanc Express would take us up the mountain. We sat and enjoyed a pizza *avec jambon et champignons* (ham and mushroom). Back on the train, it immediately started churning up a steep incline. Within minutes, I was looking out my window at cliffs and steep gorges leading us into the Mont Blanc Alps. The train tracks were cut precariously close to the edge of significant drop-offs, causing me to lean away from the window. Instead, I took in the views of the oncoming snow-capped peaks, from the safer, no-nausea, frontal vantage point.

We stopped four times at various Alp villages yet arrived again on time in Chamonix, France. This stylish and chic resort town was set in a beautiful river valley sporting views on all

sides of jagged snowy peaks and a glacier to the south. Gaping at the scene, we pulled our roller bags along bumpy cobbled roads. A swift river ran through the town, the water a blueish-gray color from snow runoff from the glacier. After a short walk, Theresa turned us onto Le Place D'Eglise next to a church. We spotted our hotel, Hotel Faucigny, a quaint three-story converted chalet. Guy (pronounced Geeeeeee), a pleasant French host, welcomed us, "Ahhh, yessss, ladies, I avve been waiting for you." The hotel was reminiscent of a ski lodge with pine, wood panels, and staircases, and Theresa and I struggled up two flights of stairs with our bags. My bag drama continued! I discovered a broken wheel, the result of the cobbles during the walk over. Theresa laughed and gave me a knowing glance—another clear sign from the universe to pack lighter. I pushed my ailing bag into the corner, put it in timeout, and

hopped up on my wood-frame bed to stretch out. The room was double the size of the SSG.

Following our itinerary instructions, we walked to the tourist office to purchase the required emergency/evacuation insurance. A bold trip, indeed, when one must purchase this type of insurance. Apparently, helicopter evacuations are quite expensive. Our outfitter, Compagnie Des Guides, required proof of this insurance before embarking on the tour. I handed over the €48 to a cheerful attendant and looked around at the stacks of brochures promoting skiing, trekking, camping, biking, and ice climbing. We were in the right place. On the steps of the tourism office, we met some of our group and our head guide, Nicholas, a handsome salt-and-pepper-haired sporto. I said *bonjour* and hello to a French couple, Dominique and Christina, and also to Ian, who was traveling with his

son Trent and daughter Becca. Patrick, from Belgium, would be joining our group the next morning.

Nicholas introduced himself and in French described our trek. Then in heavily accented English he did the same. We would only carry day packs since Nicholas's team would transfer our bigger bags as we moved from place to place. He went over equipment, clothing/gear suggestions, and how we would pack lunches. He gave us our meeting time for the next morning, and we all left in search of dinner. With the trip overview and random French verbs swirling in my head, I walked on with Theresa to find a local restaurant. Along the river, we found a quaint spot for dinner and promptly began chatting nervously over a bottle of Gamay Rouge. We savored a regional culinary favorite, called a *tartiflette*. It was an oven-baked dish of sliced potatoes, chunked ham, Gruyère cheese, and crème fraiche with more cheese baked on top. It was by far the best version of cheesy potatoes ever devised.

Le Tour de Mont Blanc commence

The next five days left me weak in the knees (thighs and all leg parts) from staggering views of the Alps. Each day consisted of 4,000 feet of climbing or descending on rocky, grassy, or snowy trails. Europeans didn't bother to cut

switchbacks or find easy routes; they just went straight up or down the mountain like goats! I was not sure my pre-trip workout regimen had adequately prepared me for the strenuous six to eight hours of hiking per day. Our group began on Sunday morning in the town center of Chamonix. There, I met everyone again and shook hands with the eager Belgian, Patrick, who I noted was wearing yellow knee-high soccer socks and orange shorts. He'd be easy to spot on the trail. We milled around and chatted about our pending adventure while our guides readied for departure and loaded the suitcases in the transfer van. We took a ride to Les Houches, where a gondola transported us to the top of the first peak. Twenty-five strangers crammed in a gondola car, admiring the rising views. The gondola ride would be our easiest summit on the circuit.

Once we were out of the gondola, the hike began in earnest, passing through grassy and rocky areas in equal amounts. Eventually, our first day would take us down a steep descent to a quaint village, Les Contamines. Along the way, we were stunned by the views from the trail that led us around a pass to a Western-style planked bridge. The narrow bridge had to be navigated to cross a steep gorge and waterfall below; it made me horribly nervous. I death-gripped the rope rails and walked quickly across the swaying rope and wood contraption. After that adventure in heights and going down a descent, we went back up. My legs were weary. Several groups passed from the other direction, who called *bonjour* in a singsongly manner, clearly not tired based on the peppy tone of their voices. At lunchtime, we stopped at a mountain version of a café nestled on a grassy plateau with fields of yellow and purple wildflowers on all sides. I joined Theresa and Patrick in the grass to soak in the 70-degree sun.

At the next flat area, a statue paying tribute to Mary was erected on a ridge overlooking a small pool of water. Looking longingly into Mary's gentle face, I hoped she could provide some healing for my ill-prepared legs. I remarked to Theresa that we had been hiking six hours. "My legs are trashed, and the last descent will be painful." She agreed, and we both tried to use the switchback technique instead of plowing straight down. The aches were worrisome, but we kept going, trying to think of other things like a cold drink at the bottom of the trail. The village below came into view. Encouraged, we became hopeful to make it through day one. Studying the village from the ridge above, we saw a steepled church with a small row of hotels, cafés, houses, and La Poste. The village was spotlighted in the bright sun just below us. At the town outskirts and out of the dense evergreens, the sun warmed our backs, and for a moment, I forgot about my achy legs. The one-block alpine village (Les Deux-Alpes) was idyllic, with its peaked roofs all accenting the dramatic snow-covered peaks.

Our tired group crossed the street and strode up to the Le Grizzli Hotel with Nicholas. Le Grizzli had a lovely patio area where Patrick, Theresa, and I settled at a table and promptly ordered beers. Patrick was talkative as ever, seemingly unaffected by the strenuous hike;

he chatted about his many travels and casually mentioned the six languages he was fluent in. I half listened as he and Theresa chatted and swapped travel stories and destinations. Admittedly, I was busy stretching my calves and quads in my seated position, hoping not to cramp. Nicholas came back outside and handed out room assignments and keys. Soon after, we all attempted to walk up a couple flights of stairs. Leaning on the guardrail, I walked gingerly up the stairs. Once in the room, I strolled to the small patio and pushed open the sliding door to see the panoramic Alps views to our south.

In dire need of showers, we noted the extreme amount of lactic acid in our legs. After a shower, I ventured out on the patio again, to admire the sunset, with a tin of sports cream in my hand to rub on my tortured legs. Distracted by the setting sun, I felt the metal tin slip from my hand. It fell two stories and bounced loudly off the hood of a parked car in the back of the hotel. Shocked, I leaned over the railing, lamenting my lost lotion, in no position to run down and grab it. It would have to wait until later—that is, if I could traverse the stairs again. I walked back in the room and announced to Theresa that I had sent our lotion tin plunging to its death. And

there was a dent in someone's car hood. She joined me on the balcony while I pointed to the impact spot. She erupted in a burst of laughter and confirmed that she could see a small dent! Blushing, I sat down on my bed and caused no further trouble until we set off for dinner. Listening to the murmurs, I confirmed everyone's legs felt as awful as mine. I saw the subtle grimaces set on faces for the very short walk to dinner down the street. Just before dinner, I snuck around back to collect my tin of lotion, hoping the car owner was not waiting around the corner to take me out at the knees.

Safely back with the clan, I shuffled to dinner like an old woman with severe arthritis. It was a small inn for a group of nine, so we piled around the biggest table they had. Offering no menus, our waiter described two choices for the meal. First, sensing our leg pains, he passed around an aperitif drink, Kir, a wine/liquor mix. He announced that dinner was a baked potato and cheese concoction in a sausage or ham option. The regional name for the dish is a *Tartiflette*, which we had tried back in Chamonix. Impossibly, this version was even more rich and delicious than the previous. Theresa and Patrick greedily dug in, well past hungry. The three of us continued the get-to-know session, talking about our various careers and where we hoped to travel in the future. Patrick spoke French to Dominique and Christina to his right, then effortlessly turned to his left and addressed Theresa in English. His language skills were impressive! This yellow-socked lad was a fine addition to our Alps quest. Theresa and I would have to share time with the lone single guy on the trip.

Dominique and Christina were mostly quiet at first. I noted that Becca and Trent were the picky eaters of our crew. Each day, I collected details about my travel mates. Christina and Dominique were vacationing and celebrating their anniversary. Ian and his two kids (Trent and Becca) hailed from Salt Lake City and had returned to France to honor the site of his former Mormon pilgrimage. We had several religious bases covered on this trip. Dinner eventually wound down, and we returned on tired legs to prepare for day two in the Alps. I desperately wished for a hot tub as I fell into a restless sleep.

Le Col du Bonhomme and Les Luge

Each day, we hiked six to eight hours, but the evening always held a culinary reward and French wine. I awoke stiff-legged, thighs actually sore to the touch. The sky looked bright and ominous, typifying how quickly the weather could change at elevation. At breakfast, our crew was chatting over bread, strong coffee, and homemade jelly that looked to be the same consistency as my thigh muscles. I munched on the same fare and hoped my legs would carry me. Nicholas and the All-Mountain crew drove us a short distance to the trailhead outside of town. The trail led up a valley to a col lined by roaring rivers fed from melting snow. My predominant memory of that day was of snow and a new deep green, sandwiched with the flip-flopping weather of sun and rain. We trekked on equal parts mud and melting snow. The first two hours were under a warming sun in shirt sleeves. The next hours brought intermittent driving rain, prompting layering with a poncho to keep our packs dry. In between our wardrobe changes, the valley held the promise of new growth, budding flowers, and an approaching summer.

After the break, the rain pelted again, smacking loudly off nylon rain gear. It became apparent that some of us were more prepared for rain than others. I pulled my hood tight and marched on, mostly dry except from my knees down. Theresa and I remarked how thankful we were that we had purchased overpriced waterproof jackets. We watched perplexed as Trent and Becca got wetter and wetter. The trail turned upward, then to long stretches of granular snow soaking our hiking shoes. We passed by another small shelter that afforded me a minute to pop some trail mix into my mouth. Nicholas turned and spoke to Dominque, Christina, and Theresa: "Ça *va?*" He asked, "How are you?" I replied back, "Ça *va bien*" ("I am doing well."), and Nicholas nodded to Theresa, searching for her response. He laughed and fluttered his eyelids when he spoke.

The fickle sun came out again, and we noticed a large dam in the valley that became visible from our elevation. A refuge also came into view, with a large porch and carved wooden chairs perched all around. At lunchtime, the refuge hosted 30 hikers all with soaked shoes.

We ate lunch with the lovely aroma of socks hanging over the wood stove. Two groups jockeyed for space to prep lunch and to find areas to drape aromatic foot covers. Lunch was tabbouleh, carrot salad, and as much bread and cheese as we wanted. There were thermoses filled with coffee or hot chocolate. We were always well fed. Each morning, Nicholas would hand us an individual bag full of snacks and lunch for our packs. Group rules: we all shared the weight of daily food rations. The only tough assignment was getting stuck with a five-pound wheel of cheese. Our lunchtime was interrupted by an announcement that an ibex had been spotted on a hill facing the lodge. That brought the lot of barefooted hikers out on the porch. I was thankful for some fresh air, instead of the damp mustiness of socks. Lunch over, we continued toward the Auberge de la Nova.

Sucking in the clear Alps air, I squished toward my group and more snow-covered trails. We came quickly to a section of hilly terrain that had been turned into a sledding hill by the French group. From across the hill, they encouraged and yelled to us, "*Les luge, les luge!*" We watched the last of their group slide—*dans les derrieres*—down a 30-foot section of steep trail. Our comrades continued to cheer, until Ian, in our group, slid down with his hands in the air, roller coaster–style. The boisterous cheers continued, and they waved to the rest of us to come down. My suspicions were confirmed: they had been drinking wine at lunch. With boisterous encouragement, I took my turn down the luge run and added a wet ass to my soaked shoes. I was surprised at how much speed I picked up down the now-packed luge run. Grinning broadly, I joined my new French friends and yelled to Dominique, Christina, and Trent to join us.

The good spirits continued, the sun came out, and the trail turned to grass. Bright yellow wildflowers popped up everywhere, and dairy cows grazed along the hillsides as we started the descent. We encountered several cows, standing or lying across the trail. Cow pastures and cow pies were prevalent on our last stint of walking. The last hour went by quickly on the downslope that led to an inviting auberge. The inn had a well-appointed courtyard with picnic tables. Theresa and Patrick magically appeared and handed me a beer.

Nicholas handed out keys and explained the community showers were set up by floor, second for women and main for men. While waiting for a turn, I bummed some shampoo from Ian. I was so thankful the shower was warm enough to shake off the

chill. Dinner was a delightful mixture of chicken cutlets with cheesy potatoes paired with a veggie casserole. Several bottles of red wine were passed around. Christina, Dominique, Patrick, Theresa, and I happily partook. Ian abstained, explaining that Mormons do not believe in consuming alcoholic beverages or other addictive substances. I shrugged and reached for a second helping of casserole and wine.

Alps Day Three (Col de la Seign to Italy)
Il a plu! (It rained.) The first hour of five was
dry. During our breakfast, I peeked outside
from the dry confines of the dining room. It
had rained overnight, and everything looked
drenched. The warmth of my coffee mug and
the crunch of French bread with jam were
quickly forgotten. Our destination was Italy
and a quiet little town called Cormayeur. Today,
instead of cows on the trail, there were herds
of sheep grazing on the ridgelines. Their gray/
white coats contrasted sharply against the wet
green grass. The clouds turned from white
to gray, and I hunched my shoulders to the
imminent rain. The group was quiet, sensing
a wet afternoon of walking. Nicholas seemed
unphased as he had seen plenty of rainy days
as a guide. When the first drops came, Theresa
wasted no time putting on her raincoat. I
followed, then we pulled the ponchos over our
packs to keep out leaks that would potentially
run down our necks. We walked on through the
chilly rain. I stared down at my sodden feet, any
views obscured by mist.

A brisk wind kicked up as we approached
the Col de la Seign. It was a challenging
weather day. I remember stopping by a stone
wall (not a wall attached to house or a roof),
which offered only partial protection from
the brisk wind. We leaned against the wall
while Nicholas made his rounds to check on
his flock. Patrick, Dominique, Christina, and
Theresa were in good spirits despite the lousy
weather. I tightened my hood and tried to
stay warm while Nicholas walked back to Ian,
Becca, and Trent. I heard him grumble as he
doubled back, *"Ou es l'equipe reve?"* ("Where
is the dream team?"—loosely translated.) They
had lagged behind, soaked and cold. I don't
recall them packing much gear for rain or cold.
Every mountain hiking list includes the same
essentials: a raincoat AND a poncho.

Nicholas ushered us onward as the rain
continued, and after another hour, this time
a small refuge with a roof appeared for a rest
stop. It was leaky and not much warmer than
outside, but I could at least pull off my hood
and gloves long enough to find snacks for a very
brief lunch. No picnic tables and tablecloths
today. Still munching on trail mix, I walked
out in the rain again. Theresa and I conferred,
then decided to embrace the weather and smile
through the rain. The shift in attitude actually
made us feel warmer. Bonus: we knew a cozy
inn was waiting down the trail. The trail leveled
out and turned into a dirt road that ran parallel
to a rushing river dotted with huge boulders.
Crossing over the bridge marked our passage
into Italy. While we walked, the rain finally
lessened to a drizzle, turning my thoughts

to food and a shower. After rounding the next bend, Isabelle and the van were waiting. Sweet! I smiled broadly and watched as everyone in our group breathed a sigh of relief while piling in the van. We steamed up the windows on the short ride.

Rufugio Monte Bianco was a three-story structure where Isabelle handed Theresa keys to our room and pointed out a small mudroom. She instructed us to take off our shoes, and then she set about stuffing the insides with newspapers. We thanked her and found our room. The room was absolutely tiny (a smaller version of my college dorm), with just enough space for bunk beds, a pedestal sink, and one set of drawers. The community showers were just down the hall. Two people could not move around at the same time in our room, so I sat on my bunk and rummaged through my bag to locate a towel and some dry clothes. We hung all our wet clothes and socks on the radiator before heading to the shower area. The refugio did not provide towels, so the lone towel I brought saw double duty. Thankful I had paid attention to the packing list, I showered and changed, then handed off the damp towel to Theresa.

The lack of towels was a catalyst for a temper tantrum. (Not everyone in our group had remembered the packing list.) En route to my shower, I caught Ian trying to console his daughter. She was frustrated, and her voice escalated while he listened to her tirade. She demanded to stay in town at a more proper motel, one that had fresh towels! Turned out she didn't bring one. I also recalled the accommodations description, which did not include spas or four-star resorts. I cringed as the argument went on for several minutes, uncomfortable to be in earshot of the heated exchange.

With our shortened hiking day, we had time to walk the streets of Cormayeur before dinner. Mother Nature finally turned the faucet off, so we explored the town and popped in and out of cafés and a grocery store. I was obsessed with snacks because of our truncated lunch. Theresa and I skipped the ice cream shop and watched a jovial group of English boys scamper around, sharing bags of chips. They skipped and munched on the salty goodness, calling to each other, "Guys, the chips are lovely." We laughed and meandered back through the town and avoided Becca at the grocery store. She was buying large bottles of Evian. I couldn't figure her out. Why buy expensive bottled water when you could refill your own bottle with ice-cold glacier water from natural springs at stops all along our hiking route? *Where do you suppose Evian water comes from?*

Back at the refugio, our group downstairs had found the snack bags and the lunch we had skipped due to the torrential rain. We happily ate chicken drummies out of a foil bag and bites of cheese with mugs of hot tea. Patrick proudly produced a chocolate bar to share. The mood was cheerful, and enthusiastic conversations sprung up in the room. Isabelle, Christina, Dominique, Theresa, and Patrick all shared stories while dinner was being prepared. The small wood stove churned out waves of heat in the dining room, where picnic tables lined an expanse of windows that looked out toward the riverbed. We played an international version of Scrabble to pass the time. We noted an Italian influence for the evening meal when bowls of pasta marinara with mushrooms arrived. With appetites fueled by all the hiking, we devoured a second course of tender chicken breasts laced with buttery green beans, followed by a crème caramel dessert. After dinner, fatigue washed over us like the rain earlier in the day. We bade one another *bon nuit* and *buena notte*, to curl up in our small bunk beds lined with luxurious down comforters. The view out the tiny bedroom window would have been spectacular, except for the fog obscuring the neighboring peaks.

Le Suisse Frontier

We left Italy for neighboring Switzerland. After breakfast, Isabelle seemed impatient to get us loaded. Her patience had been tested by another annoying public display with Becca, who wanted to take a day off. She implied it was her dad: "My dad is tired and sore and needs a day off; I'll stay back with him." Our group knew who really wanted to rest her feet. Earlier, I overheard complaints to her dad that her shoes were still wet. Isabelle tapped the wheel, and, finally, only Trent joined us for the day's trek. At the decision, Isabelle drove us through Cormayeur, past a detour and the Mont Blanc tunnel up a winding road to our start point. Watching her drive away, I figured Isabelle was in for a day of adult babysitting.

Nicholas bade us look up at the day's route toward the Col de Ferret to more rugged snow-covered peaks. Five strides in, Nicholas abruptly stopped and asked, "Where is Patrick?" No one knew. Did Isabelle forget Patrick, or was he still sleeping? Minutes later, we learned the self-sufficient Patrick had slept in (aka missed an alarm) and caught the next van with the French group. We reunited at our first rest stop, the Refugio Elena. The hike began on a dirt two-track that turned steep and switch-backed to the refugio. As we left, the Italian flag billowed in the wind set against a stunning view of the valley below.

The Italian trail was steeper than others, forcing us to plod snail-slow, leaning forward to maintain balance. Everyone was gassed by the pitch, panting mightily until we came to our first plateau. There was more snow to traverse before we passed a sign marker confirming our entry into Switzerland. That marked our peak altitude for the day. The trail led to a narrow shelf around several peaks that opened to a mountain café, lined with picnic tables and umbrellas. Each table held a unique centerpiece: a worn leather hiking boot filled with soil and bright purple wildflowers. Patrick, Theresa, and I lunched on bread, cheese, salmon pâté, crab batonettes, and chocolate bites. We dined in our bare feet while we ate in the sun and listened to the sounds of Swiss cowbells ringing up from an adjacent pasture.

Our sun-soaked lunch ended, and we were back walking down a narrowing path next to a cow pasture. The trail was cut into the mountainside, so we hugged the left side as the cliff fell away off our right shoulders. We also encountered a precarious stream (waterfall, rather) that had cut a path across our trail. Cold and swift-moving water splashed down a narrow gorge and disappeared under a blanket of snow and ice. Nicholas had maneuvered carefully to the other side and motioned for each of us to follow. He pointed out which rocks to use as leverage to cross the wet gorge to safety. I watched Patrick and Theresa push off the rocky edge, then Nicholas would grab their arms to be sure they made it across. Only Christina had a bit of trouble. We all exhaled when her first step sent her skidding several feet down on her butt. Her husband helped her up, and then carefully, she picked her way over wet rocks to Nicholas's waiting arms.

After the adventurous crossing, we stopped at a flat, grassy spot that jutted out over the gorge below. We lounged in thick green grass laced with wildflowers. We navigated along a rooted path on the descent, and I realized my legs had finally grown accustomed to the steep ups and downs. In the valley, our last river crossing (this one had a wooden bridge) took us into the next city and transport to our lodge. Isabelle's smiling face was behind the wheel of the familiar van. She drove rapidly down a winding road laid out like a single spaghetti noodle flung wildly on a dinner plate (Isabelle's Wild Ride). We abruptly rounded corners then turned up again to Champex, a beautiful town on an alpine lake. I did not judge her demeanor, considering she had been adult babysitting all day. We were deposited in front of Hotel Glacier, where our host handed out keys and dinnertime details. Hotel Glacier was considerably fancier than our previous nights' lodging.

Theresa and I were giddy at the prospect of having our very own bathroom for one night. The room was spacious, with cozy pillows and down bedding. I pulled the curtains aside and revealed a small balcony that held a panoramic view out over the lake. *The Sound of Music* was most certainly filmed right out that window. We took full advantage of the showers to scrub away hiker grime. After cleaning up, we met Patrick for our usual happy hour drinks on the deck then strolled through the small town. We dined as a group, enjoying a sumptuous four-course meal. It began with vegetable soup then a ham and asparagus appetizer. The entrée was Cote d'Agneau (lamb with carrots and potatoes) with glasses of red wine. I found room for a slice of chocolate cake that included an orange cream filling for dessert. The four-course dinner took just under two hours, putting us all into various stages of food comas. We walked back to our room and were incredibly bummed to learn the jacuzzi had just closed. *"Zut Alors!"* I settled into my bed, laden with extra pillows, and fell into a deep sleep.

Col de la Forlaz

It sounds cliché, but the views escalated with each day. On day five in the Alps, there was no wild van ride; instead, we walked out of the hotel up the road past Lac Champex residences and took a left turn on a dirt road. The road turned to trail and became heavily forested and exceptionally thick and green—an Alps version of a rain forest. We strolled easily for the first hour, lost in conversation with Patrick, the most interesting man in Europe. Listening intently to his travel rap sheet, I concluded the need to ramp up my level of travel abroad. He chatted with our group about European taxes, jobs, cars, the Euro compared to the dollar, and a bevy of interesting economic topics. Just as our path turned uphill, we caught up to the French group on the same day hike. Seven morphed into 12. I refilled water and ended up side by side with a French couple on holiday. We approached some natural steps that climbed up the first col, where we had to ascend single file.

The sun was out, and temperatures climbed along with our steps. A rising sheen appeared on all our cheeks under the alpine sun. We kept climbing and picked our way through dry and rocky creek beds. I smiled at my new friends as we stepped into a grassy opening and traversed to a rest stop. I discovered my new favorite snack, a bag of *Les Fruites Tropicale*. As we rummaged, we wondered, Who would get the game changer and get stuck with the wheel of cheese? Theresa was sure she had gotten stuck with the cheese at least twice. The sun shone all day, so we stripped down to shorts and T-shirts. Just about noon, our group made it to a rustic cottage that served as a mess hall with cover from the elements. This site was particularly memorable because of a rustic wooden cross perched on the edge. It gave way to a vertical plunge to the valley below. The wooden cross paid tribute to the journey and safe passage for Mont Blanc travelers. Seated on picnic tables, we lunched on French bread, cheese, and cherry tomatoes. Theresa and I noticed the French group drinking wine with their lunch. Envious of the wine and of their laughter, we inquired with Nicholas. *"Nous avons besoin le bouteille de vin rouge aussi,"* I encouraged. He promptly got up, and went into the refuge, and returned with a bottle! *"Merci beaucoup,"* I thumped him on the back. He was pleased we had suggested the wine and poured us a glass. Our now lively conversation got the attention of the French group. We overheard them complimenting

Nicholas on *les conversions d'Americans*, converting our lunch habits to French customs. Several bottles of wine were passed between our groups, and we traded stories. I learned a French expression that day: the equivalent of the English saying, "It's a piece of cake." In French: *Les droits dans le nez!* Literally translated, it means "fingers in the nose."

Lunch devoured, I walked to the edge of the ridge and joined several others surveying the vertigo-inducing view. Below, the entire Rhone Valley and the town of Martigny lay in a patchwork of green. The view was a 9.95, the best yet. I sat on the nearby picnic table and stared for protracted moments until a call from Nicholas broke my reverie. Just minutes up the trail was the highest point of the day. I steadied my feet for a dizzying peak to a sheer drop down to the Rhone off to the east. As we began hiking down, the ringing of Swiss cowbells became our marching music while *les veches* grazed peacefully below.

We meandered through pastures full of marked cows down to 5,000 feet and the Col de la Forclaz Hotel. The hotel was off a well-traveled mountain road with an attached souvenir shop. Theresa and I quickly grabbed our room assignment and threw in our bags. The sunny afternoon beckoned us to find an outdoor patio. Two frosty mugs arrived, well deserved after six hours of hiking, and the souvenir shop tempted us while we sipped. After a half hour, we both emerged with a bag full of goodies to bring back home. Theresa found a red Swiss hat for herself and a Swiss cowbell. I bought a mini coffee mug with Col de la Forclaz imprinted on its side and several Swiss chocolate bars. I didn't have high hopes they would actually make it back to the States.

Le dernier jour: Le Tour de Mont Blanc
Our hike would complete the circumvention of three countries and the Mont Blanc circuit in six days. I reflected on the journey over strong coffee. The mountain had been good to us, except for the drenched day in Italy, and I had finally gained some stamina in my legs. The Alps provided inspiring and majestic views, and its small valley towns graced us with hospitality and excellent dining. My favorite dish, the Tarteflette, would be a recipe to remember. I vowed to make it for friends and family back home. Also, Nicholas had been a capable guide, and Isabelle was ever patient. I would assuredly recommend them if anyone wanted to plan a similar trip. The hike on the last day was bittersweet, as it began with a steep grade to greet my legs. With familiar cowbells ringing, we followed a steep switchback trail through the trees for about an hour until an opening provided a view of a refuge. I kept walking toward the structure, which took a lot longer to reach than I thought. It was a form of alpine optical illusion, where rest areas were farther away than they appeared.

Once we stopped, we were surrounded by expansive views on all sides, and beyond the refuge was Chamonix Ski Resort. Both groups took turns posing for photos with our quest completed. The guides snapped photos with several cameras, while someone yelled, "Fromagey!" We had all eaten our share of *fromage*. After several photo opportunities, I dug out a Mars candy bar and chewed on that while admiring the view with Patrick and Theresa. On the walk down, we watched the gondola running, carrying mountain bikers, not skiers, where we caught glimpses of daredevil bikers in full gear bombing down a steep descent. In contrast, peaceful wildflowers had sprung up everywhere, lining our path down to the base. We eventually made it down to Chamonix, milling around and not sure of what to do next. Nicholas rounded the bend and began shaking hands with the men, and he kissed all the girls twice, once on each cheek.

For a final meal together, we gathered at an outdoor lodge. I was convinced that strenuous exercise heightened culinary senses. The above-average food theme continued as several bottles of wine were opened while a salad was passed around with greens, tomatoes, and corn. Seated at two picnic tables, Christina and Dominique made a toast and presented a bottle of Gamay in celebration. Christina began filling glasses while the entrée arrived in a large steaming baking dish. Heaping portions of baked white fish and rice were ladled onto plates and topped with a red cream sauce. An apricot tart arrived mid-table with candles in honor of Dominique and Christina's twentieth wedding anniversary. Happy to help them celebrate, we raised glasses in honor of their milestone. Christina had caught me saving wine labels for my journal, and she presented the label from this last bottle with a smile. It was a festive occasion with new friends on a glorious sunny afternoon.

Also, Nicholas presented us with certificates commemorating our successful traverse of the Mont Blanc circuit. After we had admired the certificate, we found lunch was finished way too soon. The last glass of wine was poured, and it was time to say goodbye. Patrick doled out bear hugs to Theresa and me as we promised to write and stay in touch. Several vans were coming to transport us back to Chamonix.

Theresa and I returned to Hotel Faucigny for one more night. We cleaned up and handwashed a pile of sweaty hiking clothes before heading out for gift shopping. It's a great tradition to bring back unique gifts from trips abroad. I found a hat for my dad, a Swiss Army knife for my brother, and a porcelain wall hanging with painted wildflowers for my mom. I found a unique French calendar for my sister and French café chalkboard for me. I had to abort additional shopping, considering the size and condition of my wounded, one-wheeled duffel. Our final errand was to check the bus schedule

for the next day into Geneva. We had settled on a restaurant called Caleche for our last supper, a suggestion from Nicholas. Our mountain family dwindled to just two. We savored a dinner of French bread and cheese fondue without a single worry about the calorie count.

stop and smell the flowers

Chapter Three
Bomb Threats and Champagne Powder

Steamboat Springs,
Colorado,
2008

Discover the simplicity of having something to look forward to (like a trip). It will brighten your days, and the sun will start to peek over your cubicle.

Like most, I have to work to get away too. I don't make a six-figure salary, and the ebbs and flows of cash flow are ever on my mind. There are schedules to consider, money to set aside, and research to complete before leaving for a destination. There is a small business to run, and new projects are not cultivated without my organized effort. But what I've discovered is that vacationing more often has made me efficient and joyful about my daily tasks. I feel compelled to pass this knowledge along to friends and colleagues who lament their 50–60-hour workweeks. I've heard many colleagues say, "Work is crazy busy, and I can't take time off right now." Then, months—years—go by, and "now" becomes three years of life. It's time to support a new movement: to stop the glorification of busy.

Busy does not mean efficient. I've learned less multitasking and more dedicated time to one task create hours to carve off schedules. Discover a mindset to be efficient and focused in 40 hours, to carve out more personal or family time. With something to look forward to (a vacation or new hobby), it's easier to find the motivation to complete work with renewed zest. Up the travel dosage, or at least start by taking a Friday off and turn a weekend into an adventure maybe just an hour from home. Let go of the guilt and fear; use vacation time and ask the boss about flextime. Offer to work longer days Monday through Thursday for a Friday early-out. Many employers understand that flexibility boosts morale and provides increased performance and loyalty. As a boss myself, I've seen this shift firsthand. Don't assume the supervisor or boss will say no, and don't leave unused paid vacation on the table. **PTO is paid time off. You are getting paid not to work!** It's a novel concept and time the mind, body, and soul need to be healthy.

What has busy done to us? Nothing good. According to *Time* magazine's article "Save Our Vacation" from June 2015 by Jack Dickey,* quality of life and vacation time have eroded along with the quantity. Technology now perpetually tethers workers to the office; the smartphone never takes time off. Most people—61%, according to a 2013 survey—say they typically keep working even if they are not at work. By 2001, a third of Americans said they were chronically overworked. Exhausting days lead to lethargic and stress-filled (and, accordingly, sleepless) nights. The body and mind take big hits; studies link overwork to depression and cardiovascular problems.

What's the formula for reaching balance in work-life-play? Work is not the bad guy; it's the guilt hurdle in our minds. We work to achieve and earn time away. Part of what makes a vacation so fulfilling is the knowledge that we've earned it and that we really deserve it. What's the right amount? At least four weeks per year; six weeks is better considering the pile of 50-hour-workweeks. Our minds need to change and grow outside of dull routine; a new place or situation can access that part of your brain. A quote from *Braveheart* comes to mind: "Every man dies; not every man truly lives." The guilt of being away from work resides in our mind, not the boss's. She has other things consuming her, like payroll taxes, the HR scandal, and making sales projections. So take the trip, lose the guilt, and return refreshed. Find a new appreciation for people or a place that holds memories much dearer than watercooler conversations. Plus, coworkers will be thankful that the perma-scowl has left your face after a break.

The corporate ladder goes up, but it has plenty of spaces between each rung for exploration. With that thought in mind, I packed and left on a ski trip.

I sat on the floor of the airport arrivals area and watched a TV13 news crew filter in the door and start interviewing waiting passengers. The whole area was a buzz of voices and commuters who were all agitated from delays and caffeine. *What exactly was newsworthy about delayed flights on a winter morning in February?* It had something to do with the undisclosed security issue that had closed our concourse 15 minutes before the suggested boarding time. They herded us back down to check-in and cleared the area. The four of us shook our heads, wondering what was going on and when we could get on another flight. Would they hold our planes? No one at Northwest had any answers. We all exhaled and hoped we could still make our connector. In relatively good spirits, considering the unnerving news, we sat by baggage claim on the floor and waited to hear the scoop. Propped up on our backpacks, we heard news start filtering in from passengers who had overheard interviews from the news crew. We were in the middle of a suspected bomb threat, and the bomb squad was on the way!

A half hour later, still waiting, a Northwest agent, with no less than a can of Aqua Net in her hair, made a passing announcement. She walked by our group with a look of disdain, "You might want to consider moving." We exchanged confused glances. Were we really in harm's way? In the event of a bomb

STEAMBOAT COLORADO

detonation, would we all be blasted to tiny bits where we sat? Nobody else moved. So, we all shrugged and stayed put. Kim and Steve produced a deck of cards, and a game of euchre sprang up much to my dismay. I am not a card player. Too bad for Steve I was his partner and my crash course in card-game strategy didn't take. I was playing horribly, and Steve laughed at my attempt to go alone with a lousy hand. Thankfully, with the euchre game over, we learned the situation had been officially cleared by security. There was no official announcement from the airline, but we received word from our own reliable news source. Theresa's sister Shelley had called her, saying, "Did you guys get held up because of the bomb scare?" She filled Theresa in on the details from the TV13 morning news. They had reported that the security issue had been caused by an engineer's concrete probe found in his briefcase. The TSA rep had mistakenly taken it for contraband and called the code red.

Crisis averted, Northwest gathered us together for some good news. Our flight was cleared, and we would leave first priority Elated, we filed back in line through security to get on board Flight 679. We smiled at the realization we could still make our

connection in Minneapolis and joked about the bomb scare and why anyone would ever pick Grand Rapids, Michigan, to plant a bomb. We taxied to takeoff and got in position to de-ice. Just as the first bits of spray hit the windows, the power and the lights on the plane flickered slightly, followed by a low humming sound that faded to silence. A minute later, the captain clicked on his speaker and gave us more bad news. Our plane had a mechanical problem, and the replacement parts were not nearby. Flight 679 was officially canceled. Our plane limped back to the gate. My smart friends were already calling Northwest on their cell phones to try to rebook instead of waiting in line at the counter. Moods soured, we were officially not in good spirits: first a bomb scare, then a pseudo-evacuation, and now a canceled flight.

I sighed and watched, ever hopeful, as my friends got agents on the line. In a flurry of activity in the next half hour, all four of us successfully booked a flight to Detroit, then on to Denver instead of into Hayden near the resort. All direct flights to Hayden were sold out. Just a day ago, I had commented to coworkers, "It's gonna be so cool to fly right in—within minutes of the resort." Denver was not minutes away. It was four hours away from Steamboat in good driving conditions. Denver was our only option, so we tried to accept our new travel fate and pass the time until our afternoon flight to Detroit. We agreed on a lateral move, exited the airport, then drove to Olive Garden for lunch. To befit our mood, we sat at the bar and tore into a basket of breadsticks like it was their fault we were delayed. After taking our frustrations out on salad, pasta, and more bread, we returned to the airport for a second time.

Things improved slightly: the flight to Detroit was on time, and we only waited an extra hour in Detroit before jetting to DIA. It was late evening now; catching glimpses of Denver lights on the descent, we had been up since 4 a.m. We tapped into energy reserves to collect bags and rent an SUV to start up the foothills at 10 p.m. Theresa drove us into the dark as the grade increased approaching Leadville. The wind and snowflakes gathered as we drove into a full-blown snowstorm and headed west on I-70. We had been punched in the gut twice, so we only winced at the uppercut (this time from the weather) and kept going.

Back in Denver, we had been informed that Rabbit Ears Pass was closed. The main route to Steamboat was blocked! I made a few phone calls while Theresa drove and tried to reach Kim, my ex-sis-in-law who lives in Frisco, hoping she would have a hotel suggestion in her hometown.

On her advice, we landed at the Silver Inn near Silverthorne. The Silver Inn turned out to be as close as we would get to Steamboat. We were exhausted, the road north was closed, and it was well after midnight. The morning would surely bring better tidings.

Looking back on that day, I thought about the origin of the word "**travel**" and took a moment to research. The word stems from a Latin root word, for torture or torment. In Old French it became (to) *travaillier*, meaning to become tired or worn from travel. The original meanings certainly fit the front end of my ski vacation. We skied the bumps before even making it to the lift lines. Our travails were almost too numerous to track, from bomb scares to mechanical failures to driving in blizzard conditions. I notched that February day (and night) as one of my top travel misadventures. Sometimes just getting to your destination can be an adventure. It only took about 36 hours to find blissful powder. Was it worth the travails? When you work so hard to get somewhere and you finally arrive, it creates a heightened sense of appreciation.

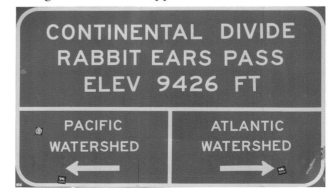

Every ski town has its own unique personality: the mountain, the resort, the village, the après-ski scene, and, of course, the locals. When we finally arrived, I was committed to soaking in the vibe.

Almost There

A bright blue light filtered through a crack in the curtain. I was not in Steamboat. Instead, I had slept fitfully on a mediocre mattress 100+ miles away. As my eyes adjusted to the light, I guessed that Steve hadn't slept much either, because the shower was running. The blue sky meant we should not be wasting time sleeping when we should have been on the slopes by now. We all took turns in the shower, skirting around each other in the small room, hurriedly repacking our bags. Then we found the SUV outside covered in eight inches of snow. We brushed it off in the blinding sun and found the golden arches for breakfast on the go. We munched on our McMuffins, with sunglasses on, trying to be patient on a two-hour trek north to Steamboat. The drive was filled with comments about the snowbanks and how awesome the conditions would be after a big dump of snow. Antsy to get there, we decided the plan was to check into the condo, throw our bags in the door, change into snow gear, and be on the mountain by noon.

A quaint little cowboy mountain town finally peeked at us ahead, making me wish I had packed a cowboy hat alongside my ski beanies. Had I been wearing boots and spurs, I would have jumped up and clinked my heels together to celebrate our arrival. We checked into the Rockies Condos and marveled at the perfectly sculpted snowbank leading us to the front office. Pumped to finally be there, I kissed the snow outside the office. Our travails were finally winding down.

Once inside, I rifled through my bag and pulled on long underwear for an afternoon of skiing. Theresa and I took the spacious loft area while Steve and Kim took the bedroom downstairs next to the kitchen. We were minutes from walking out the door when Kim picked a fight with her razor in the bathroom. While she was retrieving some lip balm from her toiletry bag on the vanity counter, her shaver jumped at her hand. She emerged bleeding and disgusted, then set about searching for bandages to cover her wound. She had taken a sizeable chunk out of her knuckle. Riffling through cupboards to find some gauze, we wrapped the bleeding appendage tight so we could get rolling. Kim was tough and undeterred from her quest for mountain air and powder—she certainly was not to be stopped by a gash on her finger.

We grinned once we finally had lift tickets, ready to head up for our first runs. Kim had one of her classic connections on this trip, landing us some discounts. An old friend JR (from her camp days) was employed at Steamboat, and he helped book our condo and lift tickets at discounted rates. Each of us saved more than $250. The afternoon was bliss on bouncy powder under blue skies and a beaming sun. Plus, all the evergreens were absolutely coated with the previous night's snow. Each tree had been transformed, limbs hidden, likening them to snow-blob creatures instead of trees. We learned the names of the lifts and found our way around and thoroughly enjoyed the snow that had previously prevented us from getting in.

I tried to find my ski legs, but instead a painful burning sensation began in my quads after the first long run. My condition is commonly known as chicken legs among my group of friends. An important ski lesson: hydrating at elevation is ever important to avoid altitude sickness. Don't wait—hydrate!

Our first half day quickly turned into afternoon, so our last run down we skied right to the Slopeside Grill for our first round of après-ski. Kim left Theresa and me with Steve so she could meet up with JR for coffee and a catch-up. She tasked us with grocery shopping while she was away. The three of us ordered Bloody Marys, and while we sipped, we marveled at our crazy adventure from the day before. Finally, the stress had been left behind in one of the snowbanks on the road to Steamboat. We toasted to the mountains, drained our drinks, then set off in search of snacks and groceries for the rest of our stay.

It was fortunate we had gotten a cart while shopping because Steve needed to lean on it to stop himself from passing out. He was experiencing a full-on mountain bonk stemming from lack of sleep, not enough water, and 10,000 feet of altitude. Theresa played doctor (She is a dentist, after all.) and had him sit down on a bench. She got him some water

and made a beeline for the sushi restaurant next door to procure carbs and protein. Back at the condo, we met up with Kim, ate our sushi snack, and got more fluids in Mr. Bonktown. We felt energetic enough to clean up and meet JR and his family slope-side for the winter carnival and fireworks. We bundled up for the frosty evening and looked forward to stretching our legs on a walk.

On the walk to meet JR, we had another incident. The sidewalks were slippery, and true to Steve's luck on an overstimulated day, he slipped. His backside and skull were introduced rapidly to the pavement below. We gasped, hoping he would not need a trip to the hospital for a concussion. We collectively exhaled when he said he was OK. Instead of rubbing dirt on it, we teased him with handfuls of snow to rub on the sore spots. Later, he admitted, "Weird—cracking my skull actually cleared my head. I feel better." The incident turned out to be the shot of natural adrenaline he needed. We walked on cautiously and met up with JR and his kids in the midst of hundreds of onlookers.

Kim made introductions, and we recollected our travel woes to JR and asked whether he would have time to ski with us during our stay. JR nodded and stood with his toddler perched on his shoulders while watching skiers on the

run carve patterns, illuminated by torches. I kept shuffling around to avoid the chill and watched JR's little girl's cheeks transform to a bright color of crimson. She started to whimper from the cold. It was a signal to close the day one curtain. The fireworks fizzled, and we said goodbyes and headed back to the friendly confines of our condo for a spaghetti dinner then more tubbing. Kim announced to Steve, while changing into her bathing suit, she would not be shaving her legs on the trip: "I am punishing my razor for cutting me!"

Laugh until You Cry

It was Sunday, our second day on the mountain, and we were rewarded with more glorious sunshine. Steve kept us on a brisk pace in the mornings because of his need to be on the mountain for first tracks. He has a confirmed condition called FOMO (fear of missing out). We shuttled over to the base, rode up the express lift, and explored the area around the Pony Express. Steamboat is not a huge resort like Snowmass or Vail, so it's easy to find your way around. My foursome skied lots of blue groomers that morning and a few diamonds once our legs were thoroughly warmed up. So far, the legend of champagne powder wasn't just Steamboat marketing. The snow conditions scrawled on the lift board in chalk listed packed powder or stashes of untouched around the

tree runs. With all the snow to push through, we tired easily. Usually, each of my runs meant several brief thigh-relieving breaks en route to the chair ride back up. Plus, it's just not possible to keep up with Theresa. She shot out of the womb on skis. If you watch her navigate a run, it's clear she's happiest making her quick and smooth signature GS turns. Kim, equally adept, rode her board. Her ability on the mountain came from the experience of being a Colorado resident in her younger days.

The day schussed by, and I lost myself in moments of searching for the sounds of my skis cutting through the snow with an almost silent swoosh. There was no teeth-clenching scraping of ski on ice that I was used to hearing on Michigan's equivalent of a ski run. The quiet skiing with the sun softening the chill remains my fondest memory of that day. We also took a moment to sprawl in Adirondack chairs, while tilting our faces up to the sun and soaking up the warmth in between quad-numbing runs. We skied all day, and, eventually, Steve and I made it down to Bear Creek first for après-ski refreshments, followed closely by Kim. Kim reported that Theresa was off tackling some expert terrain and would join us soon.

We settled at a table outside on a huge patio area that was a great vantage point to observe people coming off the hill on their last runs. Steve and I ordered my favorite après-ski snack, a plate of nachos. We shared our table with a family from England (Mom, Dad, and two young boys around 10 or 12) and chatted them up in a lovely conversation. However, I was slightly distracted by their son, who looked sad and on the verge of tears. The mum kept comforting and hugging the boy as if he was hurt. Finally, Steve and I both asked what was wrong. A story ensued about the boy's horrible toothache and their search for a dentist or a med center. Steve and I promptly turned to one another and smiled with a nod. We proudly informed our new friends from Essex that we were traveling with a dentist, who in moments would be skiing down the hill to join us. We assured them that she would not mind at all taking a look. I hoped Theresa would not be upset at our willingness to volunteer her expertise on vacation. They were thrilled, and now we had to hope Dr. Theresa was willing to take on an emergency case or make a spot diagnosis at an outdoor bar.

While we waited, our nachos arrived. They were by far the worst nachos I'd ever had, each soggy chip dripping with a watery version of yellow cheese-like goo. The chips sat at our table, swimming in that milky/cheesy mixture, until Kim and I agreed to send them away.

The beers sufficed, and moments later Theresa strode in all smiles with cheeks flushed from her last runs. We only gave her a moment to take a layer off before we introduced her and explained the boy's predicament. She raised an eyebrow at us but sat down next to the young boy and asked him where he was hurting in her best slope-side manner. Shortly after, he opened up, and she did her best to see what was going on with the suspect tooth. Dr. T made a quick dental diagnosis and suggested they head to a med center for some antibiotics and pain pills to counter the brewing infection. They headed out and thanked Dr. Theresa. The four of us were left to sip beers and recap a great day at the Boat. We didn't linger too long because we had plans to take the bus downtown for dinner.

We tubbed first, which was much needed, especially with my advanced-stage chicken legs. Showered and presentable, we took the bus into Steamboat and settled on a pub called the Smokehouse Restaurant. Red meat and barbecue looked to be the specialty as we settled into a massive wooden booth and ordered beers that came in oversized round goblets. I so looked forward to dinner, since the nachos had been such a bust. We sipped our beers while holding our large and heavy goblets with two hands. We all ordered various red meat delights, potatoes, and salads. Starting on my salad, I

began to notice a loud conversation directly behind me. I tried to pay attention to what Kim, Steve, and Theresa were saying, but I continued to be distracted by three loud Texan voices, Southern accents, and escalating laughter. Theresa watched, amused, at my curious looks over my shoulder, and she too started to key in on the conversation. It had a maddening pattern – the older Texan man of two began to tell a story, and at each pause, the woman (his companion) began to laugh like a hyena call, in short, loud bursts. I was amused at first but found it difficult to savor my dinner with the boisterous guffawing behind me.

I switched from my salad back to my beer again, and by this time, Steve and Kim had noticed the ridiculous laugh. They began giggling, watching me trying to eat my dinner with explosions of noise in my ear. Altitude may have been a factor. The Texans got drunker and louder and the ahhh, hhhhaaaa, haaaaaa, haaaa continued in more frequent bursts. My dinner was cold, and I stared at it, unable to put fork to mouth. Instead, I began to giggle, my eyes watered, then laughing tears ran down my face. At the sight of my tears, my friends imitated the laugh, trying to overtake the Texan cougar in decibels. Another 15 minutes passed, and laughter morphed to attempts to control breathing without wheezing. My dinner sat untouched, and I had our waiter wrap it while we tried to regain some composure. To this day, Steve torments me by doing his impersonation of the woman's hyena laugh, sometimes when I (we) least expect it. And it always conjures up the same response: I laugh so hard I cry.

Don't Be a Hater

Our blue skies were replaced with clouds and wind on Monday, making for a shortened day on the slopes. My legs were torched anyway, so after lunch at the base, I stayed behind begging for some extra downtime. They relented and headed off without me. Thrilled to relax indoors for a while, I clomped in my ski boots up to

the Sheraton Hotel and found an unoccupied lounge with a fireplace and two large wooden rocking chairs. Perfection. Getting comfortable, I took off the clunky boots for a while. I melted into the rocking chair, propped my socked feet up on the hearth, and promptly dozed in/out of a catnap. My cheeks flushed from the fire as I reveled in the warmth, not caring about the few passersby commenting on my doze. Eventually, I peeled myself away from my hearthside nook and begrudgingly made my way outside to meet up with my crew. They complained about the blustery wind and cold, so it didn't take much convincing to convene back at the Sheraton in front of the fire with beverages.

The result: après-ski began at 2. We concurred to begin with a bottle of champagne for the namesake powder. After sipping champagne from flutes, we walked to the nearby Gondola Pub and Grill, which was absolutely packed with warmth-seeking skiers coming off the mountain. The atmosphere was loud and energetic, factoring heavily in the selection of a shot followed by a round of beers. Still lingering in the moment, I realized Steve asked the bartender for our tab, but I beer-bullied him into staying for another round. A Fat Tire pitcher

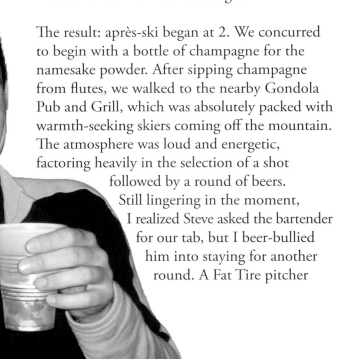

arrived, and the buzz ramped up. We drained the pitcher and shuttled back to the Rockies Condos for showers and sips of coffee. We readied to head out again.

Now adept at the bus routes, we walked to the stop where Kim and Theresa pointed out graffiti on the bus stop walls. It had a very anti-tourist sentiment.
Phrases were scrawled on the walls:
- Tourists suck
- F**k tourists up the ass

Some angry thoughts from the locals. *Why so much hatred?* We shook our heads and gladly hopped on the bus to head into town to the Ore House, probably to be served dinner by the very local who had scribbled hatred for us. It was steaks all around and bottles of wine. We had been happy since the afternoon, so we continued feeding our appetites and buzz. Our T-bones and filets were perfectly grilled medium-rare, paired with a buttered baked potato. I savored each delicious bite, thankful for a quieter dinner atmosphere. Kim had told JR we'd catch up with him for our nightcap after dinner.

We found JR and his friend Adam for Alpenglow beers at Mahogony's for our final stop. The mountain bender included hours of imbibing champagne, beers, wine, coffee, and more beer. The mountain air had infected us, and we kept riding the slope of fun. I did not turn down another cold beer from Adam while JR and Kim struck up a conversation about the old camp days. We milled around the bar and talked for hours. It was late. After a huddle, we declined the bus and called Alpine Taxi for a pickup.

When our taxi minivan arrived, we poured ourselves into the van and waved goodbyes to JR and Adam. Our driver Mike was surely overwhelmed by the stench of beer and loud, boisterous behavior. We asked Mike where he was from, and to our astonishment, he replied, "I'm from Grand Rapids, Michigan." We yelled in delight and exclaimed to Mike that we were from Michigan too. He didn't seem as excited as we were about this news, but we pressed on, asking him a bunch of questions about why he moved out West. Mike was stoic as he drove through downtown and toward the resort amid a flurry of loud, drunken inquiries about his personal life. And Theresa was adamant to ask him an important question. In a drunk yet serious voice she asked, "Mike, do you hate tourists?" Kim, Steve, and I erupted in a spasm of laughter after explaining the angry messages at the bus stop. "Nope, I don't hate tourists," he tried to assure us, smartly turning up the radio to drown us out. Spewing from the speakers, Donna Summer was singing "Bad Girls." I boldly yelled to Mike, "Turn it up! You won't be sorry!" He complied as we attempted to sing along the rest of our drive back. At Texan decibel levels, we belted out, "*Toot toot, hey beep beep. Bad girrrrls. Talking about the sad girls. Sad girrrrls. Talking about the bad girls, yeah!*" The singing morphed into giggling until the thrill ride halted at our condo development.

We dug out some cash, paid Mike, and thanked him repeatedly for putting up with us. Still

in the van, Theresa looked up and slurred to Mike, "Our condo building is the next complex just down the street. Could you pull forward a little?" He replied, "Sure," put the van in drive, and moved forward literally one foot, then put it back in park. He turned in his seat, looked back, and asked, "How's that?" Theresa nodded and winked at him with an approving glance. We all spilled out of the van in hysterics over Mike's last move. Mike had gotten the last word as we walked the extra 50 feet to our condo entrance with Donna Summer fading into the night.

No Rendezvous

Our last day at Steamboat turned out to hold equal amounts of fresh powder and wind. The Rockies had whipped up a nice snow squall and delivered it right on top of us Tuesday. I woke up wondering why I didn't have a screaming hangover considering the eight hours of drinking that had highlighted the night before. I shrugged, smiled, sipped my coffee, and pulled on my last pair of clean long underwear. We made it out on the mountain late morning and promptly split up with promises to meet for lunch at the Rendezvous Restaurant. Steve and Kim headed off to find the perfect run for knuckle draggers, and I skied with Theresa on the blues in the blinding and building snow. I tried to fine-tune some GS turns and relax my legs in the accumulating powder. Of course, on the last day I had finally found my ski legs—not chicken legs.

We had fun in the snowstorm and only encountered one problem: we couldn't find the restaurant for lunch. We consulted the map twice, skied down the run that led to the Rendezvous, and each time (twice) we ended up back at the lift with no sign of it. We were perplexed, but it was awfully hard to see the trail signs, each covered with a layer of champagne powder. On our third and final attempt, we skied down the same run, stopped at every trail and sign, and still never found it. We gave up and ended up lunching at the Gondola and the Thunderhead instead. Luckily, it was not bitter cold, so it was actually fun skiing in the snow squall, and it meant no waiting in any lift lines. We rode the lifts, skied down, repeated, and stayed out until around 3:00 (an hour before the lifts closed). We left a message for Kim and Steve to meet us at Slopeside. We met up and exchanged snowy stories of our afternoon. Apparently, the Rendezvous did exist, because they had found it. We sat around and chatted and finally enjoyed a real plate of nachos.

Kim filled us in that JR and his wife and kids were going to stop over at our condo for pizza dinner. After devouring the nachos, just

the girls set off on some power gift shopping. Kim needed cool shirts for her two boys, and I needed a gift for my dog-sitter. Steve was happy to skip that activity while the three of us sipped coffees and shopped around. Steamboat logo-wear was prevalent, and we took the time to find some deals on overpriced T-shirts and helmet stickers.

Before heading back, Theresa and I ran back to the downstairs lockers to retrieve our ski bags and shoes. As we climbed down the stairs, we couldn't help but overhear three British women in an animated conversation about a friend named Nigil. We kept quiet and listened around the corner. In excited voices, they retold a story about riding up the chairlift and watching someone try to ski down a double black near the trees in an out-of-bounds area. One of the ladies said, "What idiot would go down that?" The other woman exclaimed, "That's when I realized: Oh, my God, it's Nigil!" They cackled at the retelling. Around the corner Theresa and I listened intently to their story in perfectly accented voices.

It was a mellow night with a couple of pizzas and a chat with JR and his wife Kristin. With the pizza demolished and the kids' bedtime approaching, a wave of yawns began. Thankfully, JR gathered up the kids and their

gear and bade us goodnight, and a welcome quiet engulfed the room. The four of us sighed, collapsed on the couch and admitted we were exceptionally tired tourists. There may have been a few people in Steamboat who hated tourists, but we never found them on our trip.

Life was meant
for good friends,
great adventures,
and a few laughs

Chapter Four
Taste It with Passion

Tuscany and Rome, Italy, 2006

Italy boasts more UNESCO World Heritage Sites than any other country in the world.
Source: World Travel Statistics

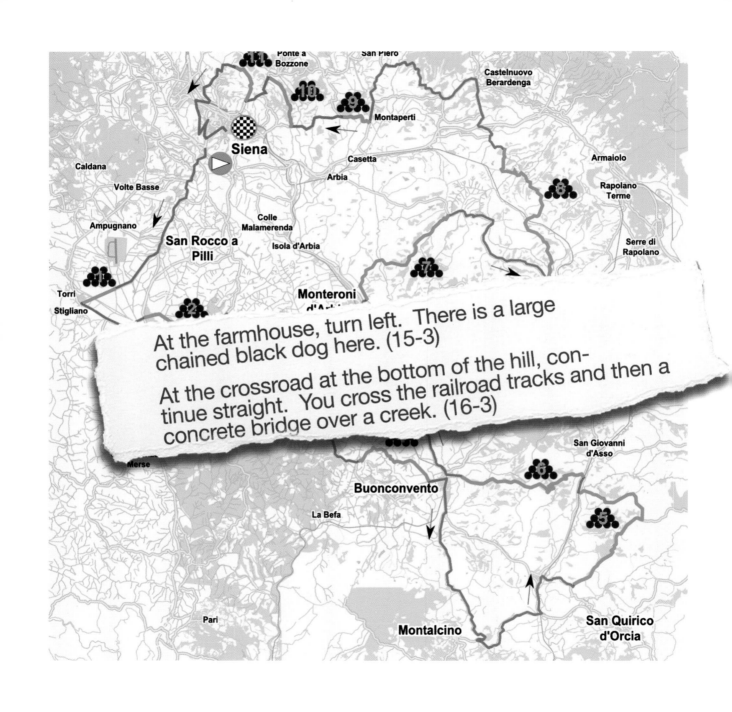

At the farmhouse, turn left. There is a large chained black dog here. (15-3)

At the crossroad at the bottom of the hill, continue straight. You cross the railroad tracks and then a concrete bridge over a creek. (16-3)

"Hey, lady, the cell phone lot is on your right—move it!" our bus driver yelled repeatedly at the car in front of her. She hammered on the horn too and banged her hands firmly on the steering wheel for emphasis. I was stirred from my reverie of checking messages and my flight itinerary on my phone to the din of yelling and honking. I looked up to see our animated bus driver going mental on a car blocking our route to the terminal. Finally, after several minutes, a traffic cop got the car moving, and our exasperated bus driver slammed on the gas. We rocketed toward Gerald R. Ford Airport, where my friends and I were abruptly deposited. She drove off, leaving a plume of exhaust and tension in the air. Thankful to be away from that scene and ready for a vacation, I prepared for a long day of travel. My head filled with thoughts of the Italian countryside, where four girlfriends would frolic. Vacation deprivation symptoms were contained with a dose of international intrigue.

Another fortieth birthday was the catalyst for this trip. For those of you about to turn a milestone age, please feel free to steal ideas from this chapter. (There are many.) On the verge of middle age, Randee informed Theresa she wanted to go to Italy and drink wine to celebrate. I offered to help by coming along. On the flight from Detroit to Amsterdam, I ate a plastic-tinged dinner, fittingly watched *Angels & Demons*, and slept a neck-cramping three hours. Theresa, her sister Andrea and I were traveling together with the plan to meet up with Randee (Theresa's college roommate) in Rome. Once on the ground in Amsterdam, Theresa got news that Randee's flight was delayed and she would miss her connection into Rome. In a sleep-deprived daze, we lamented the news and tried to get a message to her.

Three of four made it to Rome without any trouble in the afternoon. Then we promptly scurried around to find out how to get to Siena that evening. We scratched our train ride when we learned 8:30 was the last departure and Randee would just be arriving. Always cerebral, Theresa phoned Girosole Tours and asked them to help make other transportation arrangements to our hotel. Theresa hung up and exclaimed that a private driver would take us to Siena for the low price of €300. Sometimes cost is not a factor—and this was one of those times. Our threesome practically hugged and with partial relief went up a level and found Italian fast food (pizza and draft beer). Randee's flight was scheduled in at 8:15, so we hustled back downstairs to Arrivi B, just outside of customs, to wait for Randee.

Approaching 36 hours of travel, I felt comprehensively bedraggled. My spirits lifted slightly when our Girosole driver strode in wearing a black tailored suit and introduced himself as LanFranco. We made stumbling introductions in part English and part Italian, while he grinned widely at all three of us. We started pacing around, wondering where our final companion was. It was past 9:00, and our angst grew and so did LanFranco's nervousness. We checked in at the KLM desk, asked to have Randee paged, and paced around the baggage claim. We had given up. "How did we miss her?" Theresa asked. I sighed and started to think we would have to leave without her. In a last exhausted effort, Theresa walked by a nun in the baggage area while saying a final rosary. Exactly one millisecond later, Randee appeared! Thank God I was traveling with two Catholics in Rome. She happened to be walking casually by on the way to the bathroom and noticed us. Hallelujah! Praise God! All the frescos of Mary, St. Catherine, and Madonna in Rome rejoiced at finding our friend. Hysterically happy at that moment, we had our first religious experience in the Rome baggage claim. Randee was delighted to see us not nearly as haggard with anxiety.

LanFranco, with a flourish of his arm, led us to his minibus. Four greasy, tired women piled into the van to endure two and a half hours of driving through the Italian night. I would not see the hills of Tuscany approaching, falling asleep instead with my cheek bumping the side window. I woke up with a start and an urgent need to pee. Thankfully, Andrea was in my same predicament and begged LanFranco to pull over ASAP. When no rest stops appeared for several miles, she finally ordered him to pull over. In the darkened parking lot of a closed *ristorante*, Andrea and I peed behind some bushes, much to the dismay of our driver. Feeling ridiculous, I piled back in the van with a shrug to Theresa. After another 45 minutes, Hotel Alex appeared in Siena well after midnight. LanFranco, still charming at the late hour, piled our bags into the lobby and bade us a *buena notte*.

Siena and Montalcino

I awoke to sunlight creeping through the curtains and lazily turned on the firm mattress. Still in a half sleep, I heard Theresa and Randee knock on my door, ready for *colazione*. I did not want to miss breakfast, so I slid out of bed and found some clothes. Sleeping in late on day one only exacerbates feelings of jet lag. In a quaint little lounge, we sipped strong coffee and ate yogurt and cereal while trying to shake off the transportation lag. After downing my second cup, I excused myself to the shower, much needed after the epic travels the day before. The girls had agreed to meet and explore Siena, one of many hillside, walled Tuscan towns surrounded by vineyards. With my faculties returning and revived after a shower, I walked out onto the hotel's patio and took in the expansive view of the valley. Stunning views opened up, featuring rows of vineyards dotted with cypress trees lining the farm roads and catching the morning sun. I stood and gawked, smiling broadly, before setting off on a brisk walk with the girls to the center of town, called the Campo Piazza. Like all Tuscan hill towns, the entrance is a large door in the perimeter wall, and the town's gathering spot is always a square or campo lined by cafés, pizzerias, *museos*, and historical buildings.

Locals and tourists alike milled about in the campo, and we wandered aimlessly, taking in the scene, until Theresa broke the silence and suggested we tour Siena's famous duomo. We dug in our purses for the €6 to take the tour. I considered it an Italian tithe to see St. Catherine etched on the wall in Italian marble along with hundreds of frescos and carvings. The duomo had a striking façade characterized by both dark and light contrasting layers of marble on the arches and columns. Ornate paintings and carvings were everywhere, and the stained glass windows let in shards of colored light, illuminating the faces of the popes who were sculpted in the top layers. Even the floors were adorned with etchings and pictures of the saints.

We were surrounded by all the Catholic greats: the saints, the Apostles, Mary, and, of course, Jesus! The duomo is worth hours of exploration, but, limited by time, we continued moving and next toured the attached crypt before agreeing it was time for lunch.

Back at the campo, we all ordered *pizza al taglio* at a small shop and purchased small gift bottles of extra-virgin olive oil. With pizza slices in hand, we sat on the bricked floor and consumed our lunch while watching the crowd gather. We only had an hour before our afternoon pickup. So we set about to do some power shopping. Italian fashion was our theme. Andrea looked for bombshell leather boots while Theresa, Randee, and I perused sunglasses. In an attempt to fit in, we all selected large-framed, fashionable shades and took silly photos sporting our new attitude. Not only did I look more fashionable but also the glasses hid the travel bags under my eyes. We collected Andrea after dragging her out of a leather shop and briskly walked back to Hotel Alex, where yet another handsome driver waited to transport us to the next Tuscan hill town. Our driver collected our oversized bags while handing out packets that included maps, area info, and a pre-programmed cell phone. We set off again in another minibus toward Montalcino 40 kilometers away. The scenery along the way was simply magnificent.

Montalcino was equally as scenic as Siena (just slightly smaller). We arrived at our boutique hotel, La Palazzo, where we stayed for two nights. Our driver passed us off to the hotelier. She greeted us and showed us to our rooms through a maze of hallways, steps, and doors, many barely taller than my 5'9" frame. We did not linger in our cozy rooms and got lost trying to find our way back out to the street-side entrance. Our food and wine tour would commence in earnest today. It began with a café serving a typical Tuscan *spontino*, a variety of cured meats and cheese. We washed it down with a very strong double espresso that quickly became an afternoon tradition on the trip. A stocked wine shop was next, and we tried our first sips of the region's famous Brunello, along with a Verbena, the best of that grouping. Our walking tour continued into the afternoon, as we happened upon *il mercati*, a market with open-air booths and kiosks featuring local artists. I met one artist, Sylvia, who proudly displayed her original watercolor paintings. I purchased three small reprints of her work, vowing to keep one and give the other two away for gifts.

After checking the time and watching the afternoon sun sink lower, we finally walked through the gates and outside of the town to do our warm-up ring walk per our typed itinerary. Our late start made the views even more dramatic as the setting sun cast a glow on the Brunello vineyards all around us. The hills tested our legs; the route maps tested our comprehension. Our selected trip was a self-guided walking tour aided by transport only in between towns. I had a sheen of sweat under my clothes by the time we arrived back at the hotel after walking up a long hill back to Montalcino.

The ensuing evening was a blur of red wine, flushed cheeks, and handsome waiters who loved American girls! We had selected Les Barriques for dinner. Davido, a young raven-haired waiter, attended to our every need. He helped us choose a bottle of red called La Fortuna, saying that it must breathe, and then pouring the wine into a decanter and swirling it around. I received an excellent wine education on that trip, and it began that evening when Davido explained, "The reds need to open up and breathe before they hit the tongue." Along with the excellent wine, an order of bruschetta appeared, paired with pasta and a variety of sauces that we passed around and shared. Another bottle was opened, and we ate, laughed, and chatted about our first full day. The mood was festive, as the small restaurant filled with our voices and laughter from our table and the table next to ours.

Two young Italian women visiting from Milan were seated next to us, and they too had been enjoying wine, conversation, and the views. I tried to strike up a conversation with them, and despite our broken Italian and English, we were able to share a toast to birthdays. The Milan girls were celebrating a birthday. We explained our trip was in honor of Randee's fortieth. As we leaned toward their table, glasses raised, we toasted to birthday celebrations. The two girls proudly exclaimed together in English, "We drink beer, we drink wine, we are drank!" We enthusiastically clinked glasses, followed by shots of Limoncello. We snickered at the idea of being drank. Drank must be the level after drunk. The festive atmosphere continued late into the night. Before we took our leave, Davido introduced us to the chef (Angelo), and we exchanged a hug and the traditional double kiss before saying goodbye to the drank birthday girls.

To Sant'Antimo

The bustling street below meant we would not sleep in. Over a disappointing prepackaged croissant breakfast and lukewarm coffee, we looked at the maps and directions for our day's hike to the Abbey of Sant'Antimo. Hungry for real food, we packed for the day's hike and agreed to buy supplies for a picnic lunch along the way. The walking route started at Montalcino's Fort, which served as a post 100 years ago to defend against oncoming marauders. Across the street was a small shop: an *alimentari* stocked with sausages hanging in rows, stacks of cured meats, and wheels of cheese all calling out to hungry patrons like us. A jovial Italian man helped us assemble a feast including salami, pecorino cheese, and a *piccolo panne* (small loaf of bread). We stowed our edible treasures in our packs and set off north from the fort toward more Tuscan countryside.

We skirted the busy road that led into the city and tried to follow the typed directions from Girosole Tours. Our route took us quickly out of town and alongside vineyards, then through a heavily shaded, forested area. Thankfully, the trail opened back out into the sun, warming us while continuing past agritourism farms on a two-track dirt road. We consulted our directions often, and to our delight, we walked up a ridge that had great views and found a sign that read Pombaia Winery, subtitled

"Free Tasting" in English. The decision to check it out was unanimous. We walked down the driveway to the din of three dogs barking and rang the bell at the entrance to the tasting room. A bald, clean-shaven man introduced himself as Roberto, and he unlocked the door and let us in. We explained our desire to try a few wines and also purchase a bottle to go with our *pranza* (lunch). The quaint Old World tasting room held a picnic table in the middle, with bottles lining the stone walls on racks and large wooden aging casks on the opposite side. We tried three of his reds before settling on a bottle to go. Calling thank-yous after using his *bagno*, we strode back out the driveway. While walking, Andrea fashioned a creative carrying device for the wine box. She used string and looped it through and around the box handle to make a shoulder sling to transport our precious liquid.

We walked an hour down the two-track roads toward a row of winery buildings and a cute hamlet, where we spied a perfect lunch

picnic spot. We picnicked under an olive tree and sipped wine directly from the bottle. It was an idyllic and lazy lunch experience until we noted the time. We would not make the last bus back to Montalcino from Sant'Antimo, the final stop on our trek. We gulped the last drops of wine and secured our leftovers. We urgently hurried down the path, past stone storage facilities and bins of freshly picked grapes ready for processing. After another mile, we started to descend, opening up a valley view to a stone abbey and its bell tower. My most vivid memories of Tuscany will always conjure up hillside vineyards, stone cathedrals, wine, and churches!

Well past late, we toured the abbey and got a free history lesson: the church was made famous for its prayers in the form of Gregorian chants. The monks had the day off, so the chants were not live but piped in as we sat in the polished wooden pews. We spent a quiet moment paying respects watching the candles flicker off the aging stone walls and windows. We broke the reverie by leaving the abbey and walking up the final section of road to the small town—to learn we had indeed missed the last bus back to Montalcino. We milled around the bus station near the country road and discussed our options: we could call and reschedule our cooking class or try to call to get a ride. Taxis do not just randomly cruise by in Tuscany.

Randee spied two American girls with a rental car nearby. She winked at me as if to say I should go talk to them and beg a ride. Andrea and Theresa agreed with a directional nod: *Why not?* I walked casually over, said "Hi," and asked, "Any chance you two are driving toward Montalcino?" "We are heading that way," they replied. Looking into their compact back seat, they said, "It will be a tight squeeze with four of you back there!" I waved for Theresa, Andrea, and Randee to come over and happily introduced Kim and Sandy as our miracle for the day. It was indeed a tight squeeze to fit four American asses in that compact's back seat. For the short trip, I sat on

the girls' laps, my head/shoulders protruding over the console while our new friends drove. We thanked them profusely and marveled at our luck—back in town a full hour before our cooking class.

Cooking with Passion

My experiences left me a passionate believer that Italian food and wine undoubtedly possess magical qualities. So, besides absorbing lessons in Brunello winemaking, the region's superstar, it seemed fitting to squeeze in a cooking class. We met up with Chef Teresa (pronounced Ter-ee-zzzza). She had asked us to meet her in the town square at 6 sharp. After introductions, she launched into Italian foodie history while walking toward her apartment. She had stopped at the market for ingredients and vegetables from her native Rome. We had to walk up several flights of stairs to reach her third-floor apartment and earn our dinner. Once inside, I took a moment to sneak a peek out her open window. It was an amazing view of the setting sun behind patchwork vineyards and three of Teresa's D-cup bras hanging on a laundry line. We were introduced to her roommate. Then the four of us sat and listened to more history of indigenous foods of Italy, which ironically did NOT include tomatoes. Teresa was quite proud of her Roman heritage, continuing to gain flare and steam as she spoke.

Our group of five now moved into her compact kitchen. She explained we would make a group of appetizers, including roasted peppers and fennel salad, then a variety of sauces for pasta, and finishing with a mushroom risotto. She explained, "You will learn to cook with passion like the Romans did." Under her watchful eye, we became her choppers, stirrers, tasters, de-seeders, and kitchen hands. I rolled up my sleeves and happily sipped my glass of red wine, which never seemed to go empty, refilled by a magical Italian fairy that entire evening. Our chef got my trip mates Theresa and Randee started on the basic three sauces: Aglione (tomato with garlic), basic tomato (puréed tomatoes), and tomato chunks with onion.

She was adamant about not mixing onion and garlic in the same sauce. She had a firm belief the two distinct flavors competed with each other.

Somehow, Andrea and I were assigned the most difficult task in the cooking repertoire: peeling the roasted peppers. Our task was to peel and seed two roasted red peppers. As we took off the peppers' outer layers, our fingers became messy and sticky. I turned my pepper over to get a grip, and all the tiny seeds seeped out near the stem into the bottom of the pan. Ever watchful, Chef Teresa leaned over about an inch from my ear and said, "Oh, this is most unfortunate." Andrea and I looked at each other, swallowed hard, and continued on our task. Teresa handed

me a small spoon to scoop out the seeds and continued on with seed warnings saying, "You must not let any seeds get in the serving bowl. No seeds in my peppers; it is like a knife in my heart!" She continued, adding for emphasis, "When I go to a restaurant and order pepper salad, if I find one seed—just one seed—I walk out without reservation!" Was she serious, or was this part of her class performance? I wondered while raising a brow. I think the pressure was too much for Andrea because she took a big gulp from her wine glass. I wasn't feeling all that confident either after the diatribe about seeds. Theresa and Randee looked in my direction displaying smirks and suppressing grins. Our chef certainly had a flare for the dramatic, like many Romans I experienced on that trip. I convinced myself I wasn't going to get thrown out of a cooking class that I had paid for.

Thankfully, we had a moment to gather our wits as she called us all over to see the sauces being stirred and attended to by Randee and Theresa. We hovered near the bubbling pot and dipped our pinky fingers gingerly into the sauce, tasting a tiny bit on the spoon. Teresa piped in with a "No, no, no. Taste it with passion; you don't take a little bit like that; you need to really try it!" She demonstrated by spooning up sauce, dunking her finger in, and

slurping up a mouthful. Our Theresa did not need to be told twice. She followed Chef Teresa's lead with a similar enthusiastic taste. Then we all followed suit to the delight of our chef. Chef Teresa looked at Andrea after her taste and asked, "Andrea, what do you think? What does it need?" Andrea paused, looked upward, and continued to ponder for a moment too long. Teresa gave up on her offering any suggestions and said impatiently, "You think about it and you write me." I watched this exchange and suppressed a belly laugh, wondering whether Andrea and I could pass her seed test yet to come.

It was Theresa and Randee's turn to laugh next as Andrea and I finally de-seeded the peppers and presented our pan to Teresa. She was pleased. She cut them into strips, added olive oil, and placed them on crusty bread with bits of coarse salt on top. All four of us bit into this pepper bruschetta  and closed our eyes in the ecstasy of taste! It was rapturous, and all my labor and stress melted away. I grabbed another and savored the flavor of the peppery olive oil and the richness of the roasted pepper. The pepper pressure from earlier was lost in my memory, and I continued to sip, feeling a glow radiating from my cheeks.

I was full on peppers and fennel salad, but three sauces with pasta were yet to come. Our chef sat us down at her table and filled our pasta bowls with the first of three. Moving around the table, she looked directly at me as she scooped a heaping spoonful into my dish, "For you, truck driver portion!" We laughed and wondered how she knew about my tapeworm eating habits. Bowls and glasses continued to be filled at epic rates. After two more rounds of pasta, sauce, and wine, we were approaching drank and noticed our hostess seemed tipsy as well. She and her roommate had been drinking right along with us. Teresa called in her roommate, topped off glasses, and moved to the stove with a flourish of her hotpad.

She completed our cooking lesson by laboring over a pan of mushroom risotto that took much stirring, adding, and restirring. I had completely lost focus, so I let Randee and Theresa handle the mixing and the furious scramble to write the recipe down. Finally, they added the dried mushrooms, and our final entrée was ready. It was on par with or better than the peppers, rich and creamy—the mushroom flavor exquisitely

subtle. I kept thinking we couldn't possibly try another thing when Teresa appeared around the corner with a homemade bottle of Limoncello and Orangecello. Tiny shot glasses were filled with ultra-strong, citrus-infused liquors that we sipped, slipping into the next layer of liver obliteration. Our voices filled the room with toasts to health, to vacations, and also to thank Teresa for the knowledge of peppers and pasta. Time slipped beyond my grasp, and, thankfully, she ran out of things for us to drink.

We gathered our things and called more thank-yous before bumping and leaning our way out of the apartment and down the stairs in a plume of alcohol and garlic. On wobbly legs, with full bellies, we veered down the street to our hotel beds. Five hours that evening or even 10 days were not nearly enough time to taste or fully appreciate a thousand years' worth of red wine and culinary lore. The true character of the region was encapsulated that fall evening in a lively cooking class in Teresa's tiny apartment kitchen in Montalcino.

San Quirico to Hotel San Simeone, Rocca D'Orcia

The next day, I awoke with an amazing realization. No hangover. How was that possible, considering the amount of wine and booze consumption? And it turned out nobody else felt awful. Did Italian wine have a magic elixir inside each bottle? We did get some extra rest, though, before setting off on our day's walk. In our morning huddle, we agreed to skip the hotel breakfast to find better fare at a café. We piled our luggage on the front steps near the street and checked out with our hostess. To our dismay, she scurried up behind us and shoved four packaged, fruit-filled croissants into our hands. We waited until she was out of sight and promptly placed the stale pastries in the first garbage receptacle. Instead, we spotted a café on the street that beckoned us with a table for four basking in the morning sunlight. We sat and ordered coffee and lattés and fresh pastries with jam. We sipped under the sun, our mood only interrupted once when Randee tipped over reaching for her backpack, tumbling out of her chair and onto the stone street! The entire café and street passersby gave us a look, wondering what caused the ruckus. We helped her up and dusted her off, figuring that signaled time to depart on our walk toward San Quirico.

We were tested again by the Girosole hand-typed directions, which led us across pastures, turning at trees or tractors with warnings of stray dogs at certain farms. Theresa and Randee took turns interpreting the directions. We started out much the same as the previous day, but once through the arch and outside the walls of Montalcino, we turned northeast. We descended the trail, crossed the main road, then walked through a long series of connected pastures, vineyards, and farmland. Along the way, true to a note in the directions, a dog joined and followed us on the trail. We decided to name the shepherd mix Brunello, after the grapes he protected. Crews of locals were harvesting grapes near the trail. We watched them fill bin after bin of the precious wine-making fruit.

A herd of sheep grazed over the ridge beyond the trail to the south. Brunello continued with us for several miles. He interrupted our reverent walk when he spotted two baby lambs straying from the flock. A crisis erupted. Randee shrieked, and I spun around in horror as Brunello sniffed the lamb and then launched into a snarling attack, taking one lamb by the body and the nape and shaking it violently! We ran toward the scene, screaming for the dog to stop. Thankfully, he stopped his pursuit and ran away from our loud protests. The little lambs were bleating in fright while my heart pounded, hoping they were okay. On closer inspection, we saw no blood spurting out the jugular, and the lambs remained on their feet. We exhaled a huge sigh of relief. The two babies followed us down the trail for a while, finally veering off toward the herd and the

safety of their families. With the crisis behind us, we sought shade and sat on the ground to eat our purchases of pizza and sandwiches. We sipped wine again and watched bipolar Brunello swim in a nearby pond to cool off. It was much warmer than the previous day. Sweat beaded on my forehead and ran down my back and into my swoobies (sweaty boobs). We walked up and down slopes for eight miles, wearing Andrea out in the process. She complained of sore feet and toes, and although she lagged behind, she made it to the next city of San Quirico. She plunked down at the first bar.

Another stone archway marked the portal into the city, and the town square was dotted with cafés and bars. We meandered toward a sculpture park before our pickup, admiring immaculately maintained garden hedges. The sculptures were white marble, the subjects predominately naked, intertwined bodies. We raised a brow at one in particular that featured two lovers wrapped around each other in an erotic embrace. Soon after photos with the lovers in the background, our driver Andreas arrived with the minibus. He drove us to our hotel for the night, just a short 10 minutes away.

San Simeone was striking, literally built into the side of a stone cliff in the village of Rocca D'Orcia. We moved up a significant notch on the lodging star chart. Each room's door was fitted into the rock face, our rooms a combination of luxury and Old World charm. A beautiful pool one level down from the rooms was situated on the resort edge, with a far-reaching view over patchwork vineyards. Our driver had taken our bags to our rooms while we met our host Sergio. We convened in his lobby for our afternoon espresso and made small chat until we slipped away to find showers. Andrea became Sergio's instant BFF. They continued to chat about restaurants and sights we needed to see on our visit. Three days in, we switched roommates. Andrea and Randee bunked together, and I shared with Theresa for two nights, hoping the elder sister snored less.

Andrea reported back that the village had only two restaurants, and Sergio's brother owned one of the two, which was closed on that night. We were tired, so we headed to Il Borgo for an early dinner, which was memorable from the start: a huge white mountain dog lay across the stone porch entrance, serving as a lazy greeter. The pooch eventually shuffled off to find the owner. A jovial female hostess appeared and served us a complete Italian meal of pastas and wine. Theresa opted for something different, ordering

a piccolo steak that came out looking like half a roast on her plate. We all grinned as she sliced into her supersized protein feast. We splurged and ordered a bottle of Brunello, which our host suggested by year. The meal was delicious but uncommonly short. Choosing not to linger over another bottle, we walked up the steep path back to the poolside vista and slid into lounge chairs to watch the darkness blanket the vineyards below us.

Bagno Vignoni Hike

Loving our idyllic retreat, we settled in and thankfully spent two nights at San Simeone. I was delighted to actually unpack a portion of my bag and relax. Even so, staring out at the Tuscan hillsides for too long made me restless. Andrea, however, was content to muse and linger, taking up a perch with pencil and paper to sketch the scene. We breakfasted together, remarking how divine the coffee, fruit, and fresh bread tasted. Lingering over the meal with perfect amounts of sunlight and breeze, we spied a clock reading 11. Randee, Theresa, and I decided to take ourselves on a hike to Bagno Vignoni, legendary for its natural hot springs, baths, and pools. Andrea gave us a smile and a wave as we walked down the steep path to the River D'Orcia and again tried to decipher hiking directions.

We were instructed to cross a shallow river. True enough, we did so without swamping our shoes. Directly above us was an ailing old footbridge along with another to the south (a travertine bridge), both bombed during the Nazi occupation. The Girosole directions, as a bonus, provided historic tidbits. After passing the river, the trail continued past an old mining operation. Up ahead, we noticed a large line of cliffs with mineral calcifications covering the surface from the constant runoff from the spring water. We reached the outskirts of the famous historical village, once frequented by a vacationing Pope Pius II, Santa Caterina, and Lorenzo the Magnificent. The Spa at Vignoni still exists, and modern-day tourists experience much the same treatments as our predecessors.

At the heart of the village is the town square, or a large rectangular tank of sixteenth-century origin that contains the original source of water, from the underground aquifer that supplies the pools and hot springs. We walked up and through several levels of pools all colored a unique frosty-aquamarine. Tourists of all nationalities sat on the edges and soaked in the water with the sun on their shoulders. The village surrounded the landmark, which was lined with pretty potted flowers along the tank's wall and across the patios of each café.

After five miles of hiking, we settled on a stop at La Terrazza, a green-canopied eatery. We dined outside in the shade while devouring green and caprese salads. Theresa suggested we stop on the way back at one of the lower pools to soak our feet and ankles. With five more miles of walking ahead of us it was a brilliant idea.

We may have lingered too long because dark clouds loomed overhead with distant views of Rocca D'Orcia. At the river, a few raindrops fell, so we kept moving briskly. The last section was a steep climb back up our rock. The rain came faster, and thunder rumbled. I kept moving and slipped on my raincoat. Theresa pushed on even faster, trying a shortcut through a grove of olive trees, only to scramble over a stone wall and through a hedge. I declined that chess move, instead taking the long way around. Avoiding the shrubbery obstacle, I waited under the town's archway entrance. The rain continued as we half jogged the last steps, threw open our doors, and rushed inside as the thunder gathered. A full-fledged driving rain fell for a half hour while I safely watched from my window.

Our gastronomic delights would continue that evening a mere block away at Sergio's brother's restaurant. Alessio and his wife Sarah took impeccable care of us, attending to another well-above-average dining experience. We were the only group in the restaurant, confirming we had indeed missed the busy tourist season. My glass was initially filled with a Tuscan Chianti, then we were instructed to take a plate to a buffet-style appetizer table filled with thinly sliced meats and varieties of cheeses. To follow were more wine and plates of cannelloni and tortellini stuffed and covered with fresh sauces and more cheese. I was not counting calories, and I am not afraid of carbs! The four of us enjoyed chatting with Alessio and Sarah during dinner, and, eventually, we ushered them over to share some wine. To end our meal, we posed for photos with our hosts.

Pienza and Vino Tour

It was Thursday (*Giovedi* in Italian). We took a break from the long hikes to tour Pienza and wineries instead. Andrea said a teary goodbye to Sergio and Felicia; she liked the slower pace and quiet at San Simeone. She presented her pencil drawing as a gift to our hosts. They were thrilled and asked us all to sign the sketch, even promising to find a frame to set it off in their reception area. After a round of goodbye double kisses, our driver showed up (Andreas again) to whisk us off toward Pienza. He dropped us (and our growing pile of baggage) in front of Hotel Piccolo La Valle Pienza.

We had only an hour to explore because I had attempted to book a wine tour on the Italian cell phone through LanFranco. We power shopped before pickup and learned that Pienza was designed by a late pope to be the perfect city. It was darn close to perfect. The quaint and picturesque shops, boutiques, and open-air markets appealed to our senses and pocketbooks. Local cheeses were stacked everywhere alongside local meats, rows of wine, and gourmet coffee. Another duomo marked the central spot in the city, and the narrow streets were laden with culinary products calling for us to buy now and often.

The girls began a shopping spree while I was lured into a paper shop full of cards, paper gifts, and handmade journals. I walked out with two new journals and an espresso cup set. We also found an *alementari* for lunch to-go items like bread, cheese, and cured ham or sausage. We made it back to the hotel to meet LanFranco, only to discover he had sent his friend Rocco instead. Rocco did not speak English, so I struggled to confirm when each tour would

start. I stuffed the cell phone into my pocket, hoping it would not ring and fearing more instructions in rapid Italian.

We piled in Rocco's sedan, trusting he would deliver us to our vino adventure. He pulled up in front of Casa Nova De Neri Winery, and we realized we had walked through these vineyards on the way to San Quirico. Rocco hand-signaled to me that he would wait by the car. I confirmed, and we went in and sampled four reds, ending with a superbly aged Brunello. I purchased one bottle of Brunello (1998) in a decorative wooden box etched with the winery logo. I watched in amusement as my three friends settled on starting a larger box that held up to nine bottles. Rocco opened the trunk and motioned for us to stow our purchases, rattling something off in Italian.

The adventure ramped when I realized Rocco was heading toward Montalcino, where we had just spent two days. I attempted to tell Rocco, "*No, No, Montalcino … Vino tour a quindici at Fattoria de Barbi.*" He stopped the car near the fortress, shrugged at me, and explained he would return in two hours. Frustrated, I paced in the parking lot, not sure what to do, realizing the cell phone in my pocket was of no use now. Theresa suggested we make the best of our time by getting directions to Montalcino's church, where a prized fresco by Italian painter Vanni was on display. The stroll calmed us, and we milled around in yet another immaculate, ornate cathedral brimming with artifacts and art. Just as we were walking back outside, the cell phone in my pocket rang. We froze, everyone acknowledging my fear of answering it because of the language barrier. I nervously punched the green talk button and managed a weak "*Pronto.*" The voice of LanFranco came across the line. I sighed in relief. The girls huddled around me while I conversed with him in my primary language. He apologized for the miscommunication with Rocco and told us to meet him near the fort. Our enthusiasm returned when LanFranco took us to a local wine shop where the owner talked about the Brunellos and what years were best and offered us tastes of several. I fell in wine-love with this velvety smooth, rich red while more bottles were purchased and another box (made to fit six) was added to our inventory. Rocco arrived again and carried our purchases to the car. LanFranco confirmed Rocco would take us to Fattoria de Barbi, then back to Pienza later. With a plan and our transport determined, we relaxed into more touring and tasting.

Fattoria Barbi was a bustling farm, makers of Brunello, Rosso, and olive oil. We glommed on to a group tour of the Fattoria and entered the tasting room for a sampling of the three main wines produced there. First, our host filled our logoed glasses with a Rosso, a simple red table wine. Next, we tasted a flavorful and elegant 2001 Brunello, and, last, we savored the ultra-smooth finish of a 1998 Brunello. Our tour continued through the cellar, where small, medium, and large French oak barrels lined every room, each labeled with the harvest year and type of wine. The Brunello and wine history lesson became more intriguing when an older gentleman named Jacopo shared how winemaking began at that farm. He showed us to another part of the cellar called the reserve collection that houses about 100 bottles from each year, labeled and stacked. He pointed out a bottle saved from the late 1890s, well past its drinking time. A layer of dust covered all the bottles, and Jacopo explained that the area was reserved for owners to sell or drink for special occasions.

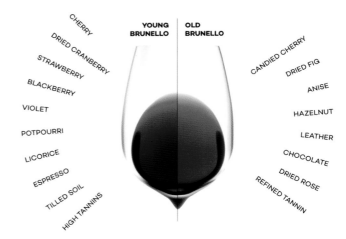

We followed Jacopo through the cellar. He explained the most optimal time to uncork a Brunello was in its tenth year from harvest. Italian regulations require that Brunellos be bottled after aging a minimum of five years. Filled with knowledge and back at the retail center of the farm, the four of us settled on more purchases. A popular choice, we selected the '98 Brunello and several bottles of extra-virgin olive oil. Laden with more wine and yet another box, we filled Rocco's entire back hatch and set off for Pienza in the early evening. Rocco encountered an Italian version of road rage on the dirt road entrance as we left the *fattoria*. He came face-to-face and car-to-car with an old woman as he turned to make his way out. She blocked our way and gave us a disgusted look (Italian stink-eye). Rocco quickly backed up to let her pass, and as he did, Theresa muttered the word *malocchia*, the Italian word for "stink-eye," meaning to curse someone. Traditionally, when the word is said, many Italians respond by pointing their fingers toward the ground three times to avoid the curse of bad luck. We made the motion and noticed Rocco smiling and laughing. He seemed thankful we were on his side.

Back safely in Pienza, we explored and continued shopping. We found a leather shop for handbags and purses for gifts. The sunset (the pink hour) was as sweet as the gelato that evening. We leaned on the outside wall to gaze at the hills around us turn from green to pink to purple and then fade to dark. We collected more items for our bulging bags, including vacuum-packed Pecorino cheeses. Andrea shopped prolifically: her shopping bag held leather goods, cheese, dried mushrooms (the kind we had used in the risotto making), and handmade pastas. After a successful shopping stint, we tried to find a restaurant for dinner, but most had chalked signs announcing they were full. Unfortunately, we had to settle for a subpar fast-food café meal because of our lack of planning. We made a quick exit to head back and assess the day's purchases in our rooms. As Andrea spread her purchases out on her bed and started packing her extra bag, a vision materialized of a cramped drive to Rome with my cheek squashed against the window.

The Eternal City
We would trade strolling walks and vineyards for the crush of people, traffic, and world-famous tourist traps in Italy's epicenter, Rome. We had agreed it was worth the battle to see the Vatican, the Coliseum, and the Forum. On Friday we elevated our stress levels immediately as the process began to load the minibus with all our purchases (70% of the pile was Andrea's). Andrea had her luggage plus an extra duffel

bag with all the newly purchased goodies. I had purposely shopped light, making room for a single wine box in my duffel. Andreas packed us up, ever patient and charming, walking with a slight limp. He shared a story about spraining his ankle in a futbol match the week prior. He talked us through the drive to Rome, pointing out village names and their wines, and on to *l'autostrada* in a glut of traffic.

We arrived during a public transportation strike, so the metros were not running. With traffic chaos all around us, we unloaded our crap on the steps of Hotel Polo near Villa Borghese and plopped down in the lobby as Theresa went to check in. We paid Andreas and said goodbye. After five minutes, Theresa strode up, red faced, with a rushed explanation of how they had booked only one room for us! We all exhaled expletives and watched the clerks at the front desk frantically try to find us other lodging. I sat on my duffel with my chin in my hands, listening in on the new arrangements being made.

Between our travel agent and Hotel Polo, we were to be sent across town to Hotel Diana in central Rome, near the termini, just north of the Coliseum. We waited another hour; the business of the city had everyone feeling nervous.

A new driver showed up in an Alfa Romeo. He looked at us and the pile of luggage and rolled his eyes. He moved with pace and loaded our loot as best he could, slamming the trunk shut. The wine boxes and backpacks were stowed on our laps. I cringed with the stopping and starting in the traffic and Andrea's attempt to make small talk with the driver. Even her eyelash flutter and charms were no match for his mood on strike day. I sat quietly until we rolled up to Hotel Diana to receive a slap on the other cheek. They did not have our reservation either, explained the young gentleman at the desk. The travel agent had not called, nor had they heard from Hotel Polo. Theresa was on the verge of a bitch attack, so I hung around with some calming words until they finally asked for our passports.

We waited some more, and thank Mary again, they found two rooms for us—the last two! Four relieved women took the lift up and collapsed on the twin beds to gather our wits and plan the afternoon. Happy the hotel debacle was behind us, we felt excitement return. We spread out a giant map of Rome on one of the beds and made a plan that included the Coliseum, the Forum, and Palatine Hill.

Theresa was eager to stretch her legs and walk off the previous anxiety. I agreed, happily packing my satchel for some power sightseeing. Once out on the busy streets, we had to convince Randee she was heading the wrong way even after the map session. Theresa snagged her from crossing a street with oncoming traffic, with her head buried and deciphering the map again. With Randee following and not leading, I glimpsed old and new Rome woven together in a weird modern twist of history. New buildings lined the street, and ahead, the corner of the Coliseum came into view. I tried not to think about Russell Crowe and the movie *Gladiator* in hopes of finding the real history of Rome. I gawked at the sight and tried to stay clear of cars, mopeds, and pedestrians. It was like being part of the mob heading to see the games, just like 2,000 years ago. Crossing streets was ridiculous. Intersections in Rome are all roundabouts with no signs or traffic lights.

Safely across and on the perimeter of the Coliseum, we watched the sea of humanity gather. We voted yes to Randee's suggestion to hire a guide. I tried to focus on the architecture instead of the street performers dressed as Roman soldiers or as emperors like Nero or Augustus. The sheer size and height of the architecture were impressive, punctuated with signature archways. We were guided by the flowing and powerful voice of Valentina, who did a great job explaining Rome's privately owned artifact. Yes, the Coliseum is not owned by the government. She bypassed the 45-minute wait line with her credentials, which made the €20 feel like a better value. We followed her steps and the rise and fall of her Roman accent. She showed her swagger by telling off another tour guide who "clearly wasn't doing it right," waving him back into position emphatically. I planned to do exactly as Valentina directed, following along like a good tourist should.

She ushered us inside the amphitheater so we could take in its architecture, the many levels, and the huge travertine blocks that held it all together. Though much of the original metal and marble had been excavated, it retained a grandeur that would make any history professor blush. Valentina spoke about ancient Rome and her industrious ancestors, who built things on such a grand scale. She doled out juicy details

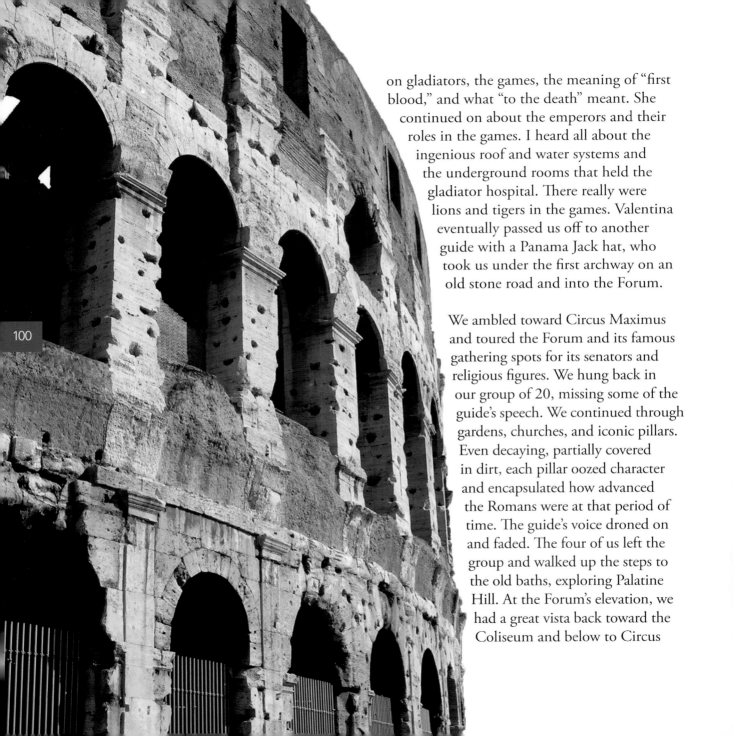

on gladiators, the games, the meaning of "first blood," and what "to the death" meant. She continued on about the emperors and their roles in the games. I heard all about the ingenious roof and water systems and the underground rooms that held the gladiator hospital. There really were lions and tigers in the games. Valentina eventually passed us off to another guide with a Panama Jack hat, who took us under the first archway on an old stone road and into the Forum.

We ambled toward Circus Maximus and toured the Forum and its famous gathering spots for its senators and religious figures. We hung back in our group of 20, missing some of the guide's speech. We continued through gardens, churches, and iconic pillars. Even decaying, partially covered in dirt, each pillar oozed character and encapsulated how advanced the Romans were at that period of time. The guide's voice droned on and faded. The four of us left the group and walked up the steps to the old baths, exploring Palatine Hill. At the Forum's elevation, we had a great vista back toward the Coliseum and below to Circus

Maximus, the stadium for chariot races: capacity 200,000 raving fans. Circus Maximus was as impressive as the Coliseum. After several hours of touring, we walked out and up the steps to a busy street, past a marble statue of a naked man and his horse.

A cold Peroni and a slice of pizza made a nice bookmark before venturing on. With so much to see, we did not linger, though I could certainly feel my legs and feet tiring. I was in heaven with pizza available at every corner; the simple and fresh ingredients made it all the more appealing. Double cheese is clearly an American add-on to pizza. Another detailed map session transpired over pizza consumption. Next stops: the Pantheon and Piazza Navona. We walked again, confirming a cab would not be a better choice in the traffic. Dusk had settled when we arrived at the piazza and the Pantheon in dim light. The majestic structure loomed toward the sky; I was unable to see the top with my neck tilted all the way back. The Pantheon was built in AD 118–125 and yet was the most preserved of any of the ancient Roman structures. The Pantheon was not crumbling and dirty but pristine and polished. Each of the main pillars that lined the entrance seemed twice as big as what I had just seen at the Forum. It was the largest masonry dome ever built, and its single oculus at 30 feet in diameter (the circular opening at the top) let in the only source of light in the temple. As I walked into the ancient temple, my sense of awe continued at our ancestors' construction abilities. A neighboring fountain in the piazza gurgled as we ended our self-tour and continued down less traveled streets in the direction of Piazza Navona.

We completed a jam-packed day with gelatos, street-side confessions, and a lucky stumble onto the Trevi Fountain. From the Pantheon, a short walk put us in the midst of Piazza Navona, which was doubly busy from both an artist market and a Sant'Agnese church service. Piazza Navona is known as a baroque delight, highlighted by the Fountain of Fuimi, designed by Bernini. Licking gelatos, we strolled around and shopped the watercolors and sketches by local artists. I lapped at my caramel cream gelato and then tasted Theresa's double chocolate and Andrea's berry-licious. The church event was gathering steam. A temporary stage had been erected for musicians, with a lectern for the bishop, who delivered a short homily. We watched as small benches became miniature confessionals; priests spoke to their members, praying with them.

Approaching 10:00, we started the long walk to Hotel Diana. Everyone was fatigued, but our guiding angel led us right into a piazza that held the Trevi Fountain. A crowd had gathered around the impressive sculpture and cascading waters. Theresa had read about the legend of the coin toss into the Trevi, so she ushered us toward the water in the front pool. We pushed our way through hundreds of onlookers. Theresa instructed us to take a coin, turn away from the fountain, then toss it over our shoulders into the fountain. Legend says that if you complete this task, you are destined to return to the Eternal City. My contribution to the Trevi Fountain was a US penny. I wondered about my return with my meager investment. After Randee and Andrea tossed in token coins, we walked around the edge and window-shopped the brightly lit stores displaying Italian national team soccer jerseys. Italy had just won the men's World Cup. It was almost midnight when we returned. On the seventh-floor veranda, we spread out our map again to plan for our last day in Rome.

Religious Icons and Losing Andrea

Religion and art are melded in Rome, most noticeably at the Vatican. Great artists such as Michelangelo, Bernini, and Raphael felt compelled to create inspiring art and sculpture for the world's most powerful church. Whether you're religious or not, the Vatican is an opportunity to see grandeur, decadence, and art—but be prepared to find out whether God has blessed you with the virtue of patience. I waited in an enormous line (much longer than the Madonna concert in Chicago) for the privilege. We were up early to take our turn with thousands of others to enter the Vatican Museum, the Sistine Chapel, and St. Peter's Basilica. With so much religious and art content, we again opted for a guide and the silly-looking earpieces to listen to the tour program. As a point of comparison, I had been to Le Louvre in Paris, and the Vatican held an even greater amount of iconic sculpture and art. The ornate carvings, art, and frescos everywhere were stylistically unlike anything I had seen before. Each pope had been carefully carved and their personas lined the Vatican halls, watching us move carefully about their sacred space. It was crowded, and our guide ushered us through quickly, so we enjoyed a rushed version of magnificence.

In the Sistine Chapel, the holiest part of the Vatican, I strained to be still and look up at the famous ceiling. Pushy tourists bumped me from either side. I felt more claustrophobic than reverent. There was an entire room dedicated to Michelangelo's work: the *Pietà*, gold-rimmed tapestries, woven maps, and marbled heads or feet on pedestals, Achilles' heel among them. Although we had four hours to see the art in the Vatican, a month would have been better to admire the collection. The basilica was last on our tour, and its enormity was only part of the grandeur—every inch of space and every piece of marble contribute to a masterpiece. Inside and out, the Vatican provided my camera with impeccable subject matter. The blue skies set off the marble, and I snapped heavenly shots of the saints on the roof of the basilica

and lining the square. This section may be best depicted with my photographs instead of my feeble attempts to describe the scene. Ironically, the last photo in my Vatican album was a photo of me taking a swig from a Peroni bottle, the basilica's spire over my shoulder.

The morning had quickly turned to afternoon, and after yet another slice of pizza, we purchased Metro tickets to head toward the Spanish Steps. The Metro was just as crowded as the Sistine Chapel. Theresa, Randee, and I stood together near the exit doors, holding rails in and out of stops. Andrea squeezed into the back of our car to a bench seat to rest her feet. Her brief moment of relief was short-lived. We confirmed we would exit at the next stop. The train stopped, the doors opened, and a wave of people pushed their way out of the compartment. Andrea, not an aggressive type, got stuck in the melee. Instead of stepping off the train with us, she stood an inch away from the closing door as three pairs of panicked eyes watched her continue down the tracks. She rode out of sight. The three of us burst into conversation about what to do. We waited at the stop for quite a while, thinking she would double back and meet us. After 30 minutes, Theresa suggested we move on and that her little sister would fend for herself that afternoon. Theresa admitted, "I'm not sure if Andrea remembers the name of our hotel or has a key!"

Slightly worried but unwilling to end our touring, the three of us embarked on an afternoon shopping adventure. An espresso near the Spanish Steps ramped up our energy levels. We skipped admiring the famous terraced steps and fountain leading up to the church, the Trinita dei Monti. Instead, Italian fashion and shoes called to Randee and Theresa. We muddled through the language barrier, having fun at a leather shop where the clerk insisted she must put the gloves on our hands. She motioned for Theresa to put her elbow on a padded circular area on the counter, explaining to extend her hand. The clerk slipped the black driving gloves onto Theresa's hands and pushed them down over her fingers. Theresa nodded in affirmation while I looked at the purses, handbags, and journal covers.

Our next stop was at a two-level shoe store, where both Randee and Theresa spent some time trying on stylish shoe-boots with Western flare. Amused, I watched as Theresa and Randee paraded around trying on pair after pair and checking them out in the mirror. The woman waiting on them was getting a workout. She eventually walked away while they discussed which pairs to purchase. My travel budget was busted, so I abstained from dropping another €100. Both of my gal pals purchased a pair or two. During the checkout process, the clerk

called to them in irritated Italian, "*Prontoooo … Prontoooo!*" Clearly, it was a version of "Hello, hello, I am waiting for you to sign your bill." The impatience and sarcasm in her voice were unmistakable. We took our leave, feeling like children who had just been sent to timeout by the shoe lady.

The last stop was back near the Trevi Fountain for the soccer jersey purchases. We thought briefly of Andrea alone before succumbing to racks of clothing. With enough shopping damage done, we collected bags, refilled water, and walked toward the hotel, hoping Andrea had done the same. Walking on exceptionally tired feet, we spied a cab off a side street and asked whether he could take us to Hotel Diana. A grungy dark-haired man nodded yes as we climbed in. I took the front seat, and within moments I realized our grave mistake. Our cabbie was crazy (or maybe all Romans drive this way), and I tried not to wince as we came within inches of pedestrians or mopeds. The car rocketed past obstacles on severely narrow cobblestone streets. He kept up the high rate of speed, banged the horn, and waved his hands when things got in his way. For good measure, he thought it was a grand idea to eat an apple in the middle of our ride, leaving one remaining hand on the wheel. In between sloppy bites, he swore *fongool* and yelled at traffic. I swiveled around in horror, asking whether my friends wanted to ride up front. They grinned in amazement as I was jolted forward again by a hard right and a narrow miss of a motorcycle coming at us. Miraculously, the Roman cab ride/video game ended with no lives lost. We were deposited, sweaty and anxious, at the hotel.

Mercifully, Andrea had found her way back too, and we reunited to share stories of our afternoons. For our last supper in Rome, we settled on a nearby restaurant with outdoor seating, and we ordered pizza once again. We savored the slices of pizza with basil, fresh tomato sauce, and mozzarella with a toast to friends over one last bottle of red. The discussion over dinner was how to get all our wine and purchases to the airport and back home. Evening fell, and we retired to our rooms to ready for an early morning pickup. We had to hire two cars for the airport transport because of the extra bags and boxes of wine. We had not only eaten and drank with passion but also shopped with passion!

Chapter Five
Trunk's Full

Spain and Pyrenees, 2010

Three busy friends and I had smartly booked 10 days for this trip to prevent a common mistake called vacation cramming.

From Project Time Off's article "Doctor's Orders: Take Your Vacation," several studies show clearly why we need to take more time off. The landmark Framingham Study, the largest and longest-running study of cardiovascular disease, revealed that men who didn't take a vacation for several years were 30% more likely to have heart attacks than men who did take time off. And women who took a vacation only once every six years or less were almost eight times more likely to develop coronary heart disease than women who vacationed at least twice per year.

At Rockwell Bar in Grand Rapids, I was sipping a vodka tonic with Jen and chatting about a fall trip to Spain and the Pyrenees. The previous night, Theresa and I had discussed hiking sections of the Pyrenees on the next big trip. Not to mention each time we watched Le Tour de France, it was impossible not to get swept up in the amazing vistas of the Pyrenean peaks the bikers traversed. I filled Jen in on ideas about where to hike, flight details to Madrid, a train ride to the mountains, and visiting the French border. The V&T vanished as the preplanning chat continued.

About a half hour later, Jen's friend Ginger showed up and joined us at the bar. We were introduced, and the trip discussion continued. I excitedly shared the information I had found on hiking and lodging. Ginger was quiet only for a short while before piping in, "Where are you planning to go?" Jen and I simultaneously chimed in, "Spain!" Ginger replied immediately,

"Well, count me in—I'll go!" I shot a glance at Jen. *Is she serious?* I gave Ginger a courtesy smile and then nonverbally communicated my inquiry to Jen: *How well do you know Ginger, and is she qualified to go on a hiking adventure?* Jen returned my questioning look with a smile and continued to offer up our tentative plans to Ginger.

Later, I pulled Jen aside and asked, "Was she serious?" Jen replied with an emphatic yes, explaining that Ginger's nickname was Guaranteed Fun. The name seemed like a good omen. After an inauspicious beginning, a 10-day Spanish adventure was born, and the cast of characters included someone I had met briefly at a bar. However, Ginger proved her worth, well before we even left on the trip, by finding us a local guide. Her coworker Enrique was based in Madrid. She contacted him and asked whether he would mind showing us around the local sights.

The Enrique connection would prove to be invaluable. Luckily, he was in Michigan pre-trip on business, so Ginger invited him to dinner so we could all meet and chat about options. Over a homemade dinner at Chez Ginger, Enrique happily volunteered to show us around Madrid, and he suggested we see the Royal Palace, the cathedral, and a local artisan market. He asked us where we were staying, and I piped in my best Spanish accent, "Hotel Petit Palace Posada del Pene in the main square." Enrique smiled politely, but a strange twist formed on his lips. Either we had made a bad choice or I had said the name completely wrong. I tried again, repeating the name and the address. This time he let a quick laugh escape, then slowly enunciated the last word. "*Peine*, not *pene*. You do not want to say that word, Laura—you will get some very confused looks!" I started to blush, realizing I had just told Enrique we were staying at the Hotel Palace of the Little Penis! The laughter spread down the table, and I had a hard time finishing my plate while giggling over my bad Spanish.

My blunder clearly broke the ice, then the conversation turned toward Enrique and his family. He told us about his wife and new baby son and where he had traveled most recently. At the close of dinner, we agreed that I would work on my Spanish phrases and that we'd call Enrique straight away upon our arrival into his home city.

Theresa, Ginger, Jen, and I thanked him in advance and continued planning our trip over dessert.

Madrid

The four us checked our packing lists and readied for our journey. Before leaving, I had talked with Jen at length about NOT bringing a huge suitcase. Instead, I suggested a medium duffel with rollers—more compact and smashable. Considering the size of most European compact cars, overpacking would be problematic. Theresa and I had learned our lesson on many previous trips.

October 22 dawned, and we jetted from Grand Rapids to Atlanta, Georgia. Jen and Ginger, by virtue of their Delta status, got us into the Sky Club before our cross-Atlantic flight to Madrid. We took full advantage of the club's Wi-Fi and snack bar and in a flurry completed a few final work emails before enjoying a glass of wine. We had smartly booked 10 days for this trip to prevent a common mistake called vacation cramming. We wanted enough time to relax, put away our devices, and actually get out of the normal daily routine. And with the time change and extra travel required, a week is simply not enough time for a trip anywhere in Europe. Certainly, a 10-day trip would keep us statistically further away from stress and heart attacks!

Our overnight flight left Atlanta in the evening and arrived in Madrid the next morning. Most flights to Europe mean a six-hour time change. A word of advice for European travel: take a sleeping pill and try to get some rest during the red-eye flights. Even with a morning arrival, it is best not to sleep once you get there. Resist the urge to nap, find coffee, and push through as long as possible.

We were mostly successful at following this advice; we hailed a cab, and I attempted to tell the cabbie where to take us. Flashing back to my blunder with Enrique, I became acutely aware in my time-change daze that I said the name wrong again! *Pene, Peine*—the words were just too similar for my brain to pull apart. We knew it was close to Plaza de Mayor, so we settled on that directional; the cabbie smirked, nodded at us, and drove off. Madrid and

its streets sped by with scarcely time to take anything in. We pulled to a stop on a narrow street. I looked out my side window to an up-close view of a shop full of cured meats all hanging at various lengths from the ceiling. I stared at all the meat (still with snouts, legs, and hooves attached) for quite a while until Ginger nudged me to get out of the car to unload our bags.

Check-in was painless, and we headed to our small room that actually had a set of bunk beds. Once in the room, with four girls and luggage, we hardly had any space to move around. We took turns washing our faces, applying deodorant, and taking stock of what to do next. Ginger had definitely packed the lightest. Theresa and I complimented her carry-on-sized suitcase. My medium duffle seemed huge compared to that, but Jen's large duffel outsized everyone's. Ginger stared at it, looking displeased. We left the bags and agreed it was time for a cup of strong Spanish coffee.

Plaza Mayor was right outside the Hotel of the Little Penis, so we strolled into the open-air plaza and sat outside at a café in the bright morning sun. It was a long wait, but the *café con leches* finally arrived from our terse waiter. I savored each strong sip. We were in Madrid! In Spain! The caffeine spurred us into action;

I went to the Museo de Jamon (Museum of Ham) with Ginger to stock up on Coke Lights while Theresa found an ATM and Jen grabbed a sweatshirt. Enrique magically appeared in the plaza, no doubt tipped off by Ginger, who had proved to be the savvy traveler thus far. He gathered us together and led us on a lovely stroll through his home city. We passed by the Royal Palace grounds, and Enrique accompanied us on a tour of the cathedral and museum, Santa Maria La Real de la Almudena. Some of the best views of Madrid can be found from the balcony or rooftop of the cathedral, including a spectacular vantage point of the Royal Palace.

We walked through the museum and galleries and took in the spectacular view while statues of the saints watched us from all corners. I tried to soak in a little history on our tour. The Cathedral of Almudena is the last cathedral constructed in Europe and the first to be consecrated out of Rome by Pope John Paul II. We walked through the galleries, and Theresa was kind enough to identify various artifacts and

liturgical objects. She stopped and pointed out a part of the church where they held perpetual adoration to the consecrated Eucharist. In contrast to her reverent observation of this tradition, Ginger piped in, "Is that where they keep the holy cracker?" In shock at the choice of words, Theresa said, "Ginger, you could not have said anything more sacrilegious!" But she still smiled affirming with a yes. She explained the holy cracker for a devout Catholic is the body of Christ taken at communion. Ginger's smile and Catholic ignorance broke our silence, and we all began laughing over Theresa and Ginger's contrasting religious backgrounds. Jen and I, the two Protestant girls, continued laughing over the holy cracker conversation. I was thankful that a sense of humor prevailed. Then, in true Catholic tradition, we left the cathedral and ended up at a bar that afternoon!

We were happy to move on and get outside in the sun again because it helped stave off the time-change daze. Enrique led us out and through some beautiful gardens and on a brisk walk to meet up with his wife Monica and their seven-month-old son. After a few blocks, we squeezed into a very cozy restaurant, Chez Farida, with Monica and Enrique's closest friends, five gay guys and their partners. The restaurant was immediately packed just with our group. Jen, Ginger, Theresa, and I double kissed them all and exchanged spirited *encantadas* (greetings) for the better part of 10 minutes. We settled into lively conversations and ended up drinking entirely too many beers for our first afternoon in Madrid. Our afternoon *comida* lasted for hours, and we drank pitchers of San Miguel and feasted on veggies, rice, and other Moroccan dishes.

It was hard to keep track of all the names, especially at a table for 16. Introductions continued well into the meal, and all the guys agreed that Jen should be called La Jenni. They explained it was the nickname for young women who wear pink and are very fashionable. Perfect! The name stuck, and Jen became La Jenni for the rest of the trip.

We chatted mostly with Enrique and Manuel, and through our conversation we kept picking up on pronunciations of Spanish words that sounded as if they were spoken with a lisp. It was odd, so I made a mental note to ask about this later. Our spontaneous afternoon happy hour was fun until we hit a time-change wall and excused ourselves to head back to our hotel. We took a much-needed power siesta for two hours.

Day one was bookmarked by venturing out near our hotel for tapas, paella, and goat cheese salad at an outdoor café. Other than Theresa getting a bad cockle in her rice, our food was delicious. With a smidge of energy left, we had a nightcap at a dance bar, where we were looked up and down by the waitstaff. A dance beat pumped out of the speakers, and we had to yell to communicate with each other. Ginger ordered a Bailey's to sip while Theresa began to do a version of salsa to the Spanish club music. Ginger earned the nickname Inebria that night, and La Jenni and I laughed as Theresa salsa-ed out the door. She announced, "I don't do figure eights; I only do figure sevens!" She danced her way out into the street, and we followed her back to the hotel.

The Palace to the Pyrenees

The time change caught us off guard on our second day in Madrid. We abruptly awoke after

La Jenni announced from her bed, "Girls, it is already 10:00!" We had slept soundly, clearly needing the downtime. We had brunch instead of breakfast before heading out. It was a jam-packed day that included more sightseeing in Madrid, then an afternoon train north to the Pyrenees. It was an epic travel day that included many incidents and a lot of laughter. We laughed so much that Jen pulled a muscle in her side. It started with breakfast at El Museo de Jamon, with Theresa and Ginger's extraordinarily large plate of eggs, ham, and potatoes. I scored some bananas and coffee at La Fruiteria inside the Super Mercado then joined the girls and Enrique in the main plaza.

Enrique had signed on for day two, and he walked with us to the Royal Palace (Palacio Real) for a tour. We shelled out €8 for an unguided tour; the massive structure, ornate décor, and artwork were well worth the price of admission. We spent two hours walking and gawking until Enrique said his goodbye, giving us directions to the El Rastro Sunday market. We walked south of Plaza Mayor and eventually walked directly into the massive open-air market, where thousands of others were shopping for clothes, jewelry, purses, trinkets, shoes, boots, and more. The market was busy, as patrons battled for space in narrow walkways, with the afternoon sun adding extra heat.

We tried on boots and handmade clothes and sized up gifts as well. I came away with a scarf, Ginger bought a cute dress, Theresa found a stylish handmade shirt, and Jen purchased a dressy lavender layering sweater. We wrapped up the power shop and headed back to the hotel to stay on schedule.

Our afternoon train was departing from Atocha station. We snacked on the way back to the hotel, retrieved our already-packed bags, and luckily had 20 minutes to pop in the bar for a blossoming tradition of *cañas* (small happy hour beers), paired with bread and ham/sausages. Satiated, the four us set off toward Atocha while pulling our duffels. On the walk over, we attracted a bit of attention. From an overpass, two local guys whistled and yelled at us, "Hey, hey, fish and chips!" We guessed at the phrase's meaning based on the content and tone. We kept moving and arrived glistening from the effort. My love affair with trains was solidified again on the high-speed AVE train to Zaragoza. We sped north at an astonishing 300 KMH, arriving in only one and a half hours.

With two hours before our next train to Huesca, we snacked and drank more beer at the station bar. We had one too many and ended up rushing from the bar out to the platform. With two minutes to spare, we finally found platform seven and climbed aboard; I panicked my crew by stopping to take an ill-timed photo of the sleek-looking train before boarding.

Huesca meant the end of the line for train travel. We arrived late in a small northeastern town that serves as a gateway to the Pyrenees. We still needed to get to Biescas, 90 miles away, where we had a hotel booked. We cabbed to another part of town to the Europcar office, finding it completely dark and very closed! The frustration was palpable. Our anxiety ramped up even more when our cabbie, his car still idled on the street, shouted at us in rapid Spanish. We waved him on, and he finally left us to assess our situation on a dark street corner.

Two of four of us had cell phones, and only one of us spoke shitty Spanish. Theresa pulled out her car rental reservation sheet and found several phone numbers that we began dialing. Finally, one of the two numbers connected, and the handset was thrust into my hands. The call disconnected, and I cursed. Standing on the curb with our luggage while locals drove by and gawked, Ginger was beginning to panic.

She pleaded with us, "Girls, it's late. Let's just call it a night and get a hotel—please!" Her pleas had the opposite effect she was hoping for. As if spurred on by a challenge, Jen, Theresa, and I responded by calling the Europcar number again, assured of a different result. Jen calmed Ginger while I attempted to explain our situation to the man who answered our second call. My panicked request went something like this, "*Hola, nosotros reservacion Europcar… la puerta ferme … por favor …* please don't hang up!" An answer in rapid Spanish followed. The line clicked, and he was gone. I cursed and rage-dialed back.

On the verge of siding with Ginger, I looked down in defeat, but just then Theresa gave a yell of delight. The lights came on, and a smiling middle-aged man opened the door for us. I was so happy, and we resisted the urge to give this stranger a lingering embrace. Thankfully, he had our reservation and a car. He sheepishly explained, in broken English, that he was just upstairs in his apartment when we called, all three times. Each time we called, he was trying to explain he would be right down to unlock the door. I blushed at my inability to decipher his instructions and mentally recommitted to my Rosetta Stone Spanish on my laptop back home. Theresa completed the paperwork, and we followed him out to the garage to inspect our extremely compact car, a Leon hatchback.

He gave us a map and verbal directions for how to exit and head out of town. Another crisis averted.

We elected Theresa as the first driver of our five-speed Leon. Jen hefted her large duffel into the hatch with a thump. Ginger's face was stoic as she stared into the trunk at Jen's enormous duffel. With a combination of disgust and disbelief, she threw her hands in the air and announced, "Trunk's full!" It was concerning to see our lack of cargo space with only one of four bags inside. But, after five minutes of rearranging and piling other bags on top and sideways, we crammed it all in. I got in the back seat and sat quietly while Theresa revved the engine and took off with a squeal.

Thankfully, it was just over an hour to Biescas, so I let Jen and Theresa handle the navigation up narrow and winding mountain roads in the pitch dark. I leaned against the window, shut my eyes, and drifted in and out of sleep. Ginger napped next to me. Nodding in and out of a daze, I overheard pieces of Jen and Theresa's conversation about the next turn. Jen randomly asked Theresa whether the car had the outside temperature display on the driver panel. In the exact moment when Theresa looked down to the display, a furry gray and white animal appeared and ran across the road in front of the car. A flurry of frenzied screams escaped, and the car jolted and air brakes were manically depressed. Jen pistoned her hands up and down, smacking the roof of the car, yelling, "Aardvarrrkkkkk!" Shocked awake, I shouted, "Sheeeeepppppp!" clearly in the midst of an Irish dreamland. Theresa had looked up in the nick of time to brake hard and swerve around the furry creature. Ginger was startled awake by our screams and only spotted the tail of the creature as it disappeared into the night. Only Theresa truly knew how lucky we were to still be on the road and not tumbling down a rocky gorge to a grisly end.

After the shrieking and OMGs tapered off, we audibly exhaled. The shock wearing off, we all began snickering at our ridiculous reactions. Theresa made fun of Jen for banging on the roof during the near miss, then we all took turns guessing what animal we had nearly road-killed. Clearly, it had not been a sheep, which brought on a wave of laughs as Ginger imitated me yelling, "Sheeeeeppppp!" I giggled helplessly at my inadvertent animal choice. The guessing continued, and we surmised a possum, a small bear, or a wild hog. Theresa mocked Jen and asked, "Are aardvarks indigenous creatures to the Spanish Pyrenees?" Jen smirked and assured us the animal was long-snouted. Then, Ginger volunteered,

"If not a sheep or aardvark, I think it was an el chupacabra!" We agreed. We would never know what the beady-eyed mythical creature was that darted in our path.

We laughed the rest of the way into Biescas, found an Irish pub, and asked for directions to our hotel. Hotel Tierra in the foothills was an oasis after our action-packed day, its modern exterior and warm lights beckoning us inside. A cheery staffer checked us in and informed they had saved us a cold dinner. We accepted, and she led us around the lobby to a small dining area where we munched on fish shooters with peppers, goat cheese salad, and some fruit. The food was a welcome nightcap while recounting our day. Soon after, we headed up one flight of stairs to our rooms. I was so happy to retire to my comfortable bed, hoping not to dream of a pair of eyes reflecting demonically off headlights.

Hiking the Pyrenees

I vividly remember sitting at breakfast, sipping coffee, and watching sleet come down sideways across the valley. In the light of day, we could see the quaint village of Biescas tucked in the tree-laced foothills. We enjoyed a lazy morning, breakfasted, and downed café Americanos with more bread and cheese. Still hungry, I rummaged until I found a yogurt and a croissant. While we ate and caffeinated,

Ginger gazed outside at the growing squall and commented, "Do we hike in this weather?" Theresa smiled and replied, "Yes, layer and bring a raincoat." Ginger looked perplexed, but as the three of us stood up and strode to our rooms to change, she eventually followed and dressed for the cold.

Late morning, we left the hotel with packs that held extra layers and our lunches. (Theresa and I had visited the Officina de Tourisme earlier for maps and found a bakery for a baguette and a half wheel of cheese.) We walked up the street in the chilly air to a stone path that took us to the town church. The town was historic and Romanesque, with stone pathways, a town square, and a city center surrounded by three restaurants. All of the buildings were made of aging stone bricks and featured wooden arched doors. The path continued up, and we could clearly see some strenuous hiking was

in our future—if only we could find the stupid trailhead. For a half hour, we walked around hunting for our trail marker, crossed the road, and had to double back. We retraced our steps and eventually found the red and white GR 11 trail partially obscured by shrubbery.

Our goal was to hike to the Hermitage de St. Elena above Biescas. The sleet and rain tapered off, and the cold mountain air actually felt good as we walked. We continued up a mild grade past a rushing mountain stream and falls that led to a plateau. On this flat area, sections of a monolith stood along with a small garden. The trail signs were more visible now, and above us we could

make out a run-down stone building that we assumed was part of the Hermitage or an old dormitory. The trail led to a gravel road that switch-backed up to the building. We passed trucks working on grading and leveling the road. Thankfully, the workers let us pass without issuing any catcalls.

We had walked two hours before lunch came calling. We found a flat spot out of the wind to sit and munch on our treats of bread and cheese. There was no signage or any indication of what the run-down building was, so we consulted our map to try to determine next steps. Theresa and Jen had packed Swiss Army knives, so they carved out slices of cheese for each of us. It was camp gourmet style as we layered crudely cut cheese chunks on torn-off pieces of the crusty bread. The taste was better than the presentation. The wind continued, but the sun peeked out and warmed us while we ate.

After lunch, Jen earned another nickname; this time La Jenni became Spur. She spied a narrow trail behind the building that led into the shrubbery and tree line to a peak. She took off on a good clip with Theresa following to see what she was up to. At lunch, we had discussed heading back soon, figuring we had at least a two-hour walk back. Apparently, Spur

had a wild hair while I was left standing in the wind with Ginger, looking uncomfortable and panicked. Irritated that Jen and Theresa had split up the group, I impatiently watched the mouth of the trail for their return and coaxed Ginger out of the wind to stay warmer. Ten minutes passed, then 15, and still no Theresa or Spur. I put my camera away, shook my head, and walked up the trail a few steps to see whether I could catch a glimpse of them. Nothing. Irritation morphed into worry, and a half hour passed before they finally appeared out of breath, full of excuses of why they had charged up the trail.

Theresa shrugged and tipped her head toward Jen as if to say, "I don't know what the hell she was up to, so I followed her." Jen muttered, "I just had to see what was up there!" as if that would make Ginger feel better. Chilled from the wind and irritated at waiting, Ginger chimed in, "I didn't sign up for this shit, girls!" I glared at them both and scolded them for splitting up the group. We huddled for a minute to review the map, realizing the Hermitage was still up the trail. Jen was feeling like she wanted to push on to find the Hermitage, so Theresa volunteered to continue hiking with her. It was evident that Ginger was done, so I volunteered to walk with her back to the hotel. She was ecstatic at this news and started sprint-walking down the trail. I waved to the girls and told them to be careful and not get caught in the dark. With the prospect of warmth and a pool or sauna in her future, Ginger paced me back into Biescas in half the time it had taken to walk up.

The two of us had a head start in the pool and spa, and about an hour later the two Spurs showed up for a soak. The mountain vistas and scenery had quite an effect on Jen, as she experienced a moment of clarity atop the last peak they climbed. Theresa filled me in on their journey and how they made a small rock monument as a symbol of Jen's thankfulness for being breast cancer free. For the past year and a half, she had struggled with her cancer diagnosis, subsequent treatment, and healing. Jen and Theresa also explained how they eventually turned around when the trail turned into a ladder built into a stone wall that led straight up to the next section of rock. They started to climb the ladder only to be blasted by the wind whipping around the corner. We whiled away the afternoon near the pool in our bathrobes before discussing our evening and dinner plans. Our bartender Madelena assisted us with a dinner reservation nearby and a few suggestions for pre-dinner drinks.

Eats and Elvers

That evening, our pub crawl in Biescas covered the town's entire roster of bars. Ginger and Jen (roommates) announced they wanted to see the town and explore. Theresa and I smirked, knowing how small the village was. Nonetheless, clean and presentable, we walked up the street to the first pub we found open. Copious amounts of San Miguel were consumed, and I marveled at how quickly Jen and Ginger downed glass after glass of the stuff. I was unable to match their pace but happily watched a growing squall. Ginger, who is fluent in French, not Spanish, volunteered to order beers and snacks from our bartender, who was clearly entertained by the table of four American La Jennis. Ginger's favorite phrase was to ask while pointing at the food options in the case, "*Que es?*" She never understood the rapid Spanish answer but merely smiled and nodded with a *si*. The choices arrived at our table, including roasted peppers on crostinis. We snacked and sipped the evening away.

We landed back near the hotel for our dinner reservation. In the basement level of Hotel Tierra was a well-appointed dining room where we joined only a few tables for dinner, since it was not peak tourist season. Ginger and Theresa selected a bottle of red wine that arrived before dinner. The menu was in Spanish, featuring a variety of local and regional seafood. The fish entrée on the menu was paired *con elvers*. Both Theresa and I wanted to order fish, so I inquired with our typical question, "*Que es elvers?*" (What are elvers?) Our waitress smiled and responded with an answer in rapid Spanish. I nodded, "We'll take that!"

Dinner proved to be quite tasty, and the flaky fish was exceptionally flavorful. The only oddity was the worm-like bean sprouts sandwiched in between the fish and a layer of potato. The rubbery texture of the worm-like bean sprouts relegated them to the side of our plates. We stuck to forking in mouthfuls of fish fillet and mashed potato. After finishing our plates, we walked upstairs to our rooms.

The four of us quickly convened in one room to make a plan for the next day and the short journey to Torla. While we logged on and checked Google Maps for our route, Jen proudly announced what our fish had been paired with. "Elvers," she explained, "are a Spanish delicacy of baby eel larvae." The four of us exhaled a loud, "Ewwwwwwwwwwwwww!" I resisted the urge to run to the bathroom to purge my dinner. Thankfully, we had only eaten one or two of the elvers before discovering the culinary surprise. We said good nights and walked to our rooms. With visions of tiny white worms slowly moving across a white dinner plate, I fell into a deep sleep.

Torla and the Faja de Pelay

We notched up the difficulty level the next day both in mountain driving and hiking. The drive north on N-260 to Torla was 35 kilometers of a bad driving video game, especially from the back seat. Theresa drove again and piloted us around s-curves and hairpin turns, all with views of the roadside cliff and valley below. The incredible views kept me from focusing on my twisting stomach as my breakfast blended inside me. The peaks became bigger and the towns smaller. Torla, a small medieval Roman village, was much smaller than Biescas. The church tower was the dominant landmark, and it towered above all the other buildings, set against snow-covered peaks in the distance. All four of us exchanged wows at the best view so far in the Pyrenees of Monte Perdido.

Hotel Abetos was on the edge of the village, and it offered unobstructed views toward the mountains, while cowbells clanked from the pastures below and south of us. The hostess allowed us to check in early—another great perk when traveling in the off-season. We discovered in this region of Spain, the locals speak Spanish, French, or English. Communication was speedy without the rapid Spanish phone conversations earlier on the trip. Ginger announced, while we unpacked our hiking gear, that she was taking a pass on hiking. She did volunteer to drive us to Ordessa National Park and drop us off before heading back to town to explore.

A short five-minute drive took us into the park entrance area, where Jen, Theresa, and I pulled on jackets and day packs. Ginger hopped back in the car while we walked to a map kiosk to plot our journey distance. Lingering at the map and looking back, we noticed Ginger was still idling in the lot. "She can't find reverse, girls," Jen mused, so she volunteered to walk back to the car. Jen's verbal instructions did not suffice; Ginger couldn't figure it out, so Jen backed the Leon up for her. As Ginger drove away, the three of us hoped she found a parking spot in town that did not require backing up.

We started later than we hoped for our planned hike on the GR 11 trail named Los Cascados (the Waterfalls). The first hour was punctuated with many stops on short spurs to vistas of waterfalls cut into the cavernous valley. Each waterfall became more dramatic as we continued up, with deep gorges below us that fed water into pools of aquamarine blue. We enjoyed the hike up, snapping many photos as the walls of the canyon rose up around us. The canyon also shielded the sun, so we added layers for a while. We left footprints in a light dusting of snow that had fallen the night before and spied icy rocks in the small streams feeding into the river. As we reached a wide plateau, we began to wonder how long before we would reach the turning point of our loop to cross

around to the other cliff wall, called the Faja de Pelay. It appeared to our south as we walked into the canyon, but the distance was difficult to gauge.

As it turned out, the Faja de Pelay is a dangerous section of trail. We had hiked in not studying the topography until, luckily, we passed a guide and his group. He warned us away from our expedition, explaining that we should not attempt the Faja at the late hour in the day. "The Faja is only passable by hikers going in one direction—up not down," he warned. He described a 600-foot narrow section that typically iced over and plunged thousands of feet into the gorge below. The guide bade us farewell as he led his group toward the Col de Caballo. The three of us sat on some rocks and stared up at the cliff wall with no choice but to hike back the same way we had come in. The loop became an out-and-back. After some water and snacks, we headed back at a brisk pace. The double-time walk back deposited a throbbing blister on my fourth toe. We tired on the two-hour return that put us back in the parking lot approaching dinnertime. All totaled, we hiked 10 miles with only views of the looming Faja.

Ginger was waiting just as the evening chill had set in. On the way into town, Ginger's double-clutch breath-of-fear continued at the wheel. We rounded bends and came within inches (it seemed) of opposing traffic on the narrow road. After we made it safely back to Torla, the depth of our exhaustion started to settle in as we found a café for tea and potato chips. Typically, the tourist T-shirt shop next door would have enticed us, but instead we set our sights on choosing a spot for dinner. Back at the hotel, we showered. Then our host suggested a dinner reservation at El Duende, handing us a business card displaying a logo and mascot resembling a funny little hobgoblin.

Restaurante El Duende

In a cozy nook of the upstairs of El Duende, four tired friends sat down for dinner. A trend continued, with little or no vegetables on the menu. Spain is hell-bent on feeding you cured meats and bread. Jen's arugula salad arrived and turned out to be slices of ham with tiny bits of arugula diced on top of the cured pork! The disappointment on her face was evident when it arrived. Fittingly, more cheese and ham arrived as an appetizer, and I decided to eat without complaint in my tired state. I ordered the pork loin with mushrooms. Jen ordered the lamb feature and Theresa a steak. Ginger decided to order from the regular menu and was rewarded with a 32-ounce extra-rare roast. She had to send it back for the level above super rare. The slab of beef took up the entire plate, except for one small purple flower that served as a garnish. We all laughed at the extra-large portion, and Ginger asked for a doggie bag when the check arrived. She had befriended several town dogs earlier in the day and even planned to give her new canine friend, Nalla, a treat before leaving town.

Dinner wound down, and over dessert, Jen and I had a rather curt exchange (a bitch attack brought on by extreme exhaustion) over my ice cream treat. I probably mentioned one too many times that it reminded me of vanilla pudding as I spooned up the mixture and let it drip back into the glass dish. Catatonically, I also asked her one too many times whether she wanted to try some. She finally took exception to my comments, gave me a stern look, and responded, "Yes, Laura, I think it is pudding: J-E-L-L-O!" I looked up just in time to see Ginger and Theresa stifling a laugh. It was time to go home to my hotel bed and offer no further commentary.

The Road to Finca Pratts

We did not have a plan and let the wind blow us this way and that. I think it was Wednesday when we sadly left the quaint Hotel Abetos to drive away from the Pyrenees. I did have a gnarly blister, so it was probably best to take a day off from hiking. Theresa manned the wheel, and the *cuatro amigas* set off on another adventurous day. We wound our way through the foothills toward Ainsa, a planned stop before lunch. Since I was not driving again, I admired the scenery and the glow the beaming sun left on all the mountain peaks around us. We made it to Ainsa without trouble and pulled into a big parking lot around another walled city with a large stone and brick gate. We needed a *bano* stop, snacks, and a bottle of wine for our lunch.

We continued south toward Lleida, following a river on our left that led us on a ridge that overlooked an impressive aquamarine mountain-fed lake. As lunchtime approached, Theresa pulled into a rest stop with picnic tables and a great vista of the lake. We lunched and drank some *vino tinto* from the bottle. We neglected to grab cups in Ainsa, and our makeshift corkscrew did not fare well either; we had to push the tattered remnants of the cork inside the bottle and into the wine. No surprise, our lunch featured salami, cheese, and more bread. We had given up on the prospect of eating any vegetables on this trip. Even with the lack of greenery, the protein and fruit (wine with chunks of cork) paired well with mountain lake views.

Packing up remnants to leave, Theresa rummaged in the front console to grab her camera. Her hand came to rest on a suspect plastic bag with mushy contents. She held it up and asked Jen, who was also leaning in the passenger side, "What the hell is this?" Jen smirked, knowing Ginger was in trouble, and replied, "That's a bag of meat." Theresa let out a howl of disgust, directing us to throw it out immediately.

Laughing, Jen deposited the bag of meat in the garbage bin, and we drove off in laughing fits once again.

After just another hour we pulled into Bestue Winery. We had the only car in the lot, so we were treated to a tour and tasting mostly in Spanish by the owner and his father, Lorenzo and Lorenzo. A very modern building held a tasting counter for sampling that led into a large attached aging warehouse. Lorenzo generously poured tastes of white then several reds. During the tour, I was intrigued to hear about the family history, and Lorenzo showed us a book of letters, records, and photos to document the winery being passed down generationally. We thanked both Lorenzos for their hospitality and purchased two bottles of their best red wine blend.

It was Ginger's turn to drive. As if to squeal in delight, she peeled out of the parking lot after fidgeting with the clutch and gears. Up front this time, I sat wide-eyed as we rocketed down the road with a nervous Ginger navigating a construction zone and tailgaters. About a half hour into Ginger's turn at the wheel, with the smell of burning clutch in our noses, we decided to revoke her driving privileges. As the copilot, I had to yell "Shift!" several times when the speedometer read 85 KMH in second gear!

More laughter spilled out the open car windows as Ginger pulled over and I became the next driver. I piloted us on spaghetti roads through the foothills toward the next town. Tremp lacked establishments and seemed exceptionally dull, so we continued south, landing at a Spanish version of a truck stop in Cellars to make a plan. We ordered snacks from the bar, tapped into the free Wi-Fi, and unsuccessfully tried to find an available B&B in the area for the night. It was school term break, so everything was full!

We pressed on as evening approached. Jen got her turn at the wheel as dusk fell on the road, and she took us through a dramatic canyon and river gorge that eventually led to a huge dam site. I kept searching for signs at the suggestion of the guy at the truck stop. He implored us to look for a place called San Barronio de Oisme. At the namesake sign, we parked and gawked at the once pristine castle, complete with outbuildings, guest quarters, and a large abandoned tower. Out of the car, we noticed the real estate sign. A castle for sale! If we pooled our resources, we could make it our castle away. My non-vertigo-affected friends got a thrill out of climbing up the tower steps (the turret steps, as Ginger dubbed them in a Monty Python voice). I watched from below and stared out over the pink glow of the sunset on the rocky river bank walls. My reverie was only interrupted by the loud voices of the girls, especially Jen, asking whether the tower steps had been inspected. I listened to them wowing over the view at the lookout, and I remained thankful my feet were firmly planted on the ground. By the time the girls came back down, the perfect sunset faded away. We were no closer to finding a place to stay.

Just before complete darkness fell, we passed over a dramatically perched bridge topping a deep chasm that tumbled to the river. The dark was cover for the next hour as we passed flat, smoggy, industrial towns spewing stinky fumes. I didn't care for the drastic transition (castles to industrial sludge) and hoped we'd find Lleida's outskirts soon. The next hour was a stressful blur of getting lost while trying to find a five-star resort Ginger had Googled.

Jen battled traffic as we called and connected to a Finca Pratt staffer, who conveyed directions in a thick Spanish accent. I tried to repeat to the girls what the gentleman kept saying. I heard, "Turn on the Viservey, off the 24 and Alpicot." In the rush of traffic and voices, instead of Via de Servei (the service road), I heard one long, unfathomable Spanish word. I tried to repeat it to the girls as we sped about roundabouts. After missing the exit twice and going through the same roundabout again, we spied the resort sign and sighed in relief. The stress level thankfully lowered quickly while we hauled our bags out of the Leon. Ginger, in lightning speed, was checking in, in the lobby before the rest of us could lock up the car. At the well-appointed counter, Ginger grinned widely and spoke a welcome "These are my people" while they checked us in. Even the junior suite was five star, and Finca Pratts lived up to the reputation we had read about in the online reviews.

The manager Carlos escorted us up to our adjoining junior suites. He opened the doors to both and revealed an immaculate, contemporary, well-appointed room. He motioned for us to follow; he showed us controls on the wall, pushed a button, and a movie-screen-style shade retracted to reveal a private deck. The deck held two shiny white lounges and a single cocktail table. He pointed out where the robes and spa towels were stored, and as he talked, I peeked in the bathroom at the double-headed shower. He volunteered to walk us down to the spa. Ginger followed his steps with an, "Of course, Carlos." Like hungry puppies following their mama, we trailed Carlos to the spa area and met Monica. Ginger resisted the urge to kiss her on the spot and promptly set up a massage appointment for the morning. The spa, hot tub area, and relaxation room were all as impressive as the suites and the opulent lobby. Carlos may have sensed our hunger pains as we waved to Monica, promising a return in the morning.

In our rooms, we freshened, changed, and once again were personally escorted to an almost empty dining room. The black-suited staff sat us at a large round, helped push in our chairs, and handed us napkins and menus with deft precision. We had four waitstaff perpetually hovering near our table. Our water glasses were always full, and my pre-dinner vodka tonic arrived in a wine goblet the size of my head. I closed my eyes during a long sip and forgot we had ever been lost. Theresa and Ginger scoured the wine menu for a suitable bottle to accompany our fancy dinner. The choice must have impressed, because moments later, Xavier Pratts (the owner) introduced himself and asked us to join him for a tour of the wine cellar before dinner arrived. Of course, we accepted, and he highlighted FP's impressive international collection alongside a series of private meeting rooms. Ginger flawlessly slipped into a conversation, complimenting Xavier on his property and hospitality. Impressed, I watched as she collected his business card and explained that her company had an office and colleague in Madrid. She suggested, "We might need to come back and visit for work or meetings in the near future."

Dinner continued in FP style; I remember spooning in mouthfuls of a rich mushroom risotto in between sips of wine. The flavors from the kitchen added to an already impressive stat sheet. The pampering continued at high levels over decadent chocolate mousse desserts. Realizing the time, we charged dinner to our rooms, ready for an intimate meeting with our pillows. Back in the suite, we were delighted to find a foil-wrapped chocolate and a mini teddy bear on our pillows, adorned with the FP logo. Ginger gushed at how remarkable this place was and started to suggest she might have to stay for another day. The only oddities were friendly iguana-style lizards that darted across the hotel floor between our

rooms. It was the only time Ginger shrieked instead of cooing during our stay.

The next morning, she nearly had us convinced to stay another day after our spa and relaxation time. Theresa, Jen, and I soaked in the hot tubs and stretched out on the chaise lounges in our robes while we sipped iced water with citrus garnishes. Ginger emerged with a perma-grin after her massage and facial. She seemed distressed by the thought of having to move on to Montserrat, away from her people. Admittedly seduced by FP and all the pampering of Finca, it would be difficult to turn in the plush robe in favor of hiking pants and shoes. But we convinced Ginger to come with us. Montserrat and Barcelona were waiting. Once the bills were presented at checkout, I felt really good about spending only one night. Pampering = pricey. At checkout, the FP staffers volunteered to find a hotel on the Montserrat campus and sent us with the details for the next leg of our journey. Ginger lingered and looked back like a crushed forlorn lover the morning after a breakup. We said goodbyes and reloaded the car in the morning sun. I was surprised to see a golf course shrouded in the morning dew that I had not seen in the darkness of our arrival. Looking around surveying the area, we realized Finca Prats was an oasis of luxury and cosmopolitan culture, fenced and protected in part from a dirty and polluted city.

Montserrat and the Black Virgin

Thursday provided a dose of religious history and culture only a short drive from Lleida. One of Spain's most famous pilgrimage destinations, Montserrat is a functioning Benedictine monastery built into the mountains just west of Barcelona. The literal translation of Montserrat means "serrated or cut mountain." With the mountains, though, came more windy roads and another brush with a bitch attack after getting stuck in the back seat again. Theresa was in rare form driving and even taunted me by holding her hands away from the steering wheel as we careened around twisting bends. Turning a shade of green, I insisted she pull over so I could: (A) puke, (B) dry heave, or (C) breathe in fresh air. Shortly, after my fresh-air stop, we pulled into the Montserrat entrance and found one lone parking spot.

We changed into hiking shoes at the car and walked up the entrance road to get our first glimpse of the basilica pressed into the side of the cliff. It was busy and teeming with crowds, including groups of kids on school excursions. People spilled out of gift shops, cafeterias, and the connecting museums. We grabbed a map of the area and scoped out our day hike options while walking around the campus. Before embarking on some exercise, we popped into the lobby of Hotel Abat Cisneros and reserved two rooms for €100 each. The cost seemed ridiculous and completely Spartan in contrast to Finca Pratts at €150. We were staying near the monk dwellings, so it seemed fitting to do without extravagances. The drab furnishings and firm mattress didn't matter; we were paying for the view. Out our window was the church bell tower with the valley nestled below. We spent little time in our monk dwellings because we were planning a two-hour hike to San Jeroni's chapel.

Our hike began with a short funicular ride that deposited us on the mountain perch that marked a day full of spectacular vistas. I stayed away from the canyon edges. Of course my girlfriends taunted me at every opportunity by hanging over the guardrails as we hiked up. Ginger agreed to hike with us only with the option to bail out at any time. La Jenni lived up to her rep by hiking in a dressy T-shirt and a small Coach purse slung around her midsection. She decided to call her new attire line "Coach Active." During the hike, Ginger pointed out some rock climbers across the gorge scaling serrated peaks. We watched them and soaked in the view of Montserrat distant below.

We stopped often for pictures, but Ginger was tiring. She motioned for us to continue up the last section without her, and she promptly sat down on a sunny spot on a rock. The three of us found the small 10-by-10 chapel and paid respects by peeking inside. We could spy the altar through the tiny windows. Hike completed, we bade goodbye to San Jeroni in favor of returning to the solo Ginger. We double-timed it to Ginger and made our way down the loop and across the other side of the gorge. On the descent, I spotted two deer (or perhaps they were mountain goats) perched across the ravine. The way down was more technical on a narrow trail with stone steps carved into the ridgeline. Our knees and ankles were tested by Montserrat's serrated rocks. By late afternoon, we made it back and agreed we'd retire to our monk quarters for some rest and a change of clothes.

I propped myself up on my twin bed with two ultra-thin pillows and tried to jot down some thoughts in my journal. Theresa was engrossed in a book. We enjoyed the quiet in the room until the bells tolled on the hour. Theresa wanted to attend the 6:45 choir service in the basilica to hear the impressive vocal talents. We sat reverent, listening to heavenly sounds while gawking at the ornate décor that enveloped the church. It was an outstanding example of religious bling—every detail and carving held a story. No doubt, the Black Virgin looked down upon us from behind the altar, holding Jesus in one arm and her orb in the other.

We would learn the history of *La Morenta* (the Black Virgin) on our short overnight stay. The revered La Morenta is a Romanesque statue of the virgin made of wood. It is believed the dark color is due to changes in the varnish or possible smoke damage over the passage of time. According to Catholic tradition, the statue of the Black Virgin was carved by St. Luke around 50 AD and brought to Spain. It was later hidden from the Moors in a cave (Santa Cova

or the Holy Grotto), where it was rediscovered in 880 AD. Montserrat and its basilica also play host to the famed 50-member choir with roots from the thirteenth century. Following the service, we walked out to a connecting area where thousands of candles illuminated a walkway. We made donations, lit candles, and said our respective prayers before retiring on a very low-key evening.

My Montserrat highlight was the next morning in the basilica; Theresa and I got up before breakfast and walked back into the basilica to find the Black Virgin close up! The sun was rising above the mountain clouds, and we quietly followed signs that led to a viewing area. We saw no one

else at the early hour as we climbed up the steps near the altar to see the virgin behind the protective glass. Both Theresa and I stood before her and touched the wooden orb in her hand through the small opening. The smooth surface was visibly worn from the many tender touches of admirers over the years. It was a cool moment to link with such important history, possibly from 50 AD.

The next day, Ginger saved us all from being locked up in a Spanish prison indefinitely! Turned out we had parked the Leon in a red no-parking zone at our arrival, and the result was a thick iron chain that hung from connecting posts and blocked any exit attempt. In our defense, the red paint on the blacktop had faded to barely pink, so none of us noticed it when we pulled in. Imagine Ginger's surprise as she gaily trotted down to retrieve the car only to realize the Leon was in hock! I imagined the look of shock on her face and could hear her saying, "Ahhh, *zut alors*." And, remember, she speaks French, not Spanish.

While Ginger encountered our car on the verge of being impounded, Jen and I were happily comparing items and chatting about how cute the souvenirs were. I purchased Santa Maria medals, and Jen found some logo wear for her son Gavin. Ginger called Jen's cell phone no less than 10 times in the span of five minutes while trying to

explain the trouble. The vibrating phone in Jen's purse went unnoticed. And, for Ginger, the situation ramped up when a very official and stern-looking Montserrat uniformed guard approached her and explained (all in Spanish) that she was not allowed to park there. He vehemently pointed to the signage and continued to berate her for not following instructions. Ginger did the best she could in the tumultuous situation, with no purse, no ID, and no parking voucher (conveniently in Theresa or Jen's purse). Even with the language barrier she sweet-talked her way into procuring a Leon-get-out-of-jail-free card.

Waiting at the hotel entrance, we wondered why Ginger was 30 minutes late. The three of us grumbled, waiting impatiently. Eventually, Ginger pulled up in front of Hotel Abat. She climbed out of the hatchback and slammed the door, then marched toward us. She threw up her arms, exasperated. "Girls, what the hell?! I called you like 10 times. Where were you? What were you doing while I was getting yelled out by the Montserrat parking police? The car got the boot!" "Whaaaattt?" we exclaimed.
"There were chains and—oh, oh—it was bad. He yelled at me in Spanish, and I didn't have the parking voucher. I was afraid I was going to have to pull out the howdy booby to get our car back!"

Jen, Theresa, and I howled at this new expression for a gratuitous boob baring and realized the guard almost got more than a talking-to. Gasping in an asthma-attack-style fit of laughter, I collapsed into the backseat. We continued laughing until we cried and Ginger's flushed cheeks transitioned from crimson to a light pink. We drove the next hour retelling the story and soothing Ginger back to normal stress levels.

Barcelona (Bar-tha-lona)

Our trip was bookended by two amazing and historic Spanish cities. The last was Barcelona, which we learned you pronounced in the regional Spanish dialect (Catalan) that sounds like a lisp. Since leaving Madrid, we had been practicing the whole week on our Spanish lisps, and we'd always find a way to weave them into our conversations. We giggled helplessly and overemphasized names and words like "Th-ere-tha" (Theresa), "grath-ias" (gracias), and "thal-tha" (salsa). The lisp dialect has had long-standing effects, and, occasionally, back home, one of us will slip a word in as reminder of our trip.

On the way to Bar-tha-lona, Jen insisted on driving, and Theresa finally obliged by pulling over and swapping to the passenger side. Jen explained, "If I can successfully navigate Manhattan in NYC, then I can handle a foreign city too." I was in the backseat again, amused at the headstrong conversation. Theresa navigated, and Jen drove us right to the Hotel Amistar in the midst of the city. We couldn't figure out where to park, so we literally pulled on the sidewalk to unload our bags. During the check-in process, Ginger snuck down to a café bar and downed a shot of Crown to calm her nerves. Once all our crap was safe in the lobby, we drove a short distance to the local EuropCar and said goodbye to our trusty steed. With the car safely returned, we had to place our trust in public transportation and a T-10 card. We walked back to our family-style room at the Amistar to make a plan for the day.

We were successful at getting a big dose of Gaudi architecture on a city tour, highlighted by a tour of the famous basilica called the La Sagrada Familia (the Sacred Family). The Barcelona Metro deposited us at the La Sagrada stop where we popped up street-side to a bustling mecca of people and a long, serpentine line to enter. The spires are as unique as Gaudi's eccentric personality. The towers and ornate spires made the church feel more like a castle that required a knight's permission to enter. At the ticket office, we hoped Jen's online ticket purchase was valid and would help bypass the ridiculous line. Jen produced her receipt and sweet-talked the security guard to let us in, even though late for our booking. She smiled and waved us in! La Jenni's fast-pass tickets saved us an hour wait.

Furious construction was going on inside and out, and several cranes obstructed our views of various sections. Mesmerized, I walked and rubber-necked at the incredible details of every arch and pillar punctuated by men in yellow hard hats. Signs were posted everywhere announcing a papal visit on November 7, just one week away. We ambled on a self-guided tour and soaked up history on Antonio Gaudi's most prestigious project. Gaudi had masterminded the theme and style, documenting construction plans until he was viciously run over by a bus on his own city streets in 1920! Spain has been attempting to carry out his vision since then, with significant amounts of squabbling over details. The arguments rage within the artistic community over Gaudi's vision, and construction specialists bicker over materials and next steps. During my visit, 50% of the structure was shrouded by caution tape, and the history placards projected La Sagrada to be perpetually under construction for 30 more years. It was admittedly distracting to appreciate its grandeur with the whir and whack of metal and stone.

We walked around for an hour then huddled and agreed to skip the hour-long wait to ride the elevator to the top of a tower. The lower level

was more museum-esque, but we grew weary of digesting more history and sought the afternoon sun. Outside, we sat on the steps and soaked up rays while the cranes moved above us. I noted a rarity in my journal—touring a Spanish gothic-modern basilica that has been under construction since 1882! We eventually said no to more touring and yes to an expensive café about a block away. We rested our feet while sipping San Miguels with La Sagrada over our shoulders. We relaxed and chatted about where to head next. Taking turns in the restroom, we discovered the city's penchant toward conservancy. All bathrooms were equipped with light timers that cut out after two or three minutes. Mid-pee, Jen and I squealed in the dark. We warned Ginger and Theresa not to dally when they took their turns.

The ladies always kept me laughing, and we ventured off next toward La Rambla, Barcelona's famous pedestrian street and shopping district. La Rambla divided the city into its east and west areas. We gained confidence on the metro and figured out where to change and connect. Shopping transitioned into researching a dinner destination. La Subina was the suggestion from the hotel's front desk staff. They reminded us that it was a holiday weekend, with most trekking out of the city, so we would not need a reservation. We had dubbed it dress-up night on our self-determined itinerary. So the four of us put on versions of a little black sexy dress. I skipped the heels and slid on flat flip-flops instead. Inspecting everyone's attire, I was impressed with how nice we all looked out of a suitcase. With the extra space in her large duffel, Jen packed silver high heels for this occasion. I've never known her to choose sensible footwear. The fish and chips catcalls resumed once again, as they had in Madrid. Team fish-n-chips walked the streets again for a short stint to the restaurant.

We clearly did not need a reservation; only one other table was seated during our two-hour dining experience. Our waitress was helpful (and bilingual) as she navigated us through the predominantly seafood menu. She suggested the paella and the sea bass then slid off to get our first round of drinks. My eyes widened when a plate of spicy octopus arrived as our appetizer; Jen and Theresa giggled as I stared at the

tentacles. I tried a small bite then squeezed my eyes shut over the texture. The owner appeared before dinner with a suggestion for a wine pairing and also reappeared later to serve the paella and fish. Our dinners arrived table-side in a steaming pot. The staff ladled out portions for each for us.

Thankfully, Ginger had noticed my indecision over the menu and had taken the liberty of ordering for me. The paella was a spicy array of rice, prawns, mussels, and veggies. Spooning in my first bites, I stared at the crawfish heads and eyes on the side of my plate. The red wine was passed and poured, a tasty choice with all the spices. A sharing theme continued as a portion of sea bass landed on my plate to keep the crawfish company. Of all the fish and seafood creatures we tried at that meal, the mild seabass was the favorite pescatarian choice. It was a

meal to savor and ponder (no baby eel larvae made an appearance). The spices, and a perfect buzz, etched memories of smiles and laughs. We remained lost in conversation recounting our adventures of the previous week and toasted to one more day of our Spanish vacation.

I convinced Jen to come out with me for a nightcap after Ginger and Theresa gave us a "hell no" with their noses in a book. Jen and I slipped into some jeans and walked back out into the night only to return to the hotel half an hour later! Earlier that night, Jen and I remembered seeing a bar with a neon sign displaying "Kiss-Me" with an outlined pair of neon-red lips. It looked intriguing, so we walked toward the neon sign and the lone bouncer on a stool. We approached. He stood up quickly and said two words to us, "Boys club," with his hand held up, shaking his head no. Jen and I laughed out loud at the prospect of almost marching in the door to a gay guys-only club! The universe had given us a clear sign to go home and to bed. Instead of searching for another alluring neon sign, we simply walked back to the hotel.

Bike Barcelona

As if to tempt fate, we chose a bike tour on our final day in Barcelona to see whether we could have a close encounter with a bus just as Gaudi did. On Saturday morning, the light filtered in through the curtains, along with some street noise. As I ambled to the bathroom, hand-washed socks and underwear hung on every lamp, door, or hook available. The Amistar did not provide laundry service on a holiday weekend. As we woke up and got moving, Theresa briefed us on the bike tour, called Bike Barcelona. The gathering spot to meet the guide was at the Hard Rock Café off La Rambla. We ended up rushing to make the deadline, blaming our tardiness on four women and one bathroom. We scrambled to the metro and made it to the meeting spot, but not before Jen was able to find us some coffee and pastries. We greedily sipped our coffees, and moments later our guide, Elizabeth, showed up wearing a red sweatshirt with silk-screened text: BIKE BARCELONA. Listening to instructions, I noticed an accent that was definitely not Spanish. She was Austrian and would be giving us our historical tour of a Spanish city on the Mediterranean.

A group of 20 followed a short distance to her office and bike storage. We all picked out a wide-seated cruiser complete with a bell and front zippered pouch. The four of us hopped on our bikes and pedaled around, noting the squirrely handling and heavy frames. They were just rentals. A crazy Brit couple also tested out the bikes, and the man weaved crazily in and out of our group in the alley—narrowly missing clipping our tires. The large group was unmanageable and our foursome made a mental note to stay clear of the Brit couple. Several others in our group looked less than experienced on two wheels. The start was delayed as Elizabeth discovered she was flying solo, perhaps while her counterpart either slept in or nursed a hangover. It was a large group for one guide (with never a mention of a liability waiver) as we set off down the narrow alley. Jen had volunteered to start out as the caboose; her job was to signal Elizabeth at stopping points to be sure we stayed together.

The planned route was from the Gothic Quarter to the beach, then along the sea to the Olympic Port, and finally north on a loop around La Sagrada Familia and other Gaudi-designed buildings. Being on two wheels instead of aching feet was a nice changeup. Everyone smiled as we pedaled and complimented Theresa on her excellent choice of activities. Plus, the sun beamed, and the temperature was perfect for biking. I kept a watchful eye and scanned for mopeds or cars that might come shooting out from an alley. At the halfway point, we stopped at a seaside café for a beer and snacks. We soaked up the beach scene and watched a huge sand sculpture being made.

People walked and jogged the boardwalk, keeping up a stream of activity. We asked Elizabeth to take a group photo with the beach behind us. Later, looking at our photos, we realized the Brits had photobombed us at the café.

The danger ramped up as the tour continued away from the beach and traffic and congestion increased. Jen, Ginger, and Theresa conferred on sticking together and being acutely aware of stray cars, buses, and people in our group who sucked at riding a bike! Our group inevitably kept getting split up at intersection crossings because of the size. I got stuck behind a girl named Summer, who was wearing nearly see-through tights, her version of an appropriate bike outfit. That view did not stack up well against La Sagrada spires that rose up in front of us on the tour route. I pedaled around Summer and managed to survive the bustling streets that took us past a Gaudi apartment building, historic plazas, and gurgling fountains. In the afternoon, we cruised back in to the bike shop unharmed. We tipped Elizabeth and had to resort to walking again.

We had the afternoon to explore, so we meandered in and out of shops boasting FC Barcelona soccer jerseys; I bought one for Yvonne, my soccer-crazed business partner back home.

We landed in a neighborhood bar for tapas and *cañas*. We made plans for dinner at any establishment showing FC Barcelona play against cross-country rival Sevilla.

Back down in the metro maze, Ginger spied a photo booth and convinced us all to pile in for a group shot. The sign indicated a €2 fee, so I slid the coins in the slot and jammed in with the girls. We pushed the start button on the display screen and smiled and waited. After a long delay, there was still no flash and no pictures. The screen just kept flashing at us to deposit €2. After piling out, disappointed, and pushing the reset button in hopes of getting our money back, I realized our mistake. Just to the right of the photo button was an option (for the same amount) to buy a Pirates of the Caribbean commemorative mini key chain. I reached into the slot at the bottom of the booth and held up our prize with a look of disgust. Ginger burst into laughter after getting screwed out of our last bit of change. We rode back to our stop with a parting gift from the Barcelona metro in my pocket. On our way home, we could choose plenty of awesome photos that would fit nicely in the ugly yellow frame!

We travel not to escape life,
but for life not to escape us

Chapter Six
In the Mitten
(The Great Lake State)

The Great Lakes contain the largest supply of freshwater in the world, holding about 18% of the world's total fresh water and about 90% of the United States' total fresh water.

Source: NOAA (National Oceanic and Atmospheric Association)

- Houghton
- Marquette
- Porcupine Mountains
- Ironwood
- Sault Ste Marie
- Escanaba
- Mackinac Island
- Traverse City
- Alpena
- Ludington
- Muskegon
- Nunica
- Grand Rapids
- Bay City
- Holland
- Lansing
- Port Huron
- Kalamazoo
- Ann Arbor
- Flint
- Detroit

Drive somewhere close, go camping, hike a trail, or pedal a bike. There are plenty of affordable options. I am on a budget too! I can't afford five-star resorts or hotels unless Hotwire is giving them away, so many times I choose a tent or a friend's couch. It's still travel no matter where you lay your head.

It turns out I grew up in paradise. I didn't realize this as a kid, and as an adult I have a newfound appreciation for my own backyard playground. I don't need to travel far from home to take in one of the United States' most stunning natural wonders. Don't take my word for it: *Good Morning America** took a poll in 2011 and asked, What natural wonder is the most beautiful in the 50 states? The title belongs to the Sleeping Bear Dunes National Lakeshore, an amazing 30-mile stretch of Lake Michigan beachfront in northwestern Michigan. I had the privilege of growing up less than 10 miles away from this magnificent pile of sand, complete with a 90-mile (can't see across) view toward Wisconsin. On many school field trips, I learned the history and geology of my hometown mountain. We can thank ancient glaciers and an ice age for carving out this marvel of sand and water. Michigan is mostly flat, but there are unique dunescapes flanked by an inland sea called Lake Michigan. And this inland ocean is all fresh water with no sharks to worry about.

In my own personal focus groups paired with research, most people say money is the primary culprit for their lack of travel. Not to oversimplify, but with so many local and in-state options for Michiganders (and I am sure this is true in most other states), why all the fuss about cash? Travel light and travel local.

As a teen, I successfully completed and survived a Leelanau County rite of passage for every kid under 15. We would trudge up the steep 400-foot face of the dune and arrive panting with hands on our knees at the top, looking over sweeping views of Little and Big Glen Lakes to the east. After our hearts stopped pounding in time to our pulse, someone would yell "GO!" and we'd take off down the dune, running at full sprint. The steep slope turned the run into physical comedy full of ridiculous head-over-heels, sandy spills, and raucous laughter. I will not forget the feeling of hurtling down the dune in my bare feet, laughing until spit came out the corners of my mouth. Everyone, including me, would inevitably lose rhythm and balance. We'd fall forward like drunks, not in control of limbs incapable of keeping up with the mighty Sleeping Bear's steep pitch. At the bottom, we'd shake our heads like dogs to get the sand out of our hair and stretch our legs from the severe trauma we had just put them through. It was great fun and kid moments I will never forget.

Now as a grown woman, I totally want to run down the dune again (hopefully without serious injury), and I have an ever-growing appreciation for my home state. With age has come some wisdom. After traveling around the United States and to lots of international destinations, I can honestly say that Michigan is a leader among sand and water destinations and—dare I say—beach destinations. Michigan has a west coast too (though we don't have much in common with California). Or I've heard Michigan called the third coast as well. Lake Michigan beaches are some of the cleanest and most scenic in the world.

What? You don't think of Michigan as a beach destination? Sure, snow blankets much of our state for at least three months out of the year. Even so, the winter beachscapes are epic and worth braving the brisk winds. Granted, no sunscreen needed for a snow and sand trip, but dressed appropriately, you can watch the whitecaps crash on the ice floes that build up on the beach. If you are more of a summer person, the beach and dunes all along Lake Michigan are worthy of a visit and the inspiration for the state's tourism campaign, "Pure Michigan." As a beach volleyball player, I've spoken to countless Californians and Floridians who marvel at our dense, deep (amazingly clean), sandy beaches on my west coast. Besides, it's hard not to notice the sand, especially when it squeaks under your feet as you walk.

Even as a Michigan resident, I find it difficult to go more than a week without getting to the beach and looking west out over the big lake. This huge body of water defines life as I know it on Michigan's west coast. It gives freely and often, and the part I admire the most is the unpredictability. Live in Michigan and you will never get bored talking about the weather. I've learned that the lake is in charge. It can inspire one day with an exotic glowing sunset and send you packing the next with 40-knot sustained winds, giving you a Michigan version of skin exfoliation called sandblasting. Winter is even more unpredictable, bringing with it a phenomenon called lake-effect snow.

For example, take one run-of-the mill average snowstorm, add Lake Michigan, and now you've got a full-blown blizzard that dumps inches per hour. It's impressive. You'll still hear people talk about the blizzard of '78 and how it rendered portions of northern Michigan impassable for the better part of a week. When a snowplow truck gets stuck, it's an above-average storm. I will never forget that storm, mostly because I got to stay home from school for one full week! How sweet for a 10-year-old. My brother and I spent hours digging a tunnel in our driveway through a 15-foot-high drift that had sealed us in. My dad drove our aging snowmobile to the store for supplies like bread and milk. The Traverse City area and Leelanau County, where I grew up, received an average of 200 inches of snow per year. Now I reside in Spring Lake, about 200 miles south down the coast of Lake Michigan

and about 45 minutes west of Grand Rapids, Michigan's second-largest city. I'll always be a northern girl, though, proud of my small-town roots and thankful for my impressive neighbor, the Sleeping Bear Dunes National Lakeshore.

Never been to Michigan but maybe you've heard Tim Allen's voice in the "Pure Michigan" commercials and you're curious? I'd suggest you add it to your bucket list and make a trip plan soon. Everyone has heard of The Great Lake State, but most people really don't understand the "great" part. I can't resist the opportunity to outline a few must-sees and give you some of my personal favorites. I have already tried to sell you on northern Michigan and running the dunes. That can serve as day one of your week-long tour in Leelanau County, just west of Traverse City. Start out by connecting with M-22 and a few offshoots if you are touring by car. M-22 has gotten so popular it is now its own brand. You can buy M-22 logo stickers for the back bumper of your car. The scenic route hugs the lakeshore and winds through quaint little towns full of pubs and boutiques. Make pit stops in the likes of Leland, Maple City, Suttons Bay, Cedar, Glen Arbor, and Empire.

You'll also encounter a bevy of wineries along the way.

Of some surprise to me, the entire Traverse City area has become a wine destination. I certainly would not grade us comparable to Sonoma, Napa, or Tuscany, but the whites and Rieslings are decent (wine snobs go elsewhere). As it goes with wine, TC is an infant, but pair a glass of wine with the scenery of west bay or Lake Michigan and it makes for an above-average tasting. To be truthful, the specialty is not wine but cherries from the self-proclaimed Cherry Capital of the World. And TC hosts the National Cherry Festival to prove it every July. The rolling hills and climate (on the forty-fifth parallel) are perfect for growing cherries, and you'll see the famous white blossoms adorn the orchards every spring. The town namesake, the Cherry Republic, is a retail dynasty, where they churn out pies, jams, and gifts and ship cherry products worldwide. Hit the Cherry Republic store in Glen Arbor in the morning on day three or four, then continue to Leland or Fishtown (as locals call it) for lunch and a lazy afternoon. Both Leland and the Leland River host a collection of weathered fishing shanties, docks, tugs, charters, and smokehouses, all playing part of Michigan's fishing heritage. Leland, the town, has the same historical cool factor, and I love to pop into the Cove or the Bluebird for a perch basket. And, as your tour guide, I'd suggest a kayak on the next day and overnight in one of several small but upscale B&Bs. Fishing is a must, either on the inland lakes or on a Lake Michigan charter.

I feel exceptionally lucky to visit and stay often with my parents and brother, who still live in the Traverse City area. In between family visits or holiday celebrations, I rediscover manicured trails like the VASA for trail biking or cross-country skiing. Golfing is another highlight, and thankfully my brother Ben (an ex-PGA golf pro) still has plenty of connections at courses like the Kingsley Club, the Dunes, Mistwood, and the new Manitou Passage at the old Sugar Loaf Ski Resort. The chairlifts still line some of the holes, and it is easy to see why the hills were once used for skiing. Michigan is oft called the Golf Riviera, boasting more than 800 public courses in the state, and is consistently named as one of the best places in the country to play golf. On trips to TC, I make sure there's room for both a bike and my clubs.

Traverse City definitely has secured its reputation as a top tourist destination in Michigan and for good reason. When you meander into downtown to walk and shop the many boutiques, you'll discover that TC has managed to keep its small-town roots while offering an above-average tourism experience (especially for dining, craft beer options, and shopping). Traverse City, much like my home in western Michigan, is defined by the big lakes that created the namesake The Great Lake State. I've watched my hometown do some growing up over the years, but it remains an idyllic and serene outdoor playground. To be up north is to be away from congestion, traffic, and the bustle of my busy life. To be in Traverse City or Leelanau County near the shoreline, the beach and the dunes warrant visitors to slow down and take a moment to admire. Even my midstate residence has plenty to keep me occupied recreationally. The Muskegon to Ludington stretch is oft called the Gold Coast. I've chosen the area for its natural resources and for the bustling economy. As a local and resident of the mitten, I am proud to say I choose to stay in my home state often for adventure trips or weekends, including biking, hiking, or camping.

Pictured Rocks and the Upper Peninsula

Being a northern girl, I inherently understand the northern call. I want to go farther up north, so Michigan's Upper Peninsula calls to me often. Labor Day weekend is extra special. I get to celebrate a birthday around the national holiday, and it always means an extra day off work too. The extra Monday off is all you need to kick-start an in-state adventure to the Upper Peninsula. Michigan may be the state that invented the concept of the weekend up north, and plenty of esteemed writers have penned prose on its inspirational qualities. Henry Wadsworth Longfellow wrote of it in "The Song of Hiawatha," describing Lake Gitche-Gumme and his reflections in the water. I'm not a poet, but I wrote down my own reflections from a summer visit in 2010.

Even as a Michigan resident, I am awed by the rugged natural beauty of the U.P. and the massive five-mile suspension bridge that connects Michigan's mitten. The state is like that pair of hand-knit gloves your grandma made for you as a kid that were connected

by a strand of yarn to prevent losing the pair. Once you've crossed the Mackinaw Bridge, you'll have more than 16,000 square miles to explore without the crowds or bustling tourist traps. Only 3% of the state's population lives among the peninsula's woodlands, streams, and waterfalls. The biggest town, Marquette, is home to about 20,000 residents and also Northern Michigan University. As a lower peninsula resident, I would be considered a troll (someone who lives below the bridge), and Upper Peninsula residents are oft called Yoopers, pronounced with a decidedly slurred backwoods accent. For emphasis, follow that up with the word "eh." The remoteness of much of the U.P. has spawned plenty of jokes and songs about what it means to be a Yooper. One of my favorites is the tune called "Sweet Home Escanaba," adapted from "Sweet Home Alabama." All joking aside about trolls and Yoopers, the U.P. is a largely unknown naturalist delight, perfect for a weekender or an extended vacation.

More than just the expanse of forests, the U.P. is also surrounded by Lake Superior to the north, the world's largest body of fresh water, boasting the Pictured Rocks National Lakeshore near Munising. This area of Michigan is worthy of exploring multiple times, so I often plot shoreline U.P. time when summer trip planning.

151

We took yet another foray into the big lake's rocky lakeshore with paddling and camping gear in tow. Michigan's colorful mineral-stained cliffs are on display for 42 miles in the park. My group's plan was to attempt to see them by foot and by kayak. I gathered three other trolls who also took a call from up north. We readied to log some time in the car to get there, about seven hours' worth.

Some of the usual PWDS crew signed up for this trip: Steve, Kim, and Theresa. We snuck out of town on a Thursday night and made it to Gaylord and a $69 room at the Alpine Inn. We drove a borrowed Suburban loaded with packs, PFDs, coolers, and paddles and towed a kayak trailer with no taillights. We should not have been surprised when the state trooper pulled Theresa over, but I had to laugh when he handed her the ticket for speeding. The next day, we alternated drivers and piloted the Suburban west on Highway 2 then north toward Munising, where we

picked up our backcountry camping permits. We agreed on two nights of camping and one day of paddling. We had picked campsites that took us along the shores of Lake Superior and then to the interior of the park closer to the access road, where we stashed the car.

I did plenty of camping as a kid, but backpacking requires a completely different set of skills and equipment. The gear takes a while to accumulate, and each item must be carefully considered for weight and space. I had gotten used to the idea of re-wearing one set of clothes instead of packing an extra T-shirt, another pair of pants, or extra socks. I did treat myself to an extra pair of underwear at least. Saving room for food and water is paramount, as well as the ever-important tent and sleeping bag/pad. A checklist is best so you don't forget things like a spork, toilet paper, coffee mug, quick-dry towel, camp pillow, hat, bug spray, first-aid kit, matches, army knife, sunscreen, Jetboil fuel, journal, and a flask with your favorite sipping liquor. It's a lot to carry, and when I first slung my pack over my shoulders, I was mildly concerned about walking six miles to Pine Bluff Campsite on the first day.

My pack didn't feel heavy until I added the borrowed tent to the bottom with the exterior straps. Theresa took the stakes and poles to split up the weight. The four us rechecked our packs and confirmed that we had stuffed a food bag on top, and then we set off for a walk in the woods toward the lake. It was unseasonably warm, which quickly turned us into hot, sweaty humans. We kept the pace slow and stopped often en route to our beach campsite. The hardpack forest trail eventually gave way to sandy beach as it meandered toward Pine Bluff. We scoped out the campsite, connected to the beach about 50 yards down a narrow trail. Our packs came off, and I lay in the sand with my head propped. Kim hunted for rocks up and down the beach, and Steve went swimming right away before scrounging for firewood. My beach lounge was only interrupted a few times by aggressive, low-flying black flies that can plague the area in summer. I peeled myself up eventually and joined the crew for a Lake Superior shower before tent and dinner setup. Superior was on the verge of warm, putting it in the safe-to-swim range.

Toweled off and dry, Theresa and I unleashed the tent (borrowed from her dad) from its bag then laid out the poles and stakes for a quick assessment. Theresa had never used this tent before. We threaded the connectors through their respective pockets, and it went up quickly. I started staking the corners and noticed how spacious the tent was. Steve watched with interest and walked over to inspect our sleeping quarters. "How many people does that tent sleep?" he asked. "Five people?" He motioned over to his small two-person compact and asked Theresa, "What did I need to bring that for if I knew you were bringing the Taj Mahal tent?" Standing back, inspecting the erected tent, Steve was right. It was huge! No wonder it was so heavy. Theresa and I piled in the Taj with our sleeping bags and gear, marveling at how much room we had.

Clearly, this tent was not meant to be a lightweight canvas home for backpackers. Not much to do except enjoy the space and hope our shoulders could stand the extra weight during the next two days. The rest of the evening was split between tending to dinner and a crackling fire. We sporked in mouthfuls of packaged noodles with chunks of chicken added for protein. Our tasty after-dinner drink became known as the Camp Rita, dubbed by Kim and Theresa. They had boiled sugar water and added it to some tequila from a flask, finishing it with a squeeze of fresh lime. It was a delightful sipper to pass around while watching the flames dance and flicker in the darkening woods. Lake Superior waves whispered to us as we slept.

Paddle Pictured Rocks

"Lucky" was the word of the day on day two in Pictured Rocks. Lucky to have unseasonably warm temperatures and lucky to have a flat Lake Superior, perfect conditions for kayaking the shoreline. Seeing the rocks by kayak offers the closest access and the best view of the colorful cliffs. On a more typical day, you would fight the wind and waves and be worried about capsizing instead of soaking up views of 300-foot-tall cliffs. After hiking out from Pine Bluff and back to the car/trailer, we drove west and pulled into Miner's Beach, a sandy and easy spot to put in for our paddle. It took a solid hour to unstrap, prep, and haul all four of the boats down to the beach. After checking for water bottles and snacks and pulling on a PFD, we pushed off our paddles, stroking in and

out of the lake and heading toward the cliffs and coves to the north. Grand Island was situated over my left shoulder as I pointed the nose of my kayak east. With no particular plan for time and distance, the four of us paddled up close to the cliffs and marveled at the array of colors layered in the walls while we explored in and out of coves. Grand Portal Point and Chapel Rock were spots we hoped to reach, but from the water, every section looked spectacular.

I'm not sure how many miles we covered, but the looming cliffs continued on out of sight for many miles. Steve and Kim pushed on ahead of me, and I took a break from paddling and floated around with Theresa while chatting about saving some energy to set up camp later. We waved Kim and Steve on signally; our arms and shoulders were tired. They continued on for miles out of our sight, but we turned to head back to Miner's Beach for book time on the beach. As T and I beached our kayaks, we realized immediately how achy and tired our backs, arms, and shoulders were. While our overzealous friends stayed out for another hour, I lay on a beach towel and split time between napping and reading.

Late afternoon rolled in quickly, and once Steve and Kim made it back, we purposefully hauled and loaded the kayaks so we could find our campsite and dinner soon. Logistics had forced us to choose a less than optimal campsite for the night. Potato Patch was to be our mosquito-infested, densely overgrown site for the evening, with barely room for both tents. To get there, we hiked on a hard-packed trail with leafy underbrush up to our waists along a slight ridge. The campsite was perched at the top on a slight plateau. With a two-sport day under our belts, we focused on dinner and then sleep with trembling arms.

Munising was close by, so over morning breakfast and coffee, we made a plan to do some car-assisted cliff viewing and waterfall hiking. And a non-Jetboil dinner had us fired up on day three, perpetually hungry from a heavy dose of sweaty activities. Part of our hike out from Potato Patch took us near Lake Superior again and a section of sandy beach perfect for a swim and washing. The big lake was even warmer now as we waded in and swam around for a while. We pulled Kim away from rock collecting and beelined for the car, where we changed into a fresh set of clothes stashed there. Using the Suburban as cover, I ducked behind a car door to make an underwear and bra change. Everyone else did the same, hoping

not to give other hikers an R-rated show. The rest of our day in the park was spent admiring Miners Falls then the famous Miner's Castle Rock from a viewing area above the cliff walls. The sandstone outcropping is the most photographed in the park, and we spied a lone kayaker paddling in the bright turquoise water.

The last highlight was dinner at Sydney's, where plates of red-meat delights were devoured with piles of salty fries. It was a less than ladylike scene when I bit into my mushroom burger. We savored dinner and opted to begin the long journey home instead of staying another night in the Patch. Splitting up the drive meant a more tolerable four hours instead of eight in the car for the next day. The journey home took us through St. Ignace, to Murdick's Fudge Shop, then across the mighty bridge again. Even though we don't qualify as out-of-state tourists, we accepted the label of "fudgie" by sampling several flavors of the dense, chocolaty treat made famous in Michigan's north country.

UP North at the Porkies

Yes, Michigan is a big state. It's mostly a positive when exploring, but timing and logistics in the Mitten are important factors when pre-planning. If you drove from the west coast straight across midstate to Lake Huron and Port Huron, it's at least three hours. It's 215 miles from Grand Haven to Port Huron. And if you start from Detroit and head north toward the Mackinaw Bridge, you'll need five hours. That distance is 300 miles plus, depending on your exact starting point. Then, if you head west in the Upper Peninsula on Highway 2 from St. Ignace toward Ironwood in the westernmost part, you'll need another five or six hours, which will net another

315 miles. That's in good driving conditions in the summer. In winter, good luck and God be with you. Michigan is not a state you can pass through quickly. It is not like Indiana, Illinois, or Ohio, where you hope to quickly pass through to get to your destination. The Great Lake State will make you earn your trip, and by the nature of its northernmost position of the US map, flanked by Great Lakes, you'll need to give the state its due.

As a resident, I love my state for keeping me perpetually on my toes, especially when it comes to our distinct four-season weather and climate. The Great Lake State always has something up its mitten. The four seasons keep the state ever in transition; as Michiganders we are always in the process of rotating tank tops for sweaters. You'll never have the opportunity to be complacent or to settle into a tropical summer routine, and just when winter doldrums start to settle in your bones, the hint of a spring thaw will warm you. If you think the only time to visit Michigan is in the summer, wrong again. I would suggest spring or fall, when there is no battle with the crowds on the roads or the beaches. The lush green of spring is worthy, especially if you like to swing the sticks on the golf course. And fall colors are brighter here, especially when you have the blue of the big lakes as the backdrop.

My seasonal Michigan exploration is a work in progress, and I find there are many places (especially in the U.P.) that still need discovering. I have yet to make a trip to Michigan's Isle Royale National Park. Every time I pick up any backpacker magazine, Isle Royale is a feature. It requires a ferry boat ride from Copper Harbor, but the reward is a rugged island full of rocky ridges, wildlife, and plenty of hiking adventures with views of Lake Superior. It's on my list, but I have made it to western U.P.'s shiny gem called the Porcupine Mountains.

I followed the northern call again, this time farther north to the Upper Peninsula into a park, home to the largest tract of virgin hardwoods in North America. My destination: the Porcupine Mountains State Park (the Porkies), where you'll see a gazillion majestic trees and zero cell towers. Michigan is a big state as we've discussed. Making the drive from my abode in Spring Lake to the Porkies, in the farthest western corner of the U.P., is a back-aching, bitch-attack-inducing 11 and a half hours. Eleven hours is just too long, not to mention it hogs two precious days of time I could otherwise be spending admiring lakes, northern lights, hardwood forests, or the catch of the day. My crew and I contemplated options and asked Google Maps for help, and then we checked the USS Badger cross-lake

ferry for rates and schedules. After our research, we added the ferry to the plan and also a state (Wisconsin) to the logistics equation. The historic USS Badger departs from Ludington and slowly steams (in four hours) to Manitowoc, Wisconsin, 90 miles across Lake Michigan. The best part of four hours is that I am not piloting the ship, nor do I have any responsibility at all except to put my feet up and sip cold beverages. From Manitowoc, it is a manageable four-and-a-half-hour drive through cheese-curd Packer-fan land up to the Porkies. Splitting nine hours between a boat and a car did not give anyone in my group a rectal ache, so we inked the plan. And our plan still left almost three full days of backpacking and camping.

The weekend fun-seekers included a few staples: Kim, Steve (and their dog Zoey), and Theresa. Theresa added her niece Rosie to make it a fivesome just a day before departure. Rosie was a rookie. She had rarely set up a tent, had never carried a 30-pound pack, nor had she ever shat in the woods. She did, however, bring the median age of our group down considerably at 24. She at least had youth and exuberance on her side. Steve called up to the park office for camping information and learned backcountry permits were limited to groups of four. We would chance it and travel in a five-pack. The journey started on the early morning crossing aboard the Badger car ferry. Rather than a movie onboard, we chose a sunset show at dusk from the main viewing deck. We all gazed at a sky turning a complete palette of pastels from pinks to purples that turned Lake Michigan blue to gray, then finally dark. To serenade our colorful departure, a police escort boat spouted a water cannon off starboard until the massive ferry cleared the channel. We now had four hours to kill. On the back lounge deck, opting not to play Badger Bingo in the main cabin, we ordered salads for dinner. We laid maps out on the table to determine our hiking routes and campsites and agreed seven miles per day with a full pack was our limit. Wide-eyed and smiling, Rosie listened and nodded her head. The tentative plan was a loop starting at Overlooked Falls trailhead, first to a cabin on Lake Superior next to Mirror Lake, then back following Little Carp River trail. We guesstimated it was under 20 miles total in three days. It was a good plan.

Who needs a tent anyway?

The next morning, the ferry gave way to hours of driving north from the Green Bay Country Inn. It was our final opportunity to be clean for several days. We passed Lambeau field, cursed the Packers as any true Detroit Lions fan should, and continued north to the park. After an initial view of Lake Superior and permits secured at the main office, Steve rocketed the minivan on winding roads to our starting point. The five of us excitedly spilled out of the van and started cramming three days of food and gear into our pack. Enthusiasm was high. Our hiking shoes were laced, straps were secured, and sleeping gear was checked. My pack seemed heavy, so I tossed out a pack of PopTarts and an extra shirt. I was ready to start walking in the woods. Rosie the Rookie was all smiles, and even Zoey had her doggie pack on, ready to run.

I tucked my water bottle into my side pocket and approached Theresa. "You and Rosie ready to go?" She walked closer to me and in low voice informed, "Steve and Kim forgot their tent." Incredulous, thinking I heard wrong: "They forgot their tent—seriously?" Simultaneously, we turned toward the open back of the van, where a perplexed Steve and Kim discussed their important missing item. They confirmed, after one final search of the van, the tent was safely packed and sitting at the front door of their Grand Haven home. Silent, I waited for a rush of finger-pointing or angry accusations. Nothing happened except for some sheepish shrugging and exchanged mumbling of "I thought you packed it." Theresa, always solution-minded, refocused our tent-less friends and reminded them that we did have two other small tents and we'd make do.

So it was, Rosie went from rookie to hero (without having taken one step) with her borrowed two-person tent, packed and present. The tent I carried would have to transition from a two-man to a three-woman tent, and Rosie's ultra-compact would become a one-woman, one-tall-man, one-dog tent! It would be cozy, but the camping mission need not be aborted. Plus, on a whim, pre-trip Steve reserved a cabin for night one on Lake Superior. In our case, another bit of luck considering we were one tent down. The crisis seemed partially averted, and our five-pack started to laugh at the forgotten tent. Theresa presented Steve with Rosie's tent bag and asked, "Would you mind carrying this?"

We crossed the Little Carp River on a footbridge and started walking. It was easier to forget the tent and my busy life once we walked with the forest closing in on a narrow path. I had not packed my mobile phone, knowing the Porkies had no cellular service. I let out a long, gratifying exhale and fixed my mind on the moment—not to be interrupted for three complete days by dings, pokes, likes, or vibrations. My mind craved simpler thoughts and choices not connected to an email chain. I just wanted to think about things like:

> *Light or dark*
> *Morning or night*
> *Hungry or full*
> *Awake or sleepy*
> *Sand or stone*
> *Sun or stars*
> *Wet or dry*
> *Still woods or a rushing river*

I had plenty of time to focus my thoughts and enjoy the beauty of a deep leafy, mossy green that enveloped the trail. We hugged the Little Carp River for miles, just like the moss did the base of reaching hardwoods. Distilled sunlight sniped through the forest branches and landed on moss, lichen, river, and rocks. It was humid, so I was thankful for the abundance of shade. We stopped aplenty, getting used to our packs, and snacked on homemade jerky, gorp, and fruit snacks. Photo ops were conveniently placed around every bend in the river. Steve, oft in front with his long strides, announced, "There might be scenery up ahead." Two river crossings made for day one highlights: one with shoes on, rock-hopping, and the second where we carefully waded in, our bare feet sliding on slippery stones under the surface of the water. The river provided our music as we walked north toward Trapper Falls.

As we tired, the conversations waned, and I felt my pack dig into my right shoulder. My first hot spot presented itself, and I shifted to release the pressure. *Keep moving.* Theresa and I checked the map for distance once we hit the Superior beach. We opted not to take the shorter Cross Trail even though the North Country Trail route was longer because it deposited us just west of our cabin. As a bonus, we hiked a mile along the shore to our cabin for a grand total of eight miles.

We were elated to take our packs off, and huge sighs of relief escaped everyone. I equate the sensation to taking your ski boots off after a full day of skiing. The sun was already low, so it was time for a dunk before sunset. Lake Superior was a refreshing camp shower that doubled as an ice pack. The view from our Superior beach and the mouth of the river held huge flat, partly submerged black boulders near the shore. The grouping looked like a pod of orcas circling in the shallows. I realized they were not whales as I watched my friends sit on them and look out toward the setting sun.

The beach is strewn with terra-cotta red stones, black rocks, and pebbles in stark contrast to the sandy dunes of Lake Michigan. The black beach of Lake Superior characterized its rugged beauty; I felt I could almost hear it flaunting its superiority and power over the smaller Great Lakes. Superior, sometimes the angry and menacing lake, was calm and serene that night. She mellowed through the evening to welcome a burning red ball of sun to her edge. The sunset perched on Lake Superior for just a moment, which gave way to hunger and taco night in the cabin. Kim (our most experienced camper) suggested we eat that meal first since it was the heaviest in our packs. We all readily agreed, acutely aware of our aches. The cabin had four bunks, a table, a counter facing north, and a potbelly stove. I lit two candles, Kim and Theresa stirred our Mexican rice mixture, Rosie retrieved some water to filter, while Steve gathered firewood. We sat down to a candlelight dinner and a bottle of wine Theresa had hauled in a portable container. We demolished the food (no calorie counting while backpacking) and the wine before our late dinner turned quickly into bed-making and using the outhouse.

Just out the screen door for my turn, it occurred to me to look up for northern lights. I looked up at a star scene that turned the black night to a twinkling mass of light. I craned my neck and yelled to the gang, "Hollllyyyy crraaaappppp you have to come and look at this." I must have sounded dramatic because within minutes we all lay on the rocky beach and looked up, captivated. The big dipper stretched out in front of us, lower in the sky, and the handle pointed to the ever-bright North Star. Straight above (It's best to lie down.) is the Milky Way, strewn with millions of stars in a surrounding halo. The sunset had been a highlight, but stargazing on a Lake Superior clear night had me feeling blessed to be up north. Full of wonder (and tacos), we could now get some rest. The good news was the tent situation was a non-factor on night one.

All the girls got the bunks, and Steve volunteered to hit the floor with his sleeping pad. We fell asleep to rodents scratching in the stovepipe, Zoey licking her paws, followed by a chorus of snoring.

Pee Like a Boy

Camping and hiking is the simple life, yes? Or is it merely trying to plot distances and time in between finding a private spot to go? We took to calling the outhouses "Crapportunites" on our three days in the park. The Porcupine Mountains have this great network of rentable cabins and nearby outhouses that made being a woman in the woods significantly easier. Although Kim and I did have new Shewees (gifts from Theresa) that made for easier woodland potty breaks. A Shewee is an ingenious funnel and tube system that allows a girl to pee like a boy, avoiding swiping our bottoms on poison ivy during squatting sessions. Theresa's tip: take a wide stance to prevent peeing on your shoes. I became a believer in this pink-sleeved contraption over the weekend. I pressed the catcher/funnel tight to my private parts and made sure the tube was securely attached at the bottom. When I tried to go, instantly I understood why guys get stage fright. I needed to get used to the equipment. Eventually, after a deep breath, I let myself go (literally), and, magically, a stream of yellow shot out the funnel and onto the leafy ground. Less mess, no soggy underpants—I was hooked. Next up, I thought I might try it in winter and see if I whether could write "Laura" in the snow. Besides well-placed outhouses, the Big Carp River Trail on our second day in the park was noteworthy and very scenic. The Big Carp Trail would lead us to Correction Line Trail for the day's route. We had a solid eight miles to traverse (up, as it turned out) to Mirror Lake and to land a campsite. It was sad to leave the views of Superior behind and the safe confines of a roof over our heads. A warm and humid day was taking shape after breakfast of oatmeal and coffee. I was dreading putting on the pack for fear of awakening the shoulder hot spot again. The Big Carp River was calling, and so was the Shining Cloud Falls; we donned packs and started up. I was damp quickly and swabbed sweat away from my eyes as I labored up the grade to make another awesome waterfall vista. The river views moved inland to muddy and soggy footpaths. I tried to split time between finding dry footfalls and soaking up the deep misty green of the dense woods. During most of my steps, I heard my heavy breathing paired with a squishy suction sound that rose up from the bottom of my boot. After a lunch stop along a river perch, with a glimpse of sun, we were back at it again too soon. With still two or three miles to go, the walk transitioned to a march, and my hot spot resurfaced. I grimaced and dug my fingers in while I walked and tried to find those simple thoughts again. Dry or muddy, dirty or clean.

I convinced the girls to take another break. Steve was well ahead anyway, scoping out campsites with Zoey. I slid my pack off with a grimace and gulped the last of my water then started bumming some from Theresa. After an all-girl tribal council, we determined it was just another mile. Thankfully, we were right. Zoey and Steve walked toward us without packs, confirming we had almost made it. Rosie, Kim, Theresa, and I were elated. Steve happily shared he had found a campsite and the other three

were all occupied. Yay, Steve! Spirits lifted, we spotted the lake through the green foliage, and the mud finally gave way to sunrays bouncing off water ahead. Mirror Lake was an oasis of clean water with an abundance of waterfowl, including some very vocal loons. They called at us as we invaded their lake with our skankiness. No one bothered with soap, instead electing to stay submerged and just scrub the mud away while cooling sore muscles yet again. Mostly clean will do when backpacking. Steve, Kim, and Theresa had hijacked the rowboat near our swimming hole and were paddling around the perimeter of the small lake in hopes of enticing more waterfowl to say hello.

Thunder Rolls

The rest of the evening revolved around fitting in dinner and in our tents. Both Jetboils were put to work, and we made two steaming pots of shells and cheese with turkey sausage. "Devoured" would be the most accurate word to describe dinnertime. In that hungry moment, shoveling in mouthfuls with my blue spork, I imagined I was in a Parisian bistro cutting up a piece of duck confit. Not able to fit in another gourmet bite, we took turns stoking our fizzing and uncooperative fire. The damp firewood kept the fire fizzling, rather than flaming, so it only partly helped to keep the mosquitos away. We still sat around our

small fire and relaxed, and Rosie queued up a game called Heads Up! that kept us entertained for a while.

Unexpectedly, we were interrupted by flashes of approaching lightning. Our game-playing quickly turned to scurrying, Shewee-ing, food collecting (It all goes up a bear pole in a bag.), and tent flap securing. The weather forecast had listed Monday as the T-storm warning, but meteorology in Michigan is educated guessing. Low, rumbling thunder started, and the lightning continued to flash over top of the wind-brushed branches. Kim and Steve reminded us to get out garbage bags and ponchos to put shoes and packs in under the tent vestibule. Frantic motion continued for another 30 minutes while the T-storm kept posturing, sending bursts of wind and heat-lightning flashes. Finally, we had all crammed into two tents, and Zoey barked at the thunder. Rosie, Theresa, and I shared the other cozy tent and zipped up the flaps just as the first drops spattered on the tarp. My Robert Frost poem recital was interrupted by rain then by two moths flitting around the two headlamps in the tent. All three of us squeaked like preteens until we shooed them out and rezipped.

Lights went out, and I lay on my back and listened to the approaching storm. The wind blew harder through the thick evergreen boughs directly above us, but remarkably it never shook the tent at ground level. I looked up and watched flashes illuminate our tent. The rain came, the tent stayed dry, and the storm moved east. Only in our minds and dreams did lightning strike a large tree branch that fell and smashed our tent with all of us in it!

Morning dawned with the realization of only five more miles to transport my pack back to the completion of our loop. I lazily stretched and checked around me for wet spots under my pad. All was dry. I hoped my tent neighbors had been as fortunate. It was just after 7:00, which seemed early until I realized we had scrambled in the tents early to escape the rain. Theresa's aluminum coffee pot got its final workout, and we boiled water to add to our MRE (meal ready to eat) egg, sausage, and hash brown mixture. Kim and I handed everyone a steaming pile of eggs on top of a tortilla for a final Porkies breakfast. The sky was gray, and more rain seemed probable. Purposefully, we ate breakfast burritos and packed up gear and damp tents. Considering conditions and the number of tents, it had been all but decided to make the rest of our stay in the Porkies the tourist version instead of the badass hiker version. We still had five miles of ultra-green to hike on South Mirror Lake to Little Carp River Trail. We would pass the southern tip of Mirror Lake on a narrow plank bridge that sent us back

into enchanted woods, past Beaver Creek and toward Lily Pond. At the pond, waterfowl abounded again; this time several herons took flight around us while we munched PBJ or PBH mini-bagels. The trail intersected again with the North Country Trail as it had on the first day. The clouds held, and the rain stayed away as we walked back to Overlooked Falls and the parked van.

Lake of the Clouds

Steve and Rosie had never seen the Lake of the Clouds, so the second half of our Sunday we dedicated to backtracking (by car) around the park and west on 107 to the packed parking lot for the viewing area. A short paved trail led us up to a view of the rocky escarpment and a

narrow lake below hemmed in by an impressive thick forest of more green. Nearby Government Peak is the highest point in the park at 1,850 feet. (Our Mirror Lake campsite had been at about 1,500 feet per the topographical map and Steve's GPS.) That afternoon we carried only cameras. My shoulders were gleeful as I leaned on the stone barrier and soaked up the view that held 60,000 acres of wilderness forest and the oft-photographed lake. I thought back to my last visit to LOC in the fall of '06 and remembered the same view with strokes of fall color on all the leaves. I couldn't decide whether the velvet green of summer was more inspiring than the reds and glowing gold of autumn. In all my travels, I could only think of one other place that was greener than the Porkies—the mythical Emerald Isle known as Ireland.

Our tourist day continued on M-45 in search of cheap lodging. In just two hours, the van landed at the Comfort Inn in Iron Mountain, hometown of two famous coaches, Steve Mariucci and Tom Izzo. Now our Monday morning drive back to the ferry was only three hours, and as a bonus, we could sleep in on beds not crammed in two tents. If you kept stats, we stayed in hotels two nights, a cabin for one, and only one night in a tent. Even so, we hauled all the gear around for over 20 miles, which still counts as a semi-badass hiking trip, right? I decided it didn't really matter where we slept: we were UP north.

Superior Views
(Marquette, Michigan, and Ore to Shore)

The U.P. continues to host more in-state adventures, this time Marquette in a condo instead of a tent. The city and its single-track have been awarded a bronze-medal designation by the International Mountain Biking Association. This designation brings plenty of mountain biking enthusiasts to the area and more than 3,000 riders to the annual Ore to Shore Mountain Bike Epic Race in August. It's worth the (nine-hour) drive if you get the chance.

The view from the Rock Cut Cabin was pristine: Lake Superior stretched out beyond our sight, golden eagles soared overhead, thimbleberry bushes lined the driveway, a rock face bordered the fire pit with two perfectly placed Adirondack lounge chairs, while waves lapped on the rocky shoreline. The reverie was only interrupted about every 10 seconds ….
… when an 18-wheeler's diesel rumbled loudly past on Highway 41! The road to Marquette was perched between our cabin and the Lake Superior view. The traffic noise was the only complaint though for a week of Upper Peninsula adventures.

It was the kind of trip that left me too tired to take notes in my journal. We covered many miles each day, mostly on two-wheeled contraptions. The sun shone every day except Friday. I smiled and welcomed the rain, which meant a break for my aching inner-ass cheeks. I did a decent job of keeping up with Josh, whose boundless pedaling energy had everyone chasing, including Steve and Kim, who joined on Wednesday. Our twosome became a foursome, and we immersed ourselves in exploring Marquette, eagle hunting, pedaling single-track, rock-hunting on our private beach, rope swing river-jumping, followed by hearty meals washed down with hand-crafted brews from Black Rocks and Ore Dock Brewing.

Kim's smile was intoxicating on this trip; she soaked in nostalgia from her NMU days as a student, marveling that some of the old places still looked and felt the same (Portside Inn, Vango's, Quick Stop Bike Shop, and the Vierling Restaurant to name a few). And crazy tourists and students still hike out to Black Rocks Beach on Presque Isle for the famous 30-foot plunge into frigid Lake Superior. My nostalgia was about looking out over enormous lakes that you can't see across. The idea of it just doesn't get stale. We traded one big lake (Michigan) for a bigger lake (Superior) on this trip. Lake Superior was warm enough to swim in August and was perfect to rid the group of daily trail grime. It served as a daily prewashing to an actual shower.

Marquette has ramped up its mountain biking moxie, also securing a top-10 world ranking for single-track, along with its bronze IMBA label. With intermediate riding credentials at best, I was humbled on the trail systems. Arriving on Tuesday, Josh and I watched a race series featuring dual slalomers on a downhill course. They went really fast and wore a lot of padding. The knee pads and elbow pads I observed should have served as intermediate biker foreshadowing. Wednesday, we set off on our own adventure on the Noquamanon South Trails. Thankfully, we had met Kate at Downwind Sports, and she thoroughly went over the trail map, pointed out several routes, and explained the difficulty level (marked like ski hills from green to double black diamond).

From our starting point, we took the blue trail (labeled difficult), which climbed to the top of Mount Marquette. Kate had warned us about the climb, but neither of us was

prepared for the rocks and roots. We did a lot of hike-a-biking, adding bruises to shins and elbows. Mountain biking is all about climbs then rewards. The day eventually led to a reward as we went from blue to the red loop and down Freakin-Nature's banked turns. We pedaled around Greywalls Golf Course and passed signs telling us to be quiet. After logging 14 miles, we found the yellow trail to finish, named Gorge-Ous for its precarious ridgeline above the Carp River. Hyper-focused, I kept my wheel on the left edge along the safe side. The river and the trail spit us out on an access road just two miles north of the cabin. After a Superior prewash, we landed at Black Rocks Brewing for beers.

They sponsor the trails, so we felt obligated to patronize them.

The next day, after a morning eagle-hunting hike behind the cabin, we tested the North Trails accessed by the paved Iron Ore Path through Marquette. After seven miles on pavement, we transitioned to dirt trails following the Dead River. We bumped over roots for a few miles then stopped abruptly, spotting a rope swing with a launching board. "Let's do it," we all chimed, simultaneously pulling off layers. Each of us took several attempts with varying levels of water-entry gracefulness. My names for the rope-swing attempts: the Backside Wedgie or the Ass-Dragger. The trick was to grasp the knots on the rope as high as you could reach and swing out while pulling up your legs to avoid dragging through the water. Still laughing, we climbed back on bikes with water squishing out our backsides from our soaked padded-ass shorts.

Spontaneity continued to rule the day after another two miles. Entering another loop heading into dense woods, Steve popped his chain. No one had an extra link or the tools we needed. We backtracked to the main trail, and Steve coasted (and got pushed by Josh and Kim) back to the main road and to Quick Stop Bike Shop for repairs. Steve got by with a little help from his friends.

Ore to Shore Mountain Bike Epic

There's romantic and historical relevance with this bike race. Two months into dating Josh, he casually mentioned a bike race tradition he'd been doing for years in Marquette. "You should come up with me and race!" he offered. First-time jitters plagued me leading up to departure, and a low-grade level of apprehension had settled in my gut. Plus, I really did not want to hurl in front of a new boyfriend. And I worried about my lack of TITS (time in the saddle). I'd never done a mountain bike race, certainly not one with a mass start of more than 900 riders, point to point over rocks, sand, gravel, single-track, road, and bridges. Josh kept assuring me on the drive up, "You'll be fine," with a knowing smile. I was not convinced of my bike fitness level. One week before we had pedaled

10 miles of trails at Luton Park in Grand Rapids, which was the extent of my trail training. The day before leaving, I stopped in to CityHub Cyclery in Muskegon for some accessories and to pick up a custom logo jersey. With my new duds, I would look sharp at the very least, even if I was found bloodied and bruise in a ditch. Julia, the owner, asked what I was up to, and I told her I was riding the Ore to Shore. She grinned and asked, "Who talked you into doing that?"
"A guy named Josh," I replied.

Fast-forward another summer and Josh and I were still dating and back again in Marquette in August. The tables had turned! I had talked someone else into doing the race and offered the same advice Josh had offered me a year earlier. So Saturday we raced 28 miles in Ore to Shore's Soft Rock option. Kim made her inaugural ride while I felt like a better-prepared sophomore. The veteran, Josh, made his fifth appearance. Steve was on the disabled list with surgery looming, so he opted for the south trails during the race. With more TITS this year, I hoped to beat my 2:25 time from 2014. Success! I shaved off 15 minutes, coming in at 2:10, but my best accomplishment was not time but rather making it up Kirby Hill. Spurred on by two women, off their bikes, they became my overzealous cheerleaders. They yelled while I furiously pedaled: "You can do it! Looking strong!

Get the hell out of her way—rider coming through!" I credit them for my success. I didn't want to let them down, and they got two young kids blocking the trail out of my way.
Thanks, Trail Angels!

Also worth noting was an ill-timed seat pack malfunction. At seven miles in, after a series of rutted hills, my seat pack Velcro picked that moment to stop working. It dragged along my back wheel, forcing me to stop. I tried to reattach it and tie it to the post. Two miles later it was dragging again. I dismounted and considered whipping it (and all my tire supplies) into the woods. Instead, I stuffed the whole pack in the back of my bike shorts. I rode the rest of the way with a large black tumor protruding from my arse! I pedaled hard to try and catch back up to Kim. At the finish area, I found Kim and Josh, and we exchanged animated stories while

watching other riders cross the finish line. Kim logged 2:06 and Josh notched 1:45, shaving almost 15 minutes off last year. Dirty, happy, and tired, we mingled around eating bananas and donut holes while rehydrating. Lake Superior called to us once again for a daily dunking.

The North Country Trail (NCT) in Michigan

Troll or Yooper, there is another gem in the state for an outdoor enthusiast. Camper or backpacker, there is an undiscovered day trip for hikers or bikers of all levels on the North Country Trail. I'll admit that I had never heard of the North Country Trail until 10 years ago, introduced by bikers instead of hikers. The trail runs through my entire home state of Michigan and was approved by Congress in 1980. It spans 4,600 miles through seven states, from New York to North Dakota. Funny: I grew up hearing about the Appalachian Trail and its epic hikes and read about it in Bill Bryson's novel *A Walk in the Woods*. Not that I am enlisting a competition, but the NCT has a long way to go to live up the AT's lore. The AT covers 2,170 miles from Georgia to Maine and of course winds through the Appalachian Mountain range. Thousands have hiked its entirety, and many more are planning as I type. In contrast, most people have never heard of the NCT, including people like me in the very states where the trail exists.

After some quick research, it appears that just 11 people have completed the entire NCT hike. Another interesting detail: the NCT is not just a traditional hiking trail; some of it parallels roads or two-tracks. But possibly the biggest difference is that the NCT lacks a magnificent mountain range on its stat sheet. Even so, after some digging I realized that the NCT is impressive in its own right, with its sights, ecosystems, rivers, Great Lakes, forests, and meadows very worthy of planning a trek. Just in Michigan the NCT passes through the Manistee National Forest and also Pictured Rocks National Lakeshore in the Upper Peninsula.

A mere half-hour drive from my condo, I can access the NCT trailhead for some much-needed time with nature. Pristine wilderness can be much closer than we all think, especially if you are a Michigander. Lucky for me, my trail-riding friends discovered the NCT is open in sections to biking, and the MMBA (Michigan Mountain Biking Association) documents trail conditions on its website. The irony of it all is that allowing biking on the NCT has been controversial, primarily because of erosion and other issues that go along with sharing. But, so far, bikers and hikers (and runners too) have found a way to share this resource in certain areas in Michigan.

In fact, one of my favorite sections to bike is near Hesperia off Highway 20, northeast of Fremont, Michigan. We gather a group and bike north on a fun hard-packed trail that rolls up and down perfect slopes, on what I like to call a pedal festival. The slight uphills give you enough of a challenge, and the ensuing downhills are thrilling as you rocket past hardwoods with just inches to spare outside your handlebars. The only problem: it sure is hard to take in the beautiful scenery from the seat of a bike that requires all your attention be paid to the trail and the tree that brushed your shoulder or helmet. My tip: pedal and enjoy the ride but be sure to dismount often enough to admire the views along the way.

Being a hiker as well, I can understand the NCT purists who would rather see the scenery from their own two feet. You'll see wild berry bushes that line the trail and hidden wetlands and marshes with deer grazing and a great number of birds and other wildlife. And I've realized that I have barely scratched the surface of the NCT in western and northern Michigan. In all honesty,

a through-hike or even tackling the Michigan section would be tough, merely to find the time. Yet I am encouraged to discover the sibling to the famous Appalachian Trail. And it is right in my own backyard and is waiting for me to continue to explore it on foot or on my bike.

For more information on the North Country Trail and local trails and access points you can visit www.northcountrytrail.org.

Michigan Leeches

To round out my Mitten adventures, I feel compelled to share a story that took place after a day of riding the NCT south of Ludington. It was a hot, sticky morning, Michigan style, with the big lake perspiring mist like all of us while we struggled to pull on tight bike shorts. Our legs and behinds turned into polish sausages stuffed in a casing ready to hold in all our juices and sweat. The North Country Trail hosted our riding group of four, starting at the M-20 trailhead. We were headed to Nichols Lake Campground near Bitely, tucked in the Manistee National Forest. The NCT single-track winds around pine and hardwood forest, bog, and inland lakes; through briar and leafy patches; and in and out of the baking sun. At the trailhead lot, we geared up, adding helmets, bike cleats, sunglasses, sunscreen, Camelbacks, and snack bags to our already simmering sausages. We needed all these ingredients to survive 15+ miles of hilly, rooted, and rutted natural terrain.

We set off and rolled over M-20 blacktop and into the woods, the trail engulfing us in a steamy canopy of leaves and tall trees. Immediately, sweat rolled off my forehead and down my nose and dripped onto the packed dirt trail below my pedals. Thankfully, a benefit of biking is the self-generation of a breeze. *Pedal faster*, I thought. *It will keep me cool.* My theory worked until my quads started to cramp at mile eight. I kept my companions in sight as we swooshed by hardwoods, around banked corners, and up a slowly ascending ridgeline. My gears went down, and my body temperature went up. Sunglasses steamed and slid to the tip of my nose, like I was a middle-aged woman, leaning forward, anticipatorily reading a seedy romance novel.

To say we arrived sweaty and tired at Nichols Lake was an understatement. We were wrecked, drenched in sweat, and starving, and we literally collapsed on a rickety picnic table. A barrage of vitamin drinks, salty snacks, and tales of trail domination eventually brought smiles and laughter from the four of us. Only nature's call to the ladies' bathroom took me away from reveling over stories of our near misses with hardwoods.

I walked a short distance and pushed my way through a wooden screen door and found a stall. Instead of my usual hover, I decided to sit and pee in order to rest my aching quads. I pulled down at my sausage casings and struggled with the spandex against my still sweating skin. Wrestling them down finally, I bent and locked eyes onto a shiny, dark, wormy-looking object, perched just above my unmentionables. I shrieked, high-pitched and horrified, like a teenager being chased in a horror film. Panicked and still yelling, I flicked my fingers at the glistening thing. *Dear god, how did a leech get in my pants?* I knocked it hastily off my body to the green-painted cement floor. Pulling in quick gasps, completely grossed out to have a varmint near my privates, I leaned down toward the floor for a closer look. Almost kneeling and watching intently, I noticed it didn't move. The shine and glisten were now gone. I was perplexed. *What was it?* Closer still, almost touching the "creature," I realized it was not a leech, rather the inanimate black rubber earpiece from my sunglasses. *How did that get there?* I picked it up and examined it for final non-leech confirmation. Shrieking turned to a loud exasperated chuckle, followed by an embarrassed admission to three friends.

Bike spandex shorts don't have pockets. Off my bike, before my foray to the ladies' room, I had stuffed one arm of my sunglasses down the front of my shorts to prevent losing them. I pulled them out and left them on the table, which deposited the culprit (rubber earpiece) unknowingly. I didn't lose my sunglasses but almost lost my wits over a leech near my minge.

What's next in the mitten and nearby?
As mentioned previously, it is not important how far you go on your getaways but rather letting yourself have some important time away from work and daily routines. I try to find a mix of traveling locally in my own state,

176

with the goal of going international once a year. Lucky for me, Canada is a mere three-hour drive from my door. For example, Lake Superior Provincial Park is just two hours north of St. Ignace in Ontario. LSPP has some amazing hikes, waterfalls, and a Lake Superior coastline that is fantastic for sightseeing. The beaches in that section are dotted with car-sized boulders that you'll have to navigate on and around on the coastline trail. And I continue to plot up-north weekends and enjoy rediscovering coast towns like Ludington, Manistee, Bear Lake, and Beulah. They are all on the way up to Traverse City, which is an often-traveled section of US-31 for me.

Chapter Seven
Five Hos and a Bro

Nevada and
California,
2009

The only thing employees gain by being tied to the office is stress. There was a clear correlation between those who have more unused PTO days and those who reported feeling "very" or "extremely" stressed at work, particularly for those employees who leave more than 11 days unused.

Source: www.Projecttimeoff.com

Thankfully, I have a wealth of friends who understand how important it is not to be tethered to your office and to your phone. Social gatherings double as getaway planning sessions. Even returning from a trip, my friend Steve is already plotting the next. He believes it's important to have the next vacation queued up to keep post-vacation depression (PVD) from setting in.

A vacation in February does not have to mean heading south to a sandy beach; search for snow instead and spring break in the mountains. The only tan I'll get on a ski trip is from the neck up, paired with a perfect pair of raccoon eyes from my goggles. On winter trips, I've traded in a bikini for merino wool tops and long underwear. I love the beach too, but there is altitude appeal to being in the mountains, like a top-to-bottom run then joining friends by a warming fire, with hot chocolate in hand.

On the way to Reno and the Lake Tahoe area, I realized I had been lucky enough to visit more than 10 US and Canadian resorts. Sitting in my uncomfortable plane seat, I tallied up where I had been. My list included Aspen/Snowmass, Vail/Beaver Creek, Copper Mountain, Breckenridge, Keystone, and A-Basin in Colorado's Rocky mountain range. Other trips included Big Sky, Montana; Park City, Utah; and Sun Valley, Idaho. And being a Michigander, neighboring Canada is always a nice choice for ski trips like Whistler in British Columbia and Blue Mountain in Ontario.

However, my journey on skis ironically started on the East Coast at the Wisp Resort in western Maryland in my mid twenties. My ski racer ex-husband, employed by the resort, snagged some rentals and attempted to tutor me on making some turns. Much like the marriage, the ski lessons were not totally successful. The good news: I've kept up with the hobby even though I didn't keep the husband. I became a passable skier and learned the nuances of an incredibly high-maintenance and expensive sport. Of any sport, I've learned that having the right equipment and gear was critically important to success and to win the battle with frigid temperatures. Off and on for about five years, I skied on hand-me-downs and moved gradually from green runs to blues. And I managed to improve my skills at après-ski happy hour sessions, also an important tradition in alpine skiing.

The thrill of the mountains in winter drew six of us together for five days of testing our fitness on mountain runs at Heavenly Resort overlooking Lake Tahoe. Heavenly is so big that the resort borders two states in part of

California and Nevada. The trip was named after the gender ratio of five women to one guy. Steve had his gloves full traveling with five women: Jen, Theresa, Deb, and Kim, plus me. We were blessed with amazing snow conditions and impeccable timing, arriving in the area a day after 64 inches of snow had fallen! On the drive in from Reno in a sparkling new white minivan, we marveled at the snowbanks along the short hour-long drive from the airport to Lake Tahoe Vacation Resort. Our condo put us close to the lifts and also to the downtown-area casinos and clubs. We had so much fun during our days and nights of snow that it spawned several original songs to commemorate our adventures. On a chairlift ride, Kim and Theresa covered a Steve Miller Band tune, "Fly Like an Eagle," and later Theresa wrote a custom song for Jen in honor of her quirky ski injury, called the "Wang-Tang."

The epic snow conditions were the story line the first two days. Theresa was thrilled to ski the double-black bowls in powder over her knees. Deb and I flew down the groomed blues and occasionally turned into the moguls or trees for short stints, then back again to groomers to save our quickly tiring legs. We found out later the

first day that Theresa (skiing alone) had kicked both shoes (lost both skis on a fall) in a steep bowl. Using one ski as a shovel, she poked and prodded uphill until she found the other. In the super deep snow, she struggled for a half hour to click them back on. Deb and I met up with Theresa that afternoon, sweaty, happy, tired, and ready to exchange spirited stories.

We made a quick trip to the grocery store to pick up supplies before the other three arrived on a later flight. The condo became cozy with six of us milling around instead of three. Deb, who is a known bathroom hog, was the only minor issue with six people and two bathrooms. Steve, Kim, and Jen were plenty jealous we had a day under our jackets, so I tried not to talk about the amazing conditions. I stuck to telling stories of how expensive the food was on mountain. We chatted excitedly and got organized to find rentals for Jen then a spot for dinner. Theresa was Jen's ski Sherpa and helped her through picking out boots and skis at the rental shop while the rest of us shopped around trying on hats, gloves, and anything on the sale rack that looked interesting. Jen, armed with her Lange boots and rental skis, signaled she was ready to find some dinner. It was easiest to let Deb choose the restaurant since she was the only vegetarian among our group. We ended up in a tasty joint with local and vegan choices,

and everybody rolled out happy and full. We had a big day of skiing ahead and a mountain covering two states.

Steve, as suspected, was not going to let anyone sleep in late. His boyish excitement prodded us to be slope-side when the lifts opened at 9:00. We managed to get everybody moving to the south entrance of Heavenly, and in minutes we were whooping like kids on our first turns down perfectly groomed corduroy snow. It's difficult to keep a group together on a mountain, especially when the abilities ranged from novice to expert. I was squarely in the middle of that range, so I was happy to head off to other parts of the mountain with Steve and Kim leading this time. Besides, there were songs to write, trees to run into, and snow drifts to fall in.

Always in search of the perfect tree run, Steve talked Kim into heading off-piste to navigate the powder and drifts. Theresa, of course, went along searching for a powder stash and led the three of them down a steep. She squeezed between two trees on her skis, while Kim and Steve followed behind trying to slow up to fit in the tight space. As they did, Kim tried to avoid Steve, who was barreling down right next to her. Unable to stop, she avoided Steve but instead disappeared into the tree well with a thump. Woman down! Abruptly looking back,

Steve and Theresa retreated to dig her out and made sure she was okay. While the boarders ran into trees, the rest of us double-plankers navigated the greens and kept an eye on Jen. She had begun to tug at the front of her boot after noticing a weird pinch on her shin. We stopped for a breather at the state line between Nevada and California. Jen produced her passport for a silly photo at her border crossing. We skied through the afternoon and made plenty of stops to rest legs and also take in views of Lake Tahoe in the valley below.

We had previously scoped out a pub at the base to have après drinks. All six of us eventually trickled in, removing snow hats and gloves and delayering in between sips of beers. With wide smiles and rosy cheeks, we took turns relaying the stories of the day, including Kim's tree encounter. Theresa had skied the bumps and the bowls, and Jen proudly announced she got to use her passport. The fun squall continued for a while until we piled in the rental van to return to the condo. We showered in shifts, so Jen and Kim volunteered to run out for more food, supplies, and beer.

The supply shopping went well. But Jen returned to the parking lot and misjudged the spacing between her parking space and a heavy-duty truck just to the right. The shiny white rental minivan logged its first dent! In a nervous panic, Kim and Jen grabbed my brand-new neck warmer off the seat and attempted to buff out the dent and the scratch. Sheepishly, they returned to the condo with my neck warmer, promising to wash it, and apologized to Theresa for denting the rental. Some of us laughed, but Theresa, who had paid for the van, informed us she had not purchased the extra insurance. Jen lost her driving privileges, and I gave my Turtle Fur neck warmer an inspection. The dent was forgotten after dinner, followed by several ibuprofen and a hot tub at the condo pool area.

Fly Like an Eagle

We brown-bagged it the next day, unwilling to spend $12 for a bad slice of pizza or a burger at the mountain lodge. Even a Cliff Bar set you back $5. Inflated food prices on mountain resorts were nothing new, so we made PBJ sandwiches for our lunches. Up top, we found a locker at the restaurant lodge and stored our food for later. The six of us crammed on the high-speed chair, our skis and boards dangling above the pitch. As we glided up the mountain, Kim and Theresa coached us through some new lyrics. We caught on quickly and sang along to the tune "Fly Like an Eagle" from the Steve Miller Band.

Verse One
Ate my breakfast
Didn't have mini-wheats
Hopped the chairlift
Headed for the trees
Met my boyfriend
His name is Steve…
Ohhhh, ooooooo he's good with computers!

Chorus
I've got blood in my urine
when I pee
Blood in my urine
Cuz I went and hit a tree
Blood in my urine….
When I pee
Ohhhhh, ooooooooo, I've got a contusion!!

The singing and fit of laughter got us off to a brilliant start, with our legs starting to adjust to the lengthy, heavenly runs. We met Steve's friend Bob that day. He was out west skiing and gambling and was nice enough to share some discounted passes to save on lift tickets. Steve had him meet us for lunch, but I think the gaggle of women scared him (and his blue one-piece ski suit) off to the next mountain. I smiled and walked toward him, offering my thanks for the ski passes. He grinned but looked down at his boots in the snow. He fidgeted nervously, abruptly moving toward Steve. "Uhhh, Steve, I will pick you up in the morning for a few runs. OK, bye, then." We chuckled at Bob's nervous nature and asked Steve if all women made him nervous. "Yup, pretty much." Steve was again stuck with all five women to himself.

We continued our lunch on a picnic table outside overlooking the city and the lake below. It was better than gorgeous as we took off a layer and soaked in the mountain sun on our arms and faces. Totally fine lingering, snacking, and resting my achy legs, I happily munched on a PBJ sandwich and savored a handful of salty chips. I also extended my lunch with a Bloody Mary at the bar and talked Jen into staying behind as well. She was thrilled to take her boots off and rest her socked feet on the barstool. We sipped, savoring the olives and staring out at the incredible view. After lazily chatting and wasting another half hour, we headed out to find our crew.

By the third day, I knew my way around the mountain.

We headed back mid-mountain near the gondola then continued to the far north side to ski some new runs. Heavenly is the only resort where I remember taking the chairlift down instead of skiing all the way in. We would need the extra energy because Deb informed us she was ready for a night out dancing.

We skipped après-ski and went back to the condo. We made spaghetti, opened a bottle of wine, and, in between shower shifts, found some casually slutty clothes appropriate for a dance club. The blow-dryer got a workout between five women and plenty of long, wet hair needing to be coiffed for a night out. Steve patiently sipped his wine and watched television. Steve has a wicked sense of humor and came prepared on this trip to play a trick on Deb. Armed with a DVD copy of *Patton* (World War II movie about General Patton), he popped it in, turned up the volume, and let it play. Backstory: two years ago on a ski trip, the same movie had been played exceedingly loudly in our tiny Park City condo, while the rest of us (including Deb) tried to make dinner. Instead of helping prepare dinner, Jeff turned up the volume, announcing what a great movie it was. We were all supremely annoyed with his selfish behavior; the movie volume was so loud we couldn't hold a conversation at dinner. During the meal, Deb shot disapproving looks at Jeff.

Fast-forward, finally ready, Deb walked around the corner and caught a glimpse of Steve and the television. Steve pretended not to notice her staring.

Incredulously, she asked, "Is that *Patton*?" He smiled wryly and said, "I just happened to find it, channel surfing."
"What are the odds?" she exclaimed, just as the rest of us jumped into the room, laughing to let her in on the joke.
"We brought it just for you," Steve exclaimed to Deb.
She let out a stream of signature laughs in relief, a cue to head out.

The mood was festive out of the gate. We piled in the van, and Jen slipped a dance mix CD into the van's player (No, we didn't let her drive.), and all six of us belted out Pat Benatar, Justin Timberlake, and Madonna tunes. We finally found a parking spot and enthusiastically walked through the brisk night into Harvey's Casino and directly into Cabo Wabo Cantina, inspired by none other than Sammy Hagar. The wine at the condo had kick-started a mountain buzz, and the tropical cocktails added to the growing squall. I was sipping on a margarita and laughing while Kim, Theresa, and Deb had a hair-flipping contest. My shoulder-length cut was not worthy of an attempt, so I hung around by Steve for that part of the show. Then, Jen challenged us all to attempt her mind-boggling stunt of tying a cherry stem in a knot inside her mouth. I made no entry into that contest either, instead photographing all the attempts.

After polishing off a round, we agreed to keep the squall moving. Through the maze of the casino we found ourselves two floors up, where a live band was playing just across from a slots/casino area. We immediately took over the small dance floor and yelled for the band to play "'Proud Mary,' and play it rough!" We grooved and spun each other around to all sorts of tunes, including our request. I noticed two guys sitting in chairs in the front row looking shy. I grabbed the cuter, dark-haired one on the right, "It's time to dance with me, don't you think?" He didn't respond but let me pull him up on the dance floor. In a swift moment, a smile spread across his face, and he slipped his arm around my waist. I didn't get his name, but we had two lovely dances, and I invited him to join us at the dance club. Meanwhile, Deb and Theresa were fending off gamblers who wanted to dance. Steve and Kim happily twirled around and let out a hoot when they played Tina Turner's best song. The dancing and the fun squall continued.

Deb got her wish: a bouncer outside of Club Blu Dance and Nightclub who was setting up the barricades handed us coupons for free entry. It was just 10 p.m., early for clubbing. We walked in and surveyed the empty dance floor, complete with a pole-dancing area. Off to the right, we were lured to a velvety, plush VIP bedroom area that featured a couch and bed in its midst, adorned with copious amounts of red satin pillows. Steve, Kim, Deb, and I ventured past the roped barricades into the dance bedroom, eyeing the lush pillows, seduced by the scene.

Meanwhile, Jen was lured to an art display that featured photographs of temporary body art on every possible place on the human body. Just as Jen was about to wave us over to take a look at the very revealing photos, the first pillow was hurled across the bedroom and struck me in the belly. I looked up to a grinning Steve, who had already reloaded with another. I bent down slowly and retrieved it, paused, then in swift motion fired back across at him. My softball instincts kicked into form. He ducked, and a full-blown pillow fight ensued. Probably not the action the club was hoping for in this area. It was hilarious, and in between hoots and catcalls, I continued to throw and duck in rapid motion and took a turn hiding behind the headboard. Kim flushed me out, and then I was bombarded by Theresa and Kim. We collapsed on the bed in a fit of

laughter, gasping for air. The pillows pummeled me, and I could only fire a few back. From my perch, I noticed Jen's shocked look as she watched us from outside the barricade. She was trying to get our attention. She noticed a security guy swiftly heading our way. A bouncer strode in with hands on hips. We were asked to leave the VIP area with a disapproving look, then he neatly restacked the pillows on the bed.

Still giggling, we sheepishly headed to the bar like kids sent to their room for a timeout. Jen grabbed my and Theresa's arms and told us she was sure we were going to get kicked out! The club eventually began to fill, including a large bachelorette party, with the bride outfitted in a veil. We people-watched and stayed inconspicuous for a while until "Like a Virgin" spurted out of the speakers. We spilled on the dance floor. We danced, laughed, and made friends with the bride and her friends and began to take turns on the dance pole. Turned out that Jen had been officially certified in aerobic pole dancing on a trip to Vegas, so she treated us to some moves. We urged her on, and the bridal party screamed in support as well. Not to be upstaged, Kim took a turn and jumped up on the pole then twirled in several full circles all the way to the floor to our delight. Impressed, I had no idea that I had two close friends who were accomplished pole dancers.

The DJ kept churning out classic dance hits, so we kept up a feverish pace and paused only for long swigs of beers or cocktails. Our fervor eventually faded, and I stole a look at my watch. It was 1 a.m. As quickly as the dance party began, we drifted off the dance floor, slammed ice waters, and nodded it was time for bed. Steve reminded us he had committed to meeting Bob for first tracks the next morning. I was already plotting a sleep-in and late arrival to the mountain.

We made it on the mountain the next day—just not in the morning. I blame Club Blu, the stripper pole, and a bachelorette party for my noon arrival at the gondola. Steve and Bob had been out for hours when we stepped off. Bob had called Steve early to remind him to be ready at 8, except that he forgot daylight saving time and had to furiously scramble to get ready. The girls slept peacefully while the boys made it first in line. We didn't care and rose late and nursed a slight hangover with strong coffee and green smoothies courtesy of Deb. In pajama pants we lazed around and took our time getting gear and boots together. It was a brilliantly sunny day, perfect for one last half day on the slopes.

We walked off the gondola platform only to look back to see Jen well behind tugging on her boots. Kim and I walked back to check on her. Jen

announced, "I don't think I can ski today; my shins are killing me. They actually hurt to touch them." She looked like she might burst into tears, so Kim and I tried to figure out what was causing the pain. The pressure of the boot tightened on her ankle was even too much for her to bear. Kim and I agreed that Jen was done for the day. I felt bad she couldn't even take a run on the last day, but the mystery condition was stubborn. Jen sent us off to have fun, and she headed back to the condo to enjoy some downtime.

Now just three, we met up with Steve for some runs. Deb and I noticed how good our legs were feeling on the last day. We happily skied the groomers, hangovers fading and having a blast on the near-perfect conditions. Turns out the only complaint I'd lodge at Heavenly was the absurd on-mountain food prices. The packed powder made up for that in the end, and we finished out our sunny day with immaculate views of Lake Tahoe. With our late start, we skied and rode right up until late afternoon. The result was a ride down the high-speed chairlift instead of up. The long winding cat-track to the south lot was tough for Steve and Kim on snowboards.

Theresa was the only one in our group who braved the steep, moguled south mountain. She tackled the bumps, and we watched from our perch on the chairlift while Kim videotaped. Her perfect rhythm was interrupted only once when she caught an edge, tipped dramatically forward, and took a face-digger into the next bump. Face full of snow yet all smiles, she yelled back to Kim, "Did you get that?" Thankfully, she was okay, so it was safe to let out a belly laugh at her unexpected face-plant. She laughed too, continued on, and met us at the bottom, where we all replayed the event again while she dumped snow out of her hood.

Back at the condo, we relayed our day to Jen while piling and organizing all our gear. She discovered the cause of her injury and that it was a known condition, at least according to one toothless ski patroller who had ridden down the gondola with her—though it was difficult to understand exactly what he said. He suggested, "You got yourself a wang-tang from your boots." Jen wasn't sure exactly what she heard, "wang-bang" or "lang-tang." He explained that her Lange boots were most likely the cause. Traveling home, we theorized he meant to say, "Lange-bang," named after the rental boot. And apparently Lange boots have a

reputation for pinching shins, feet, and ankles. Jen was pacified in this knowledge, not wanting to be the only person to ever suffer a severe shin sprain! Her injury inspired another song. Weeks later, Theresa revealed a ballad she had written for Jen, of course called "I've Got a Wang-Tang Thang!"
It went like this, to the tune of an old folk song.

> I don't know, if you can tell,
> But I cannot drive a van very well!
> I've gotta wang-tang thang......
>
> And, I don't know, if you can tell,
> But I cannot ski very well,
> When you have a wang-tang thang...

(This group of friends has a penchant for gathering post-trip to share photos, videos, and, in this case, songs! Deb hosted a gathering where we shared photos, and Theresa brought her guitar to lead us through some musical moments: "Blood in My Urine" and "Wang-Tang Thang." The latter brought most of us to tears because it was the first time we had heard it. Theresa had even taken the time to write out the lyrics and practice it before that evening.)

We spent our last night in Lake Tahoe hanging out and enjoying each other's company. To make flights the next morning, we piled into the white minivan for the drive to Reno. En route, we devised a plan we hoped would prevent the rental car company from noticing the dent on the right side. We pulled into the rental car lot and piled out quickly. In swift motion like a synchronized swim team, we slid both side doors wide open, which obscured the dent from view from the agent checking us in. In all the hurried activity of unloading and unpacking the back hatch, the agent never slid the doors closed. She walked around the perimeter of the van, recorded the mileage and sent us on our way. The dent went unnoticed, and we collected our receipt with a sigh and headed to the terminal. Theresa was relieved and Jen too, since we hadn't bought the extra insurance. Turned out we were "covered" after all.

Chapter Eight
Flat Alaska?

Alaska,
2006, 2012

*"If you think adventure is
dangerous, try routine.
It's lethal."*
- Paulo Coelho

Travel is spiritual. The vast, epic scenery inspires awe, making you realize how God, the universe, and nature are truly in charge. Find space, find quiet, and refuel your soul. It's easy to get off the grid and meditate if you visit places where there's no chance of getting a speck of a cellular signal. You can't be distracted by work when the mobile phone is rendered useless, connected only to a dark pocket in your luggage. When vacation planning, seek these places of refuge where you'll only be connected to nature. For example, try Wrangell St. Elias National Park in Alaska. On my second of three visits to Alaska, my trip

Alaska flat? Really. Certainly not if you are from Michigan, stuck at sea level in between three Great Lakes. For hardcore athletes and bikers who call Alaska home, perhaps it does start to flatten out over time.

On my third foray into the state in 2012, again it seemed steep, vast, challenging, and the opposite of flat. There was plenty of suspense and apprehension leading up to a return trip to the last frontier. Several patterns emerged that became conversation points for Steve, Kim, Theresa, and me. Our pending trip was a topic

Did you know?
- Alaska officially became the forty-ninth state on January 3, 1959.
- The state boasts the lowest population density in the nation.
- 17 of the 20 highest peaks in the United States are located in Alaska.

plan featured several epic bike rides. Before embarking on a 23-mile Johnson Pass mountain bike ride with 10 other exceedingly fit women, it seemed wise to gauge what to expect from the locals. Theresa and I inquired about the level of difficulty to one of the local riders, "How steep are the trails? Are the hill climbs rocky, shale, or hard pack?" She replied quickly and casually, "Oh, they're all flat to me," with a wave of her hand. I narrowed my eyes and resisted the urge to knock her off her bike seat.

in mixed-group conversations, and someone would always pipe in, "Oh, sounds great—are you going on a cruise?" No fewer than 10 people asked this question in various work or social settings. The four of us always responded with a resounding NO. Taking a cruise was dead last on our travel to-do lists. We'd prefer not to be sardined (salmoned would be a better illustration in Alaska) with thousands of others on a floating tube of metal stuffed full of four buffet meals per day. And what fun would it be to get dropped off at a small port town that swells with visitors all touring the same places and crowding into the same tourist attractions?

Rather, in an effort to prove that Alaska is indeed not flat, we chose excursions that would be powered by our own limbs as far as we could hike, bike, fish, and paddle. Turning mobile phones off, getting off the grid, and staying clear of cruise ships and crowds were the goals. The usual comments also surfaced: "Don't you ever take a vacation and sit on the beach?" The four of us would smile and explain that mountains, glaciers, rivers, and the wildlife of Alaska would not be found on any beach.

On the front end of 10 days, our plans included a visit to Wrangell St. Elias National Park, so called for its namesake mountain range. To follow, we'd head west of Anchorage to Aleyeska and Girdwood area, which would become home base for day trips. Our anticipation was heightened by news of bear and moose maulings, creatures stomping innocent hikers all over Alaska.

Tis the season (spring) for mama grizzlies and moose to have cubs and calves. Most mothers will do anything to protect their kids, so that time of year they were exceptionally cranky. There had been seven stompings alone in Kincaid Park and a slew of bear maulings in the Anchorage burbs. Sure, we raised a brow over this news and focused instead on reading literature that listed ways to stay safe in the backcountry. In the pro column, traveling in a group of four improved our chances. We made no solo hiking plans.

Our loose safety plan was something vague, outlined over pre-trip meetings: encounter a moose; climb up the closest tree. Or, for bears, make lots of noise while hiking or biking to avoid surprises. We practiced our signature call, "Whooooppppp, whooooopppppp," a cross between a yell and high-pitched birdcall. Theresa and I learned this signature whoop from Sue, our local connection on previous trips. After handing out bear bells to attach to our bikes, Sue reminded us that most bears stay clear if you don't surprise them. She also suggested that we carry bear mace as a precaution. Yup, mace only works at close range. The mere thought of using it seemed problematic. I conjured up a vision of dropping the can or forgetting to pull the safety pin as a 1000-pound animal shredded me with one paw swipe. While reading up on bear safety and thinking endlessly of Alaska's wild side, we packed our bags with equal parts apprehension and excitement.

Dinner Bells?

We began our adventure in a park the size of Switzerland, home to 14 peaks that reach above 10,000 feet! Wrangell St. Elias National Park is perched on the southeastern corner of the state, about a four-hour drive east of Anchorage. We named it WSE during our trip. Mount Sanford, at 16,237 feet, would be visible from our Caribou Creek public-use cabin on night one in the park. To get there we covered 300+ miles on Highway 1 and rolled into Glen Allen for supplies. The Matanuska River valley and glacier held our gaze for many miles to the south before opening up to a stand of impressive peaks. Thankful to be out of the car to stretch crampy legs, we wandered through the trading post for snacks and scouted out the anti-critter section. After much discussion, we purchased four sets of bear bells and a can of bear mace in hopes of not becoming an Alaskan statistic.

As we left, the dude at the checkout joked, "Most of the locals call them dinner bells." Grinning at the quip, we stopped once more at the WSE headquarters for our BSC (bear-safe container) required for camping in the backcountry. The BSC looks like a heavy-duty Tupperware container in the shape of a mini-keg with a tight-seal lid. Per the park rangers, all food items were to be kept inside and sealed at all times except when you were stuffing them in your own mouth.

We needed another two hours in the car to get to the interior of the park and near our trailhead off Nabesna Road. Kim was at the wheel for her turn and piloted us past rushing rivers, snowcaps in the distance, and a half-hour construction delay. The road turned to dirt then partial mud before we spotted mile marker 19. We parked the Forester off to the side and piled out to prepare for our trek up to our cabin. This would be our first experience backcountry cabin camping, five miles up a rooted, soggy trail. Somehow, I ended up with the bear mace attached to my pack after reading the instructions twice. In front of me, Kim and Theresa jingled up the trail, dinner bells attached to their packs. We took turns carrying the bulky BSC stocked with our MREs (meals ready to eat). The trail pointed toward Mt. Sanford, its white-brimmed cap staring back as we began walking. A grassy field opened to skinny evergreens then to a narrow trail that led slightly up, following the river still laced with snow and ice.

About every 10 steps, we encountered bear scat and moose poop in perfect little piles of pellets. Kim and Steve kept finding pieces of leftover bones from a kill alongside the trail. They found a rabbit's paw, a shoulder bone, and a sheep's hair in what they thought was wolf scat. After inspecting many such piles, we dubbed our hike the Crap and Carnage Trail. Though we saw plenty of shit, evidence that wildlife abounded, we saw nothing alive that evening. Steve seemed disappointed, but I was thankful to keep the mace packed away and the trigger locked.

The pine-lined trail opened to several crossings of the Caribou River. Stopping to survey the best way across, we looked for markers to guide our selection. Wide sections of snow and ice made the crossing slow as we picked our way across rocks, debris, and snow shelves. The river gurgled and rushed beneath our steps. I kept my eye on Theresa, who was leading the way. About halfway across, Theresa abruptly tumbled

sideways when a thin shelf of snow gave way and sent her down three feet to the river below. Kim, Steve, and I all let out a gasp and sprinted to the spot where she lay, half in the river like a turtle on its back shell unable to right herself. Steve hauled her up, then she took stock of her shoulder and hand, which had taken the brunt of the fall. She was dampened but mostly unharmed, so we mopped her up and continued the remaining 500 feet to the cabin. Eventually, the cabin came into view, distinct like a bright star in the clear sky. The new pine boards seemed to glow against the darkening dusk, and a single outhouse stood proudly up the hill from the cabin. They beckoned us to quicken our final steps for a late dinner. Inside, a wood stove and four plank bunks lined the cabin while outside featured a lovely front porch for potential wildlife viewing or coffee drinking in the morning. We built a fire and warmed our hands while T hung her soggy items. We dined on MRE lasagna by candlelight.

Skookum and River Crossings

Day two in WSE started early when air mattresses and sleeping bags began a chorus of rustling and squeaking. My sleepy eyes cracked open to a scene of Jetboil coffee and breakfast. Fed, changed, and packed by 8:00, Steve longingly searched the misty ridgeline for wildlife one last time. Nothing. Although on a trip back and forth to the churning river for water, he did mistake Theresa's curly mop of blonde hair for a moose for a brief milli-moment. Upon a closer look, he discovered his mistake and gave up on wildlife spotting for the morning. After taking turns in the newly constructed outhouse, we returned down the Crap and Carnage Trail.

The Forester was waiting unharmed, and it happily transported us down the road to Twin Lake Campground, where the wildlife-viewing meter finally tipped toward the good. After securing fishing gear, and in my case my journal and camera, we walked out to survey the lake. A massive bald eagle was perched in a pine watching us with interest. She was previewing the lake for a meal and seemed to preside over the other waterfowl that made appearances, like loons, wood ducks, and a trumpeter swan that flew overhead. All the winged animals talked to each other as our fisherman and fisherwoman set about their task. A gull screeched at the eagle, and it refused to move even after several close flybys. The loons swooned in a rhythmic cadence, and the ducks quacked in time to fishing line being let out and reeled in. It was a gorgeous morning with a rehearsed Alaskan bird chorus. A burst of excitement (like a cymbal) spread when Theresa yelled, "Fish on!" We all moved closer as she reeled in a wriggling fish up to shore. Without a net to scoop, it was hard to secure, so the fish eventually flopped around and freed itself, much to her dismay. We all exhaled and muttered a bummer as she cast out again. Steve did not have much luck either, and eventually hunger pulled us away from the variety of morning activities. The eagle still watched, clearly amused at our fishing skills.

Continuing down the road east, we were lured into the only retail establishment since entering the park. Seeking lunch, we pulled in to the Sportsman's Paradise Lodge with Sarah Palin signs decorating the entrance. The four of us piled in to meet Doug and Judy, our hosts for a noteworthy lunchtime visit. A bar area, a few diner-style tables, and a pool table in the front area were connected to their living room. Two recliner chairs were perched by large windows, clearly set up for bird-watching. The pool table also doubled as a drying rack for several sleeping bags. We all claimed bar stools and chatted with Doug, who was a wealth of information on Alaskan politics, fishing lures, and hunting. The conversation continued over cans of Coors Light while our $15 DiGiorno frozen pizza was heating in their oven. Over slices and beers, Doug hauled out several photo albums. He narrated a myriad of moose, bear, and fishing tales. One of the best quotables involved how to distinguish grizzly vs. black bear scat. "The grizzly scat has berries and a bear bell in it," he said with a hefty chuckle. He then turned his narration to the complete volume of Sarah Palin's political rise to fame in his state, his admiration for her evident in his passionate speech. I did a lot of nodding in between mouthfuls of cheese and pepperoni.

Steve engaged him in more conversation and admitted, "I am jonesin' to catch a fish!" after explaining the skunking at Twin Lake earlier. That led our spirited host to an explanation of the lures needed for the rivers in these parts. "Walk right

back to the creek now and catch a Grayling—
no problem," he said as he pointed to a $15
lure packet on the wall over the bar. Our two
license holders, Theresa and Steve, promptly
bought trout magnets and Grayling lures.
With directions and his two dogs in tow, Doug
sent us out back to the creek with a wave.
We sloshed through an Alaskan creek bog for
a half mile and found a sunny bend to try our
luck again. Kim and I swatted mosquitos and
watched the dogs dig for moles in the wet

riverbanks. Both Theresa and Steve had some
initial action and confirmed bites, but alas our
fishermen were again unsuccessful. Kim and
I assured them they were down but not out.
Time to move on down the road.

We packed in too many activities for one
day because of a confirmed case of FOMO
(fear of missing out). We decided to press
on and hike the Skookum Volcano trail

several more miles down a diminishing dirt road. The Forester was tested as Theresa drove us through four over-the-road creeks (creeks that had become streams). Each time, I heard nervous breathing until the tires claimed mud and rocks. It was early afternoon, but Alaskan summers were never short on light. June is warm and sunny, but most roads and trails near mountains and glaciers have plenty of snowmelt conditions.

We parked at mile marker 36.8. Water, bells, and snacks in tow, we strode to catch a view of the Skookum Volcano and leftover geological rock formations. We chose a challenging hike not because of its length. Most of the trail followed the riverbed, which required walking over a wide range of silver rocks and red boulders. Our ankles were tested, crisscrossing from bank to bank. Steve had grown weary of our constant jingling, so he sprint-walked ahead to put some distance between us. The girls shrugged and jingled along searching for flat rocks to walk on. Kim was infatuated with the porous lava rocks and picked up many along the way to examine the texture. I wondered how many were stuffed in her pockets as she wandered through this huge natural rock collection.

The hike covered 2,500 feet of elevation while the rushing river provided the music. Steve was thrilled because the noise of the river drowned out the bells. It was calculated hiking. We took turns picking a route or a tree to climb across to prevent wiping out in the churning glacial melt. After two miles, my arches and toes started a lament inside my hiking shoes. I set an example to plunk down and rest. We sent Steve on to reach the summit while the three of us snacked. His backside grew smaller as we watched him hike up the final saddle to the peak. I turned and looked back down the way we came, over past eruptions that had sent rocks and boulders flying into the river. Skookum seemed even more impressive from the top down. Realizing I had to traverse back down that, I set my teeth and added a layer as a rain cloud gathered. In the distance we looked at yet another majestic peak over 12,000 feet.

Back at the car, we returned the same way and discovered that all four creeks had become streams, now more likely rivers. Four nervous WSE tourists held the oh-shit bars on the Forester as we plowed through each crossing that sent us floating several feet downriver each time. The vehicle emerged dripping and still running. Patting our import as if to implore it to tackle one final river, we splashed forward, tires grinding for a hold, finally defeating the spring runoff.

The day slogged on. We had to drive out of the park and find a place to stay. We had determined the Paradise Lodge (and more Palin stories) was not suitable for our overnight needs. Two hours later, starving and still searching for a lodge or hotel with a lit vacancy sign, we rolled back into Glen Allen. We paid for a $169 room at the Caribou Hotel. It had two queen beds and smelled like body odor. We were exhausted. Nobody cared. The Caribou Restaurant had closed, so our last remaining option was to dine at the Freeze just around the corner. Sweaty, punchy, and starving we pounded burgers, curly fries, and milkshakes like we'd been in the wilderness for months, not two days.

Then, the giggling began, and no one could stop. It started when Theresa stared catatonically at her plate and mused, "'Sop' is such a weird word," as she dipped each fry in a pile of ketchup. It was weird, I thought, before joining the giggling party. Kim began laughing that morphed to a squeak when she ran out of air. I patted at my teary eyes with a grease-soaked napkin. Sopping up ketchup was damn funny! Thankfully done with dinner, we tried to compose ourselves and tone down the laughter spasms. Back at our aromatic queen room, we took turns working out the shower as two days of sweat and grime rolled down the drain.

Summer Sledding with Sue

The Forrester was pleased to be back on paved roads and delivered us to Sue's near Anchorage. Sue and family waved from their porch and came down to meet Steve and Kim. I'd been to Alaska three times, and I was about to hike Flattop for the third time! The Flattop tradition continued as Sue described the winter's all-time snowfall record while we grabbed our gear. Don't let the name fool you: the top is flat, not the trail up. Sue, in pristine physical condition, tested our lungs as she led us quickly up the trail to Flattop's views of Cook Inlet. Steve and Theresa used a tactic to try to slow her down. They stopped and pointed out landmarks in the distance, asking Sue to describe what it was. She obliged, thankfully, which gave us all a few extra gasping breaths. The views of the inlet and the Alaskan Range inspired us all to cover the last steep, rocky steps.

The descent stole the show on Flattop that day. Sue had instructed us all to bring a garbage bag or rain pants. The path down featured corn-snow chutes that became sledding runs. With our sleds on our bodies, Sue demonstrated first. Five adults transformed into cackling kids as we sped down the sections of snow at alarming rates of speed. Turning was difficult, so we quickly learned to dig in our hiking boots like rudders to prevent sliding into bare patches and rocks. Sue's dog chased us down each section as raucous laughter continued and snow spray pelted our cheeks. Summer sledding was riotous. We hit slide and repeat all the way down. Sue's tour-guiding ability was top-notch as always. Thanking her profusely, we took our leave to check in to the Aleyeska condo a short stint down the road. The condo in Girdwood would be our home base for the rest of the trip. We plotted our day trips that night over halibut bites at the Double Musky Inn.

Two Wheels vs. Two Legs

The end of each day in Alaska brought a deep and fulfilling exhaustion. Our legs pedaled on two wheels at the trails of Hillside Park outside Anchorage. Guided again by superstar local Sue, she piloted our troop up and around miles of trails while belting out her signature bear whoop. We made a lot of noise! (Remember the first bear and moose rule: don't surprise them.) We did not scare up any bears, but we did have to detour when a moose yearling blocked our

first descent. Steve, who had hammered down ahead, had scared him up and gone through. All four of us girls were blocked; it was like playing moose-in-the-middle. After we made a ton of noise, clapping and yelling, the moose sauntered off. Sue, ever encouraging, led on to catch up with Steve. She kept imploring, "It's just a little more up." Hillside was a great maze of trails, mostly up, except for the interrupted moose-in-the-middle downhill.

It was a balmy day for Alaska, in the mid-60s. Sweat dripped off my face as I granny-geared to the next summit. My bike added an extra level of difficulty by refusing to shift in second gear. I lost my chain twice, one that sent me off the trail over a stump and into a patch of weeds still clipped to my pedals. Clambering back on, I churned up and soaked in another spectacular water and mountain view with my pals. Our reward was another screaming downhill with s-curves, banked turns, and roots to rattle your molars. After three hours in the saddle, Sue added a final one-mile pedal-fest on a flat area past the river. Steve was all smiles after our stint at Hillside but was worried his bike needed a tune-up. Tired and muddy, we parted from Sue and headed to the Moose's Tooth for food and recovery drinks. Microbrews and two pizza pies were demolished. On the way home, we stopped at the bike shop and dropped off

Steve's and my bikes. The next day, the owner informed Steve he had cracked his stem and my derailleur had to be overhauled.

Sunday on the Sound

We drove through the longest tunnel in North America to get to Whittier, the site of our sea kayak adventure. Wheels turned to water to give our weary legs a rest. Just a mere hour from our Girdwood condo, Whittier is home to 150 permanent residents who make their living from the abundant waters. Prince William Sound opens up southern Alaska to the bordering ocean and provides a safe haven to brave the frigid waters in a tiny floating watercraft. Calm waters prevailed, but nonetheless it is important to mention (This tidbit was provided by our guide.) that if you happen to fall in, you've got two minutes to get topside or find land before a hypothermic and untimely end. Equipped with both this knowledge and the proper gear, Alaska Sea Kayakers and guide McKenzie led us on an afternoon of paddling in Passage Canal.

To get there, the 2.5-mile tunnel pushed Kim's claustrophobia into high gear as we drove through the single-lane darkness. Approaching Whittier, I smiled at a quaint seaport featuring two blocks of swaying boats, commercial docks, and a marina. The town square was the deep aquamarine of the sound. Gawking at the scenery, we geared up first with a pair of rubber bib overalls. Another rubber slicker went overhead, followed by the paddle skirt. Heavy rubber boots went on last, along with hats and sunscreen. The bluebird day had us all smiles but sweltering in our non-breathable suits. McKenzie did the obligatory safety briefing, and we shoved off into the blue/gray glacial canal waters. Epic scenery is no exaggeration as we gawked at the Billings Glacier nestled between the mountains on our left. Snapping a memory photo, I tried to focus on paddling the tandem with my kayak partner Theresa. Dipping in paddles, we listened to some tidbits from McKenzie, who assured us we would see eagles, sea otters, gulls, kittywigs, stellar jays, diving ducks, and minke whales. She was spot-on, and the day added to our growing wildlife meter.

We paddled close to the shore and rocky edge, staying out of the sound's marine highway where ferry boats had the right of way. Boat wakes are not a kayaker's friend, and McKenzie kept watch. About four miles in, McKenzie turned us into Emerald Cove for a break and picnic lunch. After beaching the kayaks, we pulled off all our rubbers, ready for a gourmet lunch. I am always amazed at what guides pull out of their packs to feed hungry adventurers. McKenzie laid out a spread that included smoked salmon with cream cheese on crackers or a choice of peanut butter with Nutella sandwiches. She produced a container of veggie pasta salad and peeled an orange and passed out slices. In between mouthfuls, we chatted with McKenzie about the usual. Where you from, how long have you been a guide, what made you come to Alaska?

She complied with answers that all seemed linked to a boyfriend in the area. She informed us we had Michigan accents and it was most noticeable when we said the words "bathroom" and "fantastic." The *a*'s were the Midwest giveaways spoken through the nasal passage. We savored lunch and the sun, thankfully not wearing the rubber tourist-cooking outfits. Leaning on logs and feeling satisfied, we tilted faces to the sun and soaked in Alaska air.

At our halfway point, we crossed the canal after checking for boat traffic to make a loop back. Shoulders were tiring, but more bird-watching dulled the settling ache. "Engage the core; rotate your belly, not just your shoulders," McKenzie suggested. Birding action ramped up with flybys from ducks, gulls, and kittywigs. They seemed to be beckoning us toward the other rocky side, as if to say, "Come and see a thousand of my friends—c'mon!" Their calls made sense when McKenzie pointed out a bird rookery on the rock shelf. Throngs roosted and created a concert of bird noise. A crafty sea otter and his mates slid in and out of sight. Several glacial waterfalls cascaded into the bay as we glided past the rookery concert. The paddles dipped in shorter and slower patterns as we rounded the cove, spotting the docks of the town square. We made it back, slid to a stop, and de-rubbered for the last time while thanking McKenzie.

It was Father's Day, so we celebrated in the lounge at the Whittier Inn. Before joining my crew, I left a message for my dad from his favorite oldest daughter. I lingered outside, staring back on our water route in the distance. Heading home, we stopped at the rocky beach just outside of town where an old fishing boat lay rotting on its side. We strolled along the beach, picking our steps carefully among the rocks, and looked up in time to see a swift tail

and rounded body surface and breach. We had missed a whale spotting on the water but caught this rare sight in the settling dusk. Back on the road, Steve celebrated by getting pulled over by a state trooper going 48 in a 45 zone. Thankfully, no ticket was issued for going three over the limit.

Two Tens

Remembering two-a-days as a college athlete, I recalled how painfully sore the training sessions left me. In Alaska, two- or even three-a-days were the norm. We biked 10 miles on the Glacier/ Iditarod Trail to the Highway junction in the morning then hiked 10 strenuous miles up Crow Pass the same day, punctuated by lunch and a nap. My predominant bike memory was the overgrown trail, crowded by the big-leaved cow parsnip and other plants known to give rashes. It was much like biking through a sea of plants, as your bike and legs disappeared in the underbrush as it bent over the narrow trail. Before lunch and a nap, we scrubbed our shins and forearms with soap and water in hopes red welts would not make an appearance.

The trailhead was not far from home base, so we drove the short distance for our second training session of the day. We walked up the 2,100 feet to the pass to gawk at glaciers, waterfalls, wildflowers, and mining ruins. The pass is the highest point on the historic Iditarod Trail. Snow still lined portions of the trail, and we watched amused as snow spiders scampered across the white patches in front of our feet. Looking up became a better choice, for a rushing waterfall down the gorge to the river below. The waterfall marked a turn to more rock and plenty of snowpack. We walked in shorts and short sleeves on top of the snow to let the sun warm our shoulders. The peak held a tiny cabin in a bowl surrounded by several other peaks. The sun was blinding off the melting snow; the cabin seemed to disappear in the glare each time we tried to spot it.

From Crow Pass Peak, we looked down an impressive chute of peaks lining a valley. Standing from this vantage point, we understood why the hike had been labeled strenuous. Eventually, the gazing had to stop, giving way to trekking back down. The sun continued to have its effect on the snowpack, evidenced by a spontaneous avalanche across the valley. Down a steep chute, huge chunks rumbled and roared down off the mountain, adding to the glacial runoff across the road we would have to cross.

Our reward was dinner at Chair Five in hometown Girdwood. The cozy local bar had free entertainment: drunk locals playing pool with cheap draft-beer-charged conversations. We didn't mind. We sipped instead of guzzling and savored all things halibut once again. The flaky and mild whitefish was always the favorite choice at mealtimes.

Gone Fishin' with the Bears

We only had to drive about an hour and a half to get ourselves in the midst of a bear encounter with a fishing pole in our hands. We piloted our trusty steed to the Kenai Peninsula and Coopers Landing. The sockeye salmon were running, and Steve wanted a piece of the action. A plan shaped up spontaneously that cost $150 each to hire a guide to hike out to the Russian River. The package included a verbal guarantee of catching our limit with some invaluable fly-rod instruction, plus our guide would filet the fish on the spot. It sounded like an exceptional deal.

We met up with Matt, the guide, who led us to a dirt parking lot where we hiked in about a half mile through some dense forest. The steep-banked Russian River was much more remote and intimate than the fishing experience three years ago on the Kenai in a float boat. And instead of hundreds of fishermen lining the banks and in boats, we only competed with about 10.

All sporting a fashionable pair of heavy-duty rubber waders, we gathered around Matt, who began setting up each pole and tying bright-colored flies. He demonstrated flossing and casting, a technique closely related to fly-fishing. He flipped the line out, let it float downstream in the quick current, then gave it a slight tug to entice the salmon to grab on.

The Russian River was rushing. A swift current forced careful and slow footfalls to secure a flat spot to stand in the river. We were mostly successful at this task, except for Theresa. She earned the nickname Soggy Bottoms. She had ventured into the river above her knees (shin-high was plenty, warned the guide), and, while casting, she slipped on a rock. She splooshed sideways using her arm to prevent a full-body fall, which swamped her waders. She had to retreat to the bank to dump out the excess water, ring out her socks, and begin again. I kept my eyes on my disappearing lure in the layers of white-capped water. I developed a case of fishing elbow. Others nearby had caught some fish, evidenced by the string of them chilling in the water at their feet. For us, the fishing remained elusive, and even Matt did not have much luck. My arm continued to tire from the near constant casting. While Matt checked Kim's pole and lure, he cast out and actually got a salmon on. We all whistled and watched him reel it in with Kim ready at the net.

Steve continued to cast, determined to make his fishing investment worthwhile. Theresa did the same, and I (with less gusto) continued to floss as Matt had instructed. I've often heard "boring" as a word synonymous with fishing. It seemed that way until I heard a voice calmly call, "Bear." It was Steve's voice. I looked up and heard him say it again. Now, on full alert, we all looked up to see Steve and Theresa freeze in the middle of the river. A sow and her two cubs sauntered downriver just 40 feet away. Alaska time stood still. We all froze, and Matt seemed slightly spooked. We watched the bear intently to see where she was headed. She moved about 20 more feet away and began snaring salmon carcasses that had floated down. At the same time, she had spotted the fishermen ogling her. To make a statement, she stood on her two hind legs and roared a warning up the river. The river was loud. She was louder. Her message was received to stay the hell away from her dinner. The roar made the fine hairs on our necks stand at attention while we frantically rummaged for cameras to document our river encounter.

Matt seemed apologetic he hadn't spotted the bear first, but in his defense, he was fileting a salmon on a rock, with his back turned, when she appeared on the river. We watched and gave Matt a play-by-play as sow and cubs moved farther downriver while gorging on salmon leftovers. I had lost focus on fishing anyway. Nervously, I watched Steve and Theresa continue to fish, undaunted. And, as if our close call wasn't drama enough, a woman appeared out of the dense trees, walking on a riverbank trail just feet from the bear and cubs. I closed one eye, squinting away a bear mauling. She walked toward us, oblivious to the animal in the river. I let out a long breath as she put some distance between her and the sow demolishing salmon. I wondered how many close calls like that happened on the river every day.

With our exit route blocked by bears, Matt led us out another way. Several grumpy fishermen reluctantly handed poles back to Matt so we could pack it out. Still in waders, we had to climb up a steep goat trail, probably the way the sow had come down. The mood was quiet and mellow. I struggled up the hill in my heavy waders, Steve pouted, and Matt rambled on about our close call. "She was really close, man," Matt drawled. Of course we had noticed he wasn't packing. Kim nodded at Matt's comment and added one of her own, "I walked up that same trail to pee about five minutes before we spotted her." Contemplating that thought, we walked on, the roar still ringing in our ears. We patronized Sackett's Smokehouse Grill yet again before driving back to Girdwood.

We didn't catch any salmon, just the one that Matt landed. They did pack it on ice so we could share it with Sue the next day. We didn't catch our limit, but the $150 was worth the real-time bear encounter. The bear chatter would go on as each of us reminisced how frightening and amazing it was to have her yell at us. It was past 11:00 when we neared Girdwood and our turn. Kim spotted more than 30 eagles meeting on the mud flats of the inlet. Final rays of dusky sun cracked through the clouds, spotlighting the mighty birds surveying the waters for a meal.

Final Day

A land and sea theme pervaded each day of activities, including our last. Heading south this time, we made a stop at the Harding Ice Field Trail for a short hike before driving to Seward on Resurrection Bay. The initial trail led from a bustling parking lot up a paved trail that morphed to gravel track then to a single dirt track. The trail held small white signs with black numbers displaying 1965, 1971, 1980, and so on. The signs represented where the glacier had rested during that year and clearly showed a disconcerting pattern: how much the glacier had retreated over the past 50+ years. We did a power walk to view what remained of the impressive ice field. Rocks and boulders formed steps to ascend, and halved logs formed slippery bridges to cross runoff rivers. The narrowing trail led us to impressive views of glacial gray river valley fed from the

Harding Glacier. Tightly watching the time with a reservation for a marine life cruise, we had to turn back before hitting the trail's highest vista. Feeling slightly shortchanged, we trudged back down past the year markers again that reminded us to be better stewards of an amazing state and planet. Doing some more reading later, I discovered that all but two of Alaska's glaciers are receding.

Again, we were victims to FOMO, trying to squeeze too much into a single day. With five minutes before departure, we scuttled onto the Kenai Fjord Marine Wildlife Cruise boat and awaited sightings of marine life that included a humpback whale with calf, sea lions, porpoises, and more eagles. The 60-foot cruiser motored out through the bay to the mouth of the ocean. The staff would announce via loudspeaker when animals were spotted, and the boat's passengers would all shift from side to side to catch a glimpse. The humpback whale received the most attention as the captain idled us around for more hopeful glances of the massive creature. Where the ocean met bay, sea lions flopped around on protruding rocks, and ocean spray shot up over them, creating a dramatic

and bone-chilling scene. The seas are always rougher once the ocean currents are in play. Rolling around, holding on to the handrails, the four of us zipped jackets, slid on gloves, and listened intently for the next creature announcement.

Our boat had a buffet meal pit stop at Fox Island, where we listened to a history lesson from Ranger Jenny. The jet-black stony island beach contrasted with the icy blue water and cloudy sky as we disembarked. Inside and fed, we listened intently to Jenny's story about the Good Friday earthquake in 1964. Measuring 9.0 at its epicenter in nearby Valdez, it caused portions of the area to drop 2,000 feet. The dead trees or ghost forests that had been pointed out were remnants of the quake. The whole area morphed, and Alaska residents reeled to try to recover after that disaster. Staring at the ghost trees, we returned to the boat and back to Seward for souvenir shopping. Seward had plenty of trinkets and trash for tourists to peruse, and we eventually met for a return drive back to Girdwood. It was late again when we rolled in for one last sleep. Tired and humbled, I walked to the blinds and pulled them tight to create dark in the midnight dusk.

CAUGHT AT SEWARD ALASKA

Chapter Nine
Vortexes and the Big Ditch

Arizona,
2007, 2013

A new health study revealed that vacation has a strong impact on both stress and immune pathways and can provide short-term improvements in overall well-being.

Source: www.Projecttimeoff.com

Get out of your workaholic rut and go somewhere warm and sunny! It's good for your health, says Project Time Off's 2016 research. Your next prescription may be for a vacation. A new health study revealed that vacation has a strong impact on both stress and immune pathways and can provide short-term improvements in overall well-being.
Source: www.projecttimeoff.com

With that thought in mind, I headed south and talked a bunch of friends into going with me. We all needed a break! I usually have a strict rule about choosing a destination where I've not been. So why did I choose to return to Sedona, Arizona, for a third time? I pondered several plausible explanations on my flight into Phoenix.

1. I had been equipped with a homing device, implanted at birth at the Fort Huachuca Army Hospital in southern Arizona.

2. A Michigan winter had left me severely vitamin D deficient, and the Arizona sun is a quick and reliable cure. (Most areas get 300 sunny days per year.)

3. The red rock formations really are universal vortexes, soaking up the sun's rays then emanating back out in waves calling to me.

4. Cheap timeshare lodging at several resorts.

5. In loosely organized focus groups, I had never heard anyone say, "Sedona sucks!" In fact, it was supremely positive. I heard things like, "Great art and galleries, cool hippies, and epic hiking. Oh, and take the Pink Jeep Tour; it's amazing."

All good reasons on their own merits, the draw of Sedona called me back for a third time. My first Sedona trip was on a family vacation, then a second and third time with friends. Arizona is the state to soak up some Southwest sun and to experience the natural beauty of red rock country. I did not go to Sedona for its proclaimed metaphysical and universal energy vortexes or to find my spiritual center. While researching, I was amazed at the predominant themes present in every piece of literature and on websites about Sedona. Once my feet were on the ground, I confirmed Sedona's reputation was all New Age. There were shops full of crystals, tarot cards and psychic readings, flute music, and starry-eyed tourists hoping to find a connection with the universe and enlightenment for their souls. So is it all a hoax? Does Sedona really have four universal energy vortexes? I set out to discover the truth.

Sisters (Theresa and Andrea) were my companions on a fall trip in '07 to red rock country and to the Grand Canyon. Andrea and Theresa had not seen the Grand Canyon (one of the seven wonders of the world), so we planned a day trip and hike during our stay. I booked a two-bedroom condo at a timeshare, the Sedona Summit, courtesy of my parents. The Summit would be home base for a week stay filled with hiking, biking, golfing, and copious salsa eating.

We flew to Phoenix in the midst of an Arizona Diamondbacks baseball playoff run, in hopes of catching a game or two during our stay. Our late arrival in the evening landed us a quick stay in a seedy motel in a Phoenix suburb near the airport. When we checked in, I noted two bullet holes at the check-in window. The three of us fell asleep with the baseball game on and woke up unharmed to a brilliant blue sky with the desert sun warming to 70°. We breakfasted in downtown Phoenix at a café near Arizona State University. Over Santa Fe wraps, we ate and drank coffee and reviewed maps planning out day one.

By late morning, we set off north on Highway 17 in our rented Jeep Compass. Thousands of stoic cacti watched over the arid and parched desert that eventually gave way to more varied terrain. We drove with the windows down

and took the pull-off at the Sunset Point rest stop and then the Camp Verde exit to check out Montezuma's Castle. It seemed fitting to start our visit with a history of Sedona and the Verde Valley's first inhabitants, the Sinaqua Indians from the early 1300s. The castle and the limestone cliff dwellings have endured time exceptionally well. After a short walk, we looked up to the five-story cliff-dwelling homes chiseled into the cliff walls. I marveled at this vertigo-inducing lifestyle. I would have made a poor Sinaqua, in a constant state of nervousness, afraid to roll over in my sleep and plunge 1,000 feet to the valley floor. Though I could see why the Sinaquas had made that area home. The valley was green and fertile, fed by the natural springs and Beaver Creek. Sycamore and acacia trees lined the valley, and their five-story view was handy to spot any approaching enemies.

After our walk through the national monument, we pointed the Jeep north on a construction-riddled Highway 179. The red rocks and buttes came into view as we entered the village of Oak Creek, moving snail-like toward uptown Sedona. I pointed out Bell Rock then Snoopy Rock, and Theresa spied two mountain bikers out on a rock plateau to our east. We also pit-stopped at Oak Creek Country Club to scope out the course and make a Monday tee time. A Danny Noonan look-alike took our reservation and assured us he had rental clubs that would meet with our approval. Battling traffic made us all hungry, so we lunched at Hillside shopping area at the Javelina Cantina. The cantina's large expanse of windows looked out over Cathedral Rock and an expanding impressive view of red rock country. Hillside was a high-end, swanky outdoor mall with shops and boutiques stocked with hand-woven rugs, Southwestern art, and expensive pottery.

After wasting an hour after lunch window-shopping overpriced everything, we continued toward west Sedona to check in. Highway 179 gave way to 89A west, and we pulled in to our home-away timeshare. The development seemed newly built, and our condo was pristine, polished, and well appointed. Check-in was simple, as a well-informed concierge, Jennifer, filled a folder full of hiking maps, spa information, and a Sedona city map. We drove to our building and settled in, exclaiming how posh the condo was. I was impressed by the sunset suite and its massive bathrooms, glass showers, and built-in soaking tubs. Thumbs-up to Sunterra Resorts, we chimed, claiming beds and wheeling in our luggage. I also discovered an adobe-bricked patio that looked west for Southwest sunsets. Precisely at 5:45, the three of us noted the change of color and the light on the rocks as the sun began to set. The red

turned orange and finally to pink, as if Sedona had turned on a vortex nightlight. The glow emanates off the rock spires even after the sun disappears. We ran out to capture a view and snap photos of our first sunset encounter.

Vortex Sunday
Instead of attending church in the morning, I was lazy and elected to stay and lounge in the congregation of Bedside Baptist. Up first, Theresa had a strong pot of coffee on to combat the time change. Sipping our morning caffeine elixir, we plotted our day over breakfast. For our Sunday in Sedona, we planned a day hike to the vortex in Boynton Canyon. We researched all four vortex sites and discovered that Boynton could channel both female and masculine energies and it was a site known to balance individual and relational energies. Armed with this knowledge and open minds, we packed a lunch for the short hike and drove to the entrance off Dry Creek Road.

The scenery was the high point. I really can't be sure whether we channeled any energy from the universe. Vortex or not, getting outside, walking, and soaking up Sedona sun were all therapeutic. I could definitely see how Sedona's natural beauty inspired inner-peace seekers. We walked on a path of fine red dirt and rock as the spires rose up around us like layered thimbles perched precariously on a base. I found myself slipping on loose rocks while I gawked up at the unique vistas. We had to sign in at the trailhead where Dead Man's Pass split off. The name seemed overtly negative for a vortex trail. *How about Wispy Fairy Pass instead?* We passed rock formations funneling to a shaded path following a dry creek bed. The sun disappeared behind the west ridge as we walked. At three miles in, the trail rose sharply up to a ridged plateau. The trail had gotten progressively narrower as two ridgelines converged, forming an arrow point in the canyon. As the gap closed, we could hear the wind whistling through the gap in the rocks. Vortex seekers might think Boynton Canyon had a voice and was willing to talk. Noting the wind observation, we scrambled up to a flat vista and sat and relaxed on the sun-warmed rock shelf.

All was good except for Andrea's hand; she had accidently swiped it on a prickly pear cactus on the last section of trail. She had 20 small spikes in her hand that she worked to remove while we rested. We stretched out like lizards on the rocks and ate bagel sandwiches and tropical trail mix. The trail was an out-and-back, so from our

perch we had a great view of the valley below us. We took our time and joked we were sitting on top of the vortex. We agreed to try to channel some energy. We sat yoga style in lotus pose, closed our eyes, and placed our hands in our laps. Remembering a directive of many yoga Mondays, we touched index fingers and thumbs, known as a symbol of tapping into the universe and exposing the true soul. We heard the wind blowing again. The sky did not go dark, and there was not a crack of thunder. *What do people expect at a vortex site?*

Instead, the sun shone on my shoulders, and I touched the warm red rock where I sat. Why not tap in to nature too? We eventually moseyed back down. The sun sliding down the sky was our cue to double-time it back. On the walk back, we ran into a group of three middle-aged women heading up the trail in search of the vortex. They stopped us with a smile, and one woman asked, "How much farther?" Her cohort piped in, "How much farther to the vortex?" Grinning at the question Theresa chimed, "Oh, it's right around the corner, about a half mile up the trail. You can't miss it!" I smirked and imagined the ladies at the end, facing the canyon wall hoping to see some sort of a physical monument to represent the vortex. We waved and continued laughing at their enthusiastic naivety. We walked with

views of Lady Kuchina Rock and a sprawling Enchantment Resort as we leveled out back near the Jeep in the afternoon. We toasted a successful vortex hunt with a happy hour on our patio facing another magnificent red-rimmed sunset.

Golf Clubs and Earplugs

On one of our vacation days, we spent five hours chasing around a little white ball. We were slightly late for our tee time due to a combination of squeezing in sun time at the pool then making a stop at the Euro Deli for sandwiches. We arrived in a flurry, noted by the golf pro at Oak Creek Country Club. He smartly pushed back our tee time. It was a blessing so we could take a few practice swings with our rented King Cobra clubs. On the range, I settled into the space next to the course superintendent also out hitting. I inspected my clubs and unsheathed the driver, amazed at its oversized face. I took a few practice swings then teed one up, excited to see how the big-faced driver would perform. I made solid contact but was startled by the loud metallic TINGGGGGGGG that emanated after contact. The sound was unnerving as I looked over at the super with a surprised smile. He smiled back, "Do you want to borrow a set of earplugs for your round?" Laughing, I agreed with his assessment of my loud golf clubs. We teed off a half hour later and ended up rushing to get the round in before dark. For the first three holes, red rock formations framed each hole, so Andrea snapped as many photos as she took golf swings. We started slowly getting used to our new weapons and the startling sounds. With no one behind us, we settled in and didn't encounter other golfers until hole 7. Plus, Andrea preferred to take her time with club selection and lining up shots. Theresa and I learned to be patient. At the turn, I ordered an iced tea and continued to gawk at the stunning red rock views set against the deep green of the OCCC fairways. Our loud clubs kept us amused throughout the day, but it was a second-place highlight to the views.

At 14, Theresa and I realized it was going to be tight to fit in 18 before dark. We spurred Andrea on and began a version of speed golf to finish our round. Andrea, Theresa, and I sprinted across the fairway to approach shots, then speed-walked back to the cart. I'm not sure whether our scores suffered as a result, but we managed to finish in the fading red glow. On 18, Fritz and Bernie (a German couple) invited us to hit along with them instead

of waiting. We accepted, and the five us putted in our last balls before heading back to the clubhouse.

Hiking the Big Ditch, a Petrified Walk!
The next couple of days, we traded golf spikes and collared shirts for hiking shoes and backpacks. The three of us huddled over coffee and decided to do a warm-up hike before our Grand Canyon Grandview Trail hike. The trail map boasted the A.B. Young trail as steep and strenuous in Oak Creek Canyon, just south of Slide Rock State Park, north of uptown Sedona. Following the maps, we pulled into Bootlegger Campground to cross the river to find the trailhead. We headed upstream while navigating around huge boulders that had been deposited over time in the riverbed. A small eight-inch metal trail sign proudly proclaimed the A.B. Young Trail.

The trail description was accurate. It listed more than 30 switchbacks and 1,600 feet of elevation gain. We pushed Andrea's hiking ability, and A.B. Young was the prelude to some dizzying heights the next day. The switchback trail led us into varied greener terrain, much like an enchanted forest might look devoid of the arid dessert, cactus, and red rocks. It also held a whitetail deer, spooked at the last turn toward the top. The top of the ridge looked back on the river gorge and impressive views to the south. I might have lingered longer on my rock perch, except for the rumble of approaching thunder. The three of us were spurred into action. We squatted out of sight for a quick pee in the trees. Then we navigated the switchbacks quickly, only interrupted by a brightly colored snake that slithered across the trail just in front of an Andrea footfall. With only a mild shriek, we continued to scurry as thunder rumbled and ominous dark clouds rolled in. It would have been lovely to admire the unique canyon wall colors on the descent, but the curvy trail required focus. I counted each switchback out loud so we could track our progress to 33 and the finish. The fizzling storm only deposited a few drops on our heads. We were down at the river after just 40 minutes. Again, we tried our feet at some amateur bouldering and leaping. Andrea handled the hike well, and we talked about the more demanding hike on the docket for the next day.

We celebrated finding and completing A.B. Young with drinks at the Junipine. Still early evening, uptown Sedona was peppered with shoppers coming in and out of the Red Dirt Shirt Co. We made a stop at this tourist trap and also at the Tlequepaqe (Guadalajara knockoff) shopping area. We had been warned to be wary of the quantity of art and sculpture dominated by horses, frogs, and Indian pottery. And Arizona (not just Sedona) is full of pottery, jewelry, and paintings depicting the famous Kokopelli, a flute-playing Indian/Pueblo god with feathers protruding out of his head. He represented fertility, music, and agriculture, and his profile is oft used for Southwestern art inspiration. After 30 minutes, I was weary of browsing and admitted to Andrea that I sucked at shopping without a plan. She consented to my pleas to leave. After a brief Safeway stop for supplies, we retired to the condo for a spaghetti dinner with garlic bread. We agreed, in between bits of pasta and sauce, to rise at 3:30 a.m. in order to be at the lesser-known east gate of the Grand Canyon at sunrise. Theresa had researched a less touristy plan and read that the east entrance was a must to avoid the crowds and congestion. The guidebook touted the sunrise over the canyon. Lights went out at 10:30 in preparation for an alarm at an ungodly hour.

We had tested Andrea's physical and hiking limits, but it was I who struggled on the big ditch hike. I was petrified at many points while peering over a 4,000-foot cliff wall to the floor. It's strange to be so fond of climbing mountains (or into canyons, in this case) yet so fearful when bouts of vertigo strike. My mind is eager, but my body displays emotions and subconscious reactions on elevation adventures.

The next day, I played the "I suck in the mornings" card to get out of driving to the canyon in the murky darkness. Instead, I laid in the back seat listening to radio conversations and a four-cylinder engine churn upward. Groggy described how we all felt at that hour, but we perked up at the first speck of light, along with a glimpse of a massive elk alongside the road. I sat up quickly and rubbed my eyes as one elk materialized into many and then a bona fide herd! They all turned to look at us as they finished crossing the road, as if to say, "What the hell are you doing up at this hour!" Now, reasonably awake, we pulled over and took a photo posed in front of the national park entrance sign. The chill of the morning hit me.

Back in the car, I confirmed why when I read the display at 40 degrees. We followed the road into the park, and we were indeed alone except for the elk. In the expansive lot, our car was the solo vehicle. We had escaped the throngs of onlookers, so the sunrise would be our moment.

Spurred by the spreading light, Theresa and I actually ran down to the watchtower overlook to see the sun peeking over canyon walls. I was awestruck to watch the wave of sun move slowly down the wall toward the Colorado River below. The steep cliff walls remained hazy as the sun and cool air met head-on while the river valley floor remained obscured. After 10 minutes, we noticed a park employee, and another couple had joined in our sunrise reverie. The park employee approached us with a tidbit of insight. With a humble yet wise voice he explained, "I've worked at the canyon for over 30 years, and each morning, well, it is always unique. Every day is different." He walked off with a knowing grin. He had solidified for all of us that our early-morning sacrifice had been a better choice. The sun's rays grew brighter and spread into the whole canyon, displaying the serpentine twists and turns of the river. We continued our canyon gazing after finding coffee and a soggy microwaveable breakfast burrito at Lipan Point. It was still early when the watchtower opened, and I went up the first level while the sisters continued up to the penthouse level to peer over the guardrails. In some places, you could look down sheer walls more than 5,700 feet from top to floor.

We learned a few important statistics about the Grand Canyon:

- It averages 10 miles in width, rim to rim.
- Its depth is up to 5,700 feet.
- The park includes over one million acres of land.
- The highest point at the South Rim at Grandview Point is 7,400 feet (ironically, where our hike began that day).
- That translates into almost one vertical mile of depth.

And, of course, it is noted as one of the Seven Wonders of the World. We drove the 12 miles west to Grandview Point and readied (I pondered hurling.) for our day hike. I confirmed the serious nature of my fears and vertigo that day. I gulped, peering nervously at the trail start and a view that plunged 4,000 feet. I knew better than to look twice to the bottom, which caused an instant wave of stomach flips and dizziness. I proceeded down a narrow, steep trail cut into the side of a cliff. Andrea started in the lead, with me in the middle and Theresa last, keeping up a stream of pep talks. We walked at a snail's pace down, especially around narrow ledges and corners and a few rock overhangs. I kept one hand on the rocks to steady my nerves and focused on each foothold. My head tilted down, I kept my eyes from looking into the rock chasm. My mind remained panicked until the sheer cliff trail gave way to the Coconino Saddle, where the drop-offs lessened dramatically. Our hike destination was a plateau with views of the Horseshoe Mesa.

It took just over two hours to traverse down 2,600 feet, where we sat and rested on old mining rocks/ruins and copper- and green-colored stones. We had actually followed two forest service women on a patrol hike. We chatted them up, and they were continuing past the mesa and down to the floor to camp overnight. They snapped a picture for the three of us and wished us (really me) good luck on the return. My favorite part of the hike, besides the panoramic view from the relatively safe mesa, was my bagel sandwich and fruit snacks.

Andrea noted, in between bites, three very distinct layers and colors of rock we had passed. First, white limestone, then yellowish sandstone, and, finally, an orangey-red shale. Unique to the canyon, hikers can witness millions of years' worth of rock formation in one single glance. Thankfully, there were several points, and lunchtime, where I could enjoy the geological marvel without being scared shitless.

After lunch, Theresa suggested we start back and asked Andrea to take the lead to set a comfortable pace. I took a brief opportunity to walk in front on the less intimidating area going up the mesa plateau. We had to cross the rock saddle (I wanted to crawl across.) and ascend again on narrow ridge-cut trails. Theresa and Andrea grinned at me at times when I faced the rock wall and pressed my chest and legs against the wall to shimmy sideways. I also have a vivid memory of Andrea stretching her quads on a section of narrow trail. I watched in horror as she leaned forward with one leg/ankle in hand, clearly oblivious to how close she was to tipping over the edge.

Theresa noticed as well and suggested to her sister that she find a better spot to wobble around on one leg. I didn't need any more visions of people plunging to their death while on vacation! The last steep section had me breathing hard and ragged from exertion and from worry. I almost ran up the last section of four switchbacks, overjoyed to make it back to flat ground. I hugged a nearby pine tree. I sighed in deep contentment then collected myself to photograph the girls' heads as they appeared above the line of the rim. There were

three sets of wide smiles in our traditional upside-down-lean-in self-portrait. We drove down to the village and enjoyed survival beers in the El Tovar Lounge. We considered having dinner, but the first available reservation was 9 p.m. We skipped dinner, but Andrea found a gift shop and treated herself to a necklace charm to commemorate her epic and successful hike. We drove through the evening dusk back through Flagstaff and to Sedona. We ordered takeout pizza at Picazzo's and settled back in safely at the Summit.

Hiker in Every Biker

The words of the bike shop mechanic echoed true in my head each time I have biked in the Sedona area. After handing us maps and wishing us happy trails, he described the trails and suggested we not worry if we encountered difficult terrain. He calmly suggested with a sideways grin, "There's a hiker in every biker, girls!" I should make a point to look him up and mention how many times I've borrowed his catchy little phrase. Absolute Bikes is the shop I can thank for rentals, maps, and advice on both of my biking visits. There is literally one beginner trail that I would not label as easy. Perhaps the distinction that should be defined is trail biking vs. mountain biking. Sedona has mountains and rocks; thus, mountain biking certainly applies. Michigan has dirt, roots, trees, and mix in some sand, so let's call that trail biking. Turns out I am a trail rider, not a mountain biker. Biking in Michigan is a pedal festival compared to my hike-a-biking on red rocks. I was humbled.

Vortex hunting, golfing, hiking, and now biking: Arizona was a true multisport vacation. The big ditch behind us, we turned to mountain biking, and to my amazement and certainly Theresa's, Andrea announced she wanted to join us. A look of shock and dismay would be putting it lightly at this unexpected turn of action. Clearly, fueled by her hiking prowess, Andrea decided she would give biking a try too. Both Theresa and I had assumed we'd be biking as a pair, not as a threesome. We walked next door to inspect (and ride) our bright green Specialized full-suspension bikes around the lot. Andrea, still on a mission to prove to Theresa and me that she was a capable adventure junkie, rented a basic hard tail bike, informing, "I can handle a few hours at my own pace; we can start together but no need to wait." After we had water, helmets, and padded-ass shorts on, off we rode with Andrea in tow. To my knowledge, she had not done any trail biking, even in pancake-flat Michigan. Andrea hopped on her bike and started to follow us up the Bell Rock Pathway. It was ever so slightly uphill, but at the first main trail intersection, we stopped and waited for the pink-cheeked and flushed Andrea to arrive to be sure she felt comfortable on her bike. She was still smiling, so we pedaled on another mile or two and eventually separated near the intersection of Llama and Little Horse trails.

The sun was bright and hot, and I was sweating profusely through my red short-sleeve dryfit. Red seemed an appropriate color to wear on that day. Theresa pedaled on, happy not to be responsible for baby sis anymore. I had to hustle to keep pace. We marveled at riding over smooth sections of rocks and rolling up and over these sections until we came to a wash-out riverbed. So began the pushing of bikes rather than riding. We shouldered the bikes on actual rock steps that greeted us more than twice. Off and on the bikes we went that day, the rock formations and Bell Rock watching over us. We were also riding without our clip-in pedals, so the shoe cages made it difficult to navigate the uphills and on/off escapades. We both slipped on and off the pedals and knocked our shins. The trail was mostly rideable after navigating around the riverbed, and we enjoyed the rolling

rock trail with views of Crested Butte and the Bell. The Llama loop deposited us back at BRP. It had been about two hours, so T and I rode downhill toward the bike shop to find Andrea, hopefully in one piece. I stayed cautious on the descent, knowing the fine red dirt layer over the rocks made for slippery conditions, especially when cornering fast.

We coasted into the parking lot to find Andrea hanging out near the car. I pulled up next to her, "How'd it go, and where did you ride?" She blinked her blue eyes twice for emphasis and replied, "Llama trail, same as you." Theresa and I inquired again, knowing we had just ridden Llama. It seemed preposterous that she would have finished before us. Theresa determined she must have taken one of the cutoffs on the map that took her back to BRP. We loaded up just two bikes. Andrea elected to turn her rental in to forego another day of biking—apparently, just a taste was all she needed. The back seat was a tight fit for me with the two bikes loaded in. I survived a short drive with a pedal in my side and a handlebar pressing my shoulder.

The next day, Andrea had her fill of adventure-junkie fun. She announced she was headed to Jerome to explore the historic city and to do some shopping. Two biker babes remained, and we chose the Cockscomb to

Girdner trail system suggested at the bike shop. We had mapped it, and the loop showed it would deposit us right on the edge of our condo development. Andrea dropped us off on the trailhead on Dry Creek Road before heading south. We were buzzing with excitement as we started on a slight downhill with plenty of loose rocks and boulders. We persevered in the beginning, and the rolling up/down trail was a super fun pedal for the first couple of miles. Cockscomb wound and gave us equal amounts of uphill and downhill and led us along a power line to a latched gate. We had to dismount, push bikes through, then secure the latch before riding on to a lunch spot. I sat with my back to a boulder and tilted my face to the warming afternoon sun. I took off my shoes and dumped out a stream of fine red dust. My bike buddy was napping in the shade while I enjoyed my moments in the sun. Eventually, I stretched and pulled my padded shorts out of a self-induced wedgie from sitting too long. Still tugging on my shorts, I tossed a few hackberries at the sleeping Theresa until she lazily moaned for me to stop.

Lethargically, we packed our lunch remnants away, slid on packs over shoulders, and gingerly placed our cheeks on the saddle. Girdner was our second-half trail, where a pattern quickly emerged. We pedaled down to a dry, dusty, and bouldered creek bed then crossed by either pushing or shouldering our bikes up the bank to the far side. We'd get back on and pedal a short way, then the trail would turn again back to the river, devoid of water. The trail traversed 10 times over and back, which only allowed for short sections of pedaling. Pushing or carrying a bike is brutal work, and at each crossing, our frustration grew along with our use of colorful language. I pushed more than I pedaled in the span of an hour. We were exasperated and incredulous that anyone would suggest Girdner as a bike trail. *Ridiculous.* We complained to each other, hiked our bikes, and drank most of our water. There was a last agonizingly long push up a hill on the ridgeline where we could see familiar formations near our condo. I watched sweat drip down the tip of my nose as I hopped on to actually ride the last stretch to the parking lot. I rode right up to the front door and deposited my bike against the stucco wall and marched to the refrigerator for two beers. We sat outside on our steps, cracked a beer, and gulped. We admired our red-dirt-caked legs and shins and the line of demarcation above the sock. Too tired to change into a bathing suit, I talked Theresa into walking down to the pool. We stripped down to sports bras and biking shorts while passing the sign: PLEASE SHOWER BEFORE ENTERING THE POOL. I plunged in and befouled the Sunterra pool.

Part Two: Sedona Return

I returned to recurring themes. I did more hike-a-biking, vortex exploring, and hiking, and the same fine red dirt caked on my skin and clothes. I am still unclear about the hubbub swirling around vortex sites, but enough evidence exists that I cannot dismiss it as complete tomfoolery. For example, we stayed at Sedona Springs Resort, where the nearby airport plays host to a masculine energy vortex site. I was perplexed to hear that both Maureen and Theresa had dreams about violent encounters between boys and girls. Pure oddity? Or did the masculine vortex vibe torture a sleeping girl's mind? We also found plenty of the telltale twisted Juniper trees on the Airport Loop hike. Jim reminded us that he had a weird experience as well when he and his ex-wife flew over two vortex sites on a helicopter tour. The pilot had queued Jim to watch the instrument panel as they flew over the Airport and Bell Rock vortexes. Jim watched wide-eyed as the instruments went wacky and moved back and forth over the full spectrum in rapid motion for several seconds. Nonchalantly, the pilot confirmed it happened regularly on his route. It certainly was a conversation piece, so we agreed to add vortex hunting to our Sedona itinerary. The return trip included Theresa, Maureen, Jen, and her boyfriend Jim.

Easy Hikes and Beginner Biking

Before the trip, I had promised Maureen we could find some easy hikes that were not extreme. She called me several weeks before departure, wondering, "I am a little worried about this trip. I've heard about your adventure trips, you know."

"Oh, no worries; we don't need to do extreme or difficult stuff. Plus, I really want to play golf and sit by the pool."

"Okay, but Jen and I will skip the mountain biking day."

"Probably a good idea; Jen doesn't like mountain biking anyway."

She seemed mostly assured during our phone conversation, so I reminded her by saying, "All activities are optional!"

On our first morning in Sedona, the condo was filled with the aroma of strong coffee. We sipped and made a plan to stretch our legs and ease into our vacation. I described a hike called Devil's Bridge. Though the name was ominous, the guidebook listed it as easy; we were promised epic views, one short rock scramble, and only 0.9 miles of length. I pitched the idea to Maureen, who had been nursing a sore knee and foot from years of abuse on the volleyball court. She enthusiastically agreed we should do the hike. This sent everyone into a bustle to find shorts, hiking shoes, and water bottles.

The Sedona sun shone, warming to almost hot that day. We arrived at the trailhead to a packed parking lot that led off to several trails and also served as a launching pad for jeep and ATV tours. Our crew of five set off down the rolling two-track and immediately got dusted by several Jeeps heading out. The fine red dust was always a staple. We walked on while Jen and Jim tracked our progress on their GPS watches.

After walking about a mile, we arrived at a junction and a sign that marked the beginning of the Devil's Bridge trail. Oops, so much for our short hike. Maureen looked slightly exasperated at this news. I caught her eye with an apologetic grin and explained that the trail guide had promised easy. Jen and Jim conferred at the trail sign, confirming we still had a mile to Devil's Bridge Overlook. Feeling frisky, Maureen assured it was okay to continue on. The walk continued as the sun's intensity increased. Near the top, one short, steep scramble deposited us to our first panoramic vista, looking west. Several other groups milled around snapping photos for one another on the narrow rock archway suspended between two points of the formation. At its narrowest, the rock bridge was about three feet wide. For those sans vertigo, you could stand and peer down 500 feet on either side. I felt more comfortable sitting on the bridge and avoiding the exact middle.

Instead, I volunteered to snap photos of all my fearless friends. Jim, Jen, and Theresa even made a cheerleader pyramid. Everyone in my group badgered me to take my turn. All the other hikers laughed as I crawled out to the bridge walk, whimpering, "I don't like this!" On the hike back, I am sure I heard Jen and Mo talking about being wary of my "easy" activity rating.

As promised, we fitted in a golf day. Our group split into two different activity choices. Maureen, Theresa, and I booked a noon tee time at Sedona Golf Resort in Oak Creek Village. Team J & J reserved a spot on a half-day river trip that included paddling inflatable kayaks down river, a box lunch, and a wine tour. This time, we arrived early (Andrea was not on this trip) and were impressed with a bag full of shiny new Titlest woods and irons. Mo and I loaded up the carts for a golf adventure.

We spent just over five hours on the course as the temperature climbed to the mid-80s. We focused hard on the final five holes while trying to avoid the dreaded snowman on the card. There were only a few miscues. I hit a 350-yard drive with an assist off the cart path. The highlight was a request to play through by a foursome of guys playing slow. I am sure they had lost a couple sleeves of balls at that point. They waved at us to pass through on a par three. With an audience, each of us hit a 130-yard shot that landed safely and accurately on the green. Our audience applauded, clearly impressed by our display. "Are you girls professionals?" they yelled from their cart. We smiled and waved our thanks in anticipation of putting for birdies.

The next morning, I searched online to review biking maps and found one single beginner trail. To my surprise, Jen told me she was joining the biking excursion. "Jim rented a bike for me, so I think I should try it." My shocked look did not deter her decision. Calamity Jen lived up to her nickname that day. Maureen wished us well on her way to the pool as the four of us headed toward Absolute Bikes and the Bell Rock area. Mo called to Jen as we were leaving, "Give me a call for a pickup if you decide to call it early."

We had quite a lengthy session at the bike shop choosing bikes, switching out pedals, and getting tutorials on the trail maps. It was Groundhog Day for Theresa and me (just five years later): embarking on a ride and worrying about someone falling off a bike. I hoped Jim would provide an additional voice of reason and talk Jen out of tackling too much. Bell Rock Pathway was just north of the bike shop, so once again we pedaled uphill. At the first junction, I knew right away I should have paid more attention to the map discussion. Theresa suggested we go under the road and then circle back toward Llama loop. Jen piped in, "The guys at the bike shop said DO NOT cross the road; all the trails are more difficult on that side." Somehow Theresa's eagerness won out and under the road we went, with a promise

that the section connected back to BRP after a short stint. We pedaled, Theresa in the lead, me next, followed by Calamity and a worried Jim. After a couple of slide-offs, several minor falls, and a flat, Jen announced she had had enough.

It was better for all since we could only pedal for a short section then wait, hoping Calamity would emerge non-bloodied. Jim was an accomplished biker, but I was worried about Jen and Jim spatting over the misadventure. After some hike-a-biking we eventually returned to BRP. Jen told us she would find her way back and rode off after texting Mo to meet her at the bike shop. Without incident, Jen rolled in and met up with Mo at Blue Moon. Mo asked, "How'd it go?" Jen replied, "I had a great time after I left Jim, Theresa, and Laura." Jen and Mo plotted the rest of their afternoon without us. My threesome connected back up to Llama, Templeton, and the HT connector and rode another hour. Jim's GoPro captured our biking on video but missed Theresa's first fall. Rocks and picker bushes found their way into Theresa's route while my more cautious riding style saved me from any major bruising. Just my sit bones were getting raw from the bumpy, rocky ride. It's impossible for a flat lander to build up the appropriate ass-callouses for red rock riding.

The biking adventure ramped up the next day. Jen and Mo smartly made their own plan to visit Slide Rock State Park. Team Bike never found Max's favorite trail the next day. We did more trailhead hunting than biking on another gloriously sunny Sedona day. Theresa had done the research on a trail loop off Upper Red Rock Road just west of Sedona Springs. We mapped it, found a biking app, and yet never found Max's trail. *Really, Max?* I logged a mental stat sheet for the day: three miles of pedaling, four miles of hike-a-biking, one bitch attack, and five spectacular red rock views. The three of us were exasperated with Max's directions but good naturedly rode around on unnamed trails, more than likely for hiking, not biking.

In classic fashion, on a section of hike-a-biking we arrived at a steep uphill section where a trail sign read, "WARNING: This trail is unauthorized and not sanctioned for use by the Red Rock Forest Service." With no choice, we turned the opposite way, which meant more uphill and another steep-stepped section of un-rideable rock. I watched in shock as my two lunatic friends shouldered their bikes and began striding up the trail. I was convinced we were on a hiking trail. I folded my arms around my chest, planted my feet, and let my bike fall to the dirt. I was not going up that trail any farther carrying my bike. I left it on its side by

a cactus and walked up 200 feet to inform Jim and Theresa I was turning back to follow the trail back to the road.

At the top of the ridge, I caught Theresa looking back at me perplexed.
"Where is your bike?"
I pointed, "It's down there."
"What? Why? What are you doing?"
"I am not carrying my bike up this trail anymore."
"Well, it's got to come out on the other side. C'mon."
"No, this is the road to nowhere."
"I will go down and get your bike, then."
"Nope. I'm done and am biking back on my own."
"No, you can't split us up."
"Yes, I can. This is NOT a biking trail—I think that is pretty clear."
"Fine, we need to tell Jim."

The conversation continued in terse, short bits until Jim reappeared, clearly sensing the tension. I gave Jim my condensed story, that I was headed back to the road to find the car. With a pending argument in the air, Jim moved toward me and seemed agreeable not to continue up the ridge. Thankfully, Theresa conceded or thought splitting up would be more dangerous. So, retracing our wheel marks, we went back down the formation. I was quiet in my victory retreat until a slight downhill on a river washout section. I lost control of my bike and super-womaned over my handle bars. I let out an anguished, "Laura down!" My front tire had slipped on loose stones and turned 90 degrees, my momentum sent me skidding across the dusty red rocks. My bike landed on the back of my legs for good measure. And, in the rush to break my fall, I had instinctively extended my hands. Calling to Jim (I didn't think T was in a mood to help me), I lay there assessing limbs and looking for blood. Jim pedaled back and dusted me off, and we rode again on Cockscomb.

Theresa took a turn next, adding another fall to her growing hip bruise. Jim retrieved her from a thorny picker bush just moments from done. She had attempted to bike up a short yet steep rocky section that popped out to the road. Jim shook his head, suggesting we call it a day. We ended our ride looking out over Cathedral Rock, wondering about Jen and Mo. In the car, Theresa and I began inspecting our maladies on hips, shins, hands. Jim looked at our wounds and pronounced, "You girls bruise like a peach!"

Final Vortex Research

A mere two miles from our front door, we had to explore the Airport vortex site for final clues about the red rock phenomenon. Plus, the hike was an easy loop that would suit everyone in our group. I bet Maureen looked up the hike to confirm the details. The four-mile hike around the airport perimeter was perfect to stretch our legs and let the sun bake on our tan lines. And awesome continuous views on all sides of the city gave us a vantage point of formations we had not seen. We counted many more twisted Juniper trees, signs that vortex energy was near.

About halfway around the loop, we walked next to the perimeter fence on the edge of the main landing strip. We agreed, "It would be cool if a plane was landing while we were on the edge of the tarmac." As if by magic or by vortex pull, a small plane appeared, and we heard its engines grow louder as it made its descent. We all excitedly realized it would fly directly over us and make a landing. "Perfect timing!" Riveted to the approaching plane, we readied cameras. The closer it got, the more nervous we all became. Turned out we underestimated how close it would get, how loud it would be, and how much wind and jet wash it would create. Five normal adults were transformed into screaming idiots as a regional jet zoomed by hundreds of feet overhead. The pilot had a bird's-eye view of us, ducking and protecting our heads with our hands. Only Mo had smartly sat down on a rock to take her picture and did not participate in the squealing and running. Yes, the shrieking included Jim too. Thankfully not mowed down by the jet, we erupted over our stupidity. No one had thought to videotape the landing. Jim reviewed his photo and informed us he had a close-up shot of his thumb.

Team J & J left us that afternoon on Thursday for an early Friday flight out of Phoenix. They packed it up and waved goodbye, saying, "We'll see you back in the Mitten." Just MoTLo remained for one extra night and day.

S Is for Strenuous

The three of us bustled around the kitchen while finishing off the last of our coffee, yogurt, and toast. Mo suggested we do an easy hike with her in the morning at the Oak Creek Canyon Bridge as a warm-up to something more strenuous later in the day. Theresa and I had commiserated, planning to hike Bear Mountain. Mo volunteered to drop us off at the trailhead. She smartly planned to spend the day at the pool with a book while T and I labored up a steep trail in the sun.

A consistent sun shone brilliantly as Theresa and I set off from the Bear Mountain Wilderness trailhead after lunch, armed with water, sandwiches, and salty chips. The trail sign at the beginning promised a challenge.

Warning! Be prepared to meet the wilderness challenge. Do not put yourself or others at risk and do not be a lost or injured visitor. Plan a minimum of 5 hours for the round trip.

After reading that pep talk, I smiled and strode off. In the first section of trail we passed another hiker who was returning from his hike. He looked gassed, dusty, and sweaty. As we passed, I nodded hello and smiled. He returned with a tired smile, "That one was definitely an S!" It took me a few moments to realize he meant, S = Strenuous, referring to the trail rating system on the Forest Service maps. E is for easy, and M is for moderate.

It featured a 2,000-foot elevation gain on sun-exposed terrain and three false peaks before the actual top. Theresa and I found the ascent challenging and steep and were careful to stay away from the trail-crowding prickly pear cactus. The trail was innocuous and flat at the start, but an imposing red rock spire rose up in front of us as we approached the first steep section. Most other hikers were coming back down, having chosen to tackle the Bear not in the heat of the day. Several hikers gave us advice as we strode up the trail. "You are about a quarter of the way up, but it's worth it," said one couple. "Watch out for loose rocks and the false peaks, but the view is worth the climb," exclaimed a group of four women.

We both smiled and continued. I heard my breath in my ear as I leaned in to the angle of the climb. Thankfully, the steep rock scramble sections gave way to flatter sections for a few strides before angling back up. That pattern continued, and at an hour in, Theresa and I decided we should fuel up with our turkey sandwiches and chips. Theresa found one lone shade tree on the first large plateau, and we looked out over the valley below, spotting the parking lot at the start. I devoured the salty chips paired with turkey on sourdough and sipped water from my Camelback hose. We did not linger, figuring we needed plenty of time to make the summit. I let Theresa lead while I captured video clips to document the terrain and level of difficulty for Mo. We scooted and scrambled up narrow rock steps. We pushed out the bad air when the grade lessened a few times. I gawked at impressive views at two false peaks and peered down into a 1,000-foot gorge below the trail.

The weird Laura feelings reappeared near the top because I had to walk within two feet of the edge of a canyon wall to make the summit. I looked the opposite direction and leaned into the hill on pure instinct for the final steps. Theresa immediately held her hand up for a congratulatory high five. Then, I took a deep breath in and scanned a panoramic vista of snow-capped mountain peaks to the north and then Sedona's famous formations like Bell Rock, Courthouse Butte, and Castle Rock to the southeast. It was indeed worth it, as the other hikers had promised. I took a quick personal inventory before the descent and confirmed I had some water left, my legs were wobbly, my shoes and shins were caked with more red dust, and my shoulders were sunburned. It was a good day of hiking, as we began the thigh-burning walk back down. We completed our wilderness experience in four and a half hours, by the way.

Mo was pleased to see us and handed us cold drinks from inside the car. I greedily gulped while taking off my shoes and socks before hopping in the car. From my spot lounging in the back seat, I stared at the red rock formations, which seemed increasingly odd at ground level. We notched one more dip in the pool that night and received several "oh dears" from the elderly women, aghast at Theresa's thigh bruise that had turned a shade of deep purple rimmed in a lime green. Later, uptown Sedona and the Taos Cantina hosted our last supper. We enjoyed favorites again, fish tacos with plenty of guacamole.

On the Wings of Angels

The Frontier flight from Phoenix to Denver turned our adventure drama to black comedy, featuring an evangelical not-so-frequent flyer. I would have preferred to notch my earbuds in, to be transported by some mellow tunes while recounting some trip highlights. It didn't happen. A middle-aged, large-bellied, and large-bosomed woman with a preteen daughter on her arm made a scene at check-in and on the plane. It began with a tirade in a loud outdoor voice with announcements of how the kiosk was not working: "I just can't figure this dang thing out." She repeated as an appeal for help. The daughter eventually checked them in with help from an attendant.

The woman continued her stream of prose while looking around searching for someone to acknowledge that the kiosk was broken and how dang hot it was in Phoenix. Theresa was closest to her at the next check-in counter and caught a whiff of another alarming feature. She reeked of body odor on top of her obnoxious loud talking.

Escaping the check-in area, we distanced ourselves from her for a while in a local cantina before boarding. But we were reunited in close quarters on a flying tube of metal. Mo, T, and I had teased one another about how one of us would get stuck sitting next to her. That sent a wave of anxiety through me as we walked onboard. I could already hear the din of her voice as she tried to find her seat. Thanking my vortex luck, I was not seated next to her, but close enough, one row up to her right. Anyone on the plane heard her tirade continue as I tried to yoga breathe my way to the flight's merciful ending in Denver.

To start, she sat in the wrong seat. Then, her nervous chatter continued, directed at several blushing Frontier flight attendants. "I can't read these seat cards. How am I supposed to find my seat? Now, look, I am going to have to move my bags. How am I supposed to figure this out!" She continued, "Oh, lucky day, I don't need the seatbelt expander. I was worried about that, ya know." She chattered on to no one in particular. My seatmate to my left and I shared a knowing glance of exasperation. This woman single-handedly held up the already late flight with her antics and inability to read a seat assignment card. *Sigh.*

The plane eventually taxied, and we tried to tune out the chatter as we took off and flew north. Some air pockets and turbulence sent her off again on yet another wave of loud outbursts. The turbulence continued, as did she. "Oh dear Jesus! Oh Lord! We are flying on the wings of angels." I couldn't help but peek backward and watch her rock in her seat and rub her armrest violently. And the poor daughter just looked ahead. She was surely praying silently for her mother's untimely end. "Dear Jesus, thank God we were bathed in your waters. Oh dear Jesus!" The women bellowed at God and at all of us. As we bounced along, my seatmate looked over at me and we nonverbally communicated how ridiculous the scene was. With a half grin and a shake of my head, I looked outside my window, not searching for angels in the clouds but praying for silence.

Our tribulation finally ended in Denver. As I stood up to retrieve my backpack, I wished my new friend next to me safe travels. She returned the same to me and leaned ever so close to my ear with a final message, "You know, she gets to vote in the next election!"

Chapter Ten
The Liver Dance

Ireland,
2011

If you want to save some green, go in November and rent a cottage that sleeps six for only $750 for a week. Break that out between four or five people and you've got yourself a travel pot of gold (potatoes).

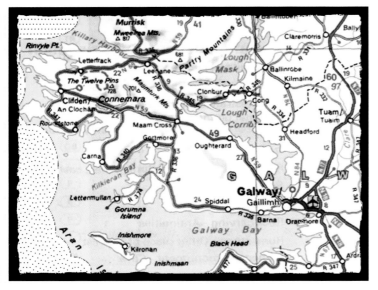

To a Town called Letterfreck

A group of nine travelers is too large to effectively manage. Nine people mean nine opinions on a dinner selection, nine ideas for activities, and nine butts that need to sit on a plane, on a train, or in three cars. A group of nine assembled when my group of four combined with Theresa's kid brother Jimmy for his thirtieth-birthday tour of Ireland. Jimmy's family entourage included his mom (Julie) and sisters Andrea, Shelly, MaryBeth, and Theresa. Add Jen and my mutual friend Karla to the equation for a bona fide troop of tourists. Aer Lingus deposited us on the isle in Dublin, then we switched modes, taking a train to Galway. We continued by car to Connemara in western Ireland to a town with three pubs, a grocery store, a hardware store, a Catholic church, and one petrol station. It was perfect. Letterfreck was perched two short miles from the mystical crashing Atlantic coast.

Aer Lingus made it difficult to sleep as we crossed the ocean. The staff never dimmed the lights and were hell-bent on feeding us or pouring tea every two hours. The constant interruptions made sleep scarce. Bleary, I was deposited through customs and whisked by bus to Dublin's train station. Desperately seeking coffee, I was jerked to attention when the sisters (Sherpa Shelly and MaryBeth) suggested we

To experience true Ireland is to immerse oneself in a rural community, its stone walls, and its green pastures and to make yourself at home. Learn to be happy about driving on the wrong side of the road. Stay in a local cottage in a town called Letterfreck for a few days of immersion into the culture and the local pub scene. Be sure to drench every piece of clothing you own in the sweet smell of peat from the fireplaces. There will be cows, sheep stampedes, castles, and toasts to your health. Stop in at local pubs, have some veg soup, down some pints, make some new friends. The legend of Irish hospitality will be confirmed on many friendly smiles from lads and lassies.

swap the 11:30 train for 9:30. The subsequent rush got me moving faster, with Jen imploring Karla and me to hurry and exchange tickets. We had five minutes to swap tickets and board the train! I was last on, stowing my luggage and collapsing into a window seat. It began to rain.

I leaned my head on my travel pillow and fell into sleep, bumped awake occasionally to see 50 shades of green fields passing by. The rain only slightly obscured row after row of stone walls and grazing, spray-painted sheep. A three-hour rail journey deposited us at Galway City over the River Shannon and across expansive views of Galway Bay. Off the train, roller bags in tow, we milled around the busy station to gather the crew for the next phase. There was a significant line to the unisex restroom, where Julie and Shelly waited their turn. MaryBeth, just off the train, perhaps still in the clutches of her post-Ambien nap, bolted to the front and pushed her way to the stall without a word to the people in line. The next woman exclaimed to Shelly, "Well, I guess she had to take a shit."

The Wrong Side of the Road

MaryBeth, relieved of her burden, led the way into the light of day. Our crew of nine zombie-walked to a pub for a lunch that felt more like breakfast. Despite the mealtime, Guinness was served along with a round of chips (the Irish equivalent to fries). Budget Car Rental got a dose of the family clan when MaryBeth and her entourage entered the tiny office to claim even tinier cars. Andrea seemed miffed when she was denied driving privileges. I watched amused as the stress level rose. I stayed still in the corner while Jen secured our car, a Ford Focus. Jen reported that the car insurance was more than the rental fee for the week. We began a process to learn to drive on the wrong side of the road. Our motto for driving became "Keep the bitch in the ditch" to remind us of the swapped driver/passenger roles.

Jen volunteered to drive one car that held Karla and me. From the back seat, I warned Jen to keep MaryBeth in her sights. "Don't lose her!" I barked. Getting out of the car park was pure madness. Galway is not a large metropolis, but pair it with Ireland signposts and the wrong side of the road and it felt like the Flyin' Ryan in downtown Chicago. Only a double rainbow perched on Galway Bay distracted me from a nervy escape out of Galway west toward Connemara. Karla and I scanned for signs displaying N59 then directed Jen on turns.

Following MaryBeth proved difficult and ultimately unsuccessful. Her car went from slow and getting used to the clutch to rocketing 80 KPH toward a highway heading west.

"Jen, you have to keep up with her!" I yelled. She responded by hammering the gas and tailing her as best she could. With one eye on the map, I saw their car pull up in the wrong lane to head east. "Where the hell is she going?" I exclaimed. Jen pulled up next to the car to flag them down only to discover a bearded young man at the wheel. He peered over with an inquisitive look. We had been following the wrong car. And, of the nine, only two people had working cell phones. As the car's chief navigator, I consulted the map and confirmed with Jen that we were headed west. Wide-eyed, Karla sat up front and nervously checked her cell phone. Around each corner, I leaned into the center of the car, my perception telling me my left side would scrape the bushes or stone walls flanking the narrow roads. Ireland's road commission does not save room for shoulders.

Jimmy and MaryBeth's carloads had gotten slightly ahead, so they stopped at a pub along our commute, the Boat Inn. They kept an eye out and tried to get a text message to Jen's phone. In the driving mist, our car completely missed them standing near the road and flagging us as we passed. Thankfully, a text came in just a few miles down the road, so we turned around and joined for a round of Guinness. The logistics challenge continued into the misty night as the three cars set off again to find

Heather Hill Cottages, just a short walk from Molly's Pub in Letterfreck. Our car arrived first. I didn't know which of the seven cottages belonged to us. Jen and I developed a system: she navigated the car to shine headlights on each entrance until 7 displayed a note and key that opened a door. Cottage found, we started hauling in our gear. Eventually, the other car arrived and dropped off bunkmates Theresa and Andrea. The rest of the crew had a cottage in Tully, a wee bit down the road.

I selected a room upstairs to myself and listened to Jen and Karla's constant chatter, lamenting about chargers and cell phones while checking in on Facebook. My cell phone was stowed away, and without an international cellular plan, it would not be used on this trip. I smiled about unplugging, being off the grid, and unpacked a few things as I settled into my nook. Theresa, who was across the hall in her room, listened incredulously as well to the ongoing struggle with devices, internet connections, and charger adaptors. That evening, our crew

eventually made it down to the Dew, across from Molly's Pub, for dinner before collapsing into a jet-lagged sleep.

During our stay at Heather Hill, the first evening after sundown the lights abruptly went out. A scramble in the dark developed to figure out what happened. Eventually, we found an electric meter (like a gumball machine with a turn knob) set up in the main parlor to accept a €2 coin to continue electric usage for the house. The electrical apparatus was watched with great care after the first incident. We gathered extra coins and stacked them nearby in case the lights went out again.

Diamond Hill and Kylemore Abbey

Theresa had loosely organized a hike the following day in nearby Connemara National Park. The idea was to meet in the grocery store parking lot around 10. Nobody showed up, and Andrea opted to be dropped off back in Tully instead. While we waited for the no-shows, Jen and Karla popped over to the hardware store and procured a roll of duct tape for an adventure race they signed up for later in the week. Their race kit suggested taping shoes to your feet, lest they get sucked off into the bog. The race, the Turf Guy Challenge, is a 10K adventure/obstacle race complete with bog traversing, a frigid water plunge, and a peat toss. The Killary Adventure

Center hosted the event just up the road 10 miles. Staring at the rolls of duct tape, I was still in shock that Jen and Karla were planning to run it on our holiday.

The November timeframe turned out to be a brilliant choice for the trip. We did not have to jockey for position with tour buses or hordes of visitors. We saw only three other hiking groups as we piled out of the Focus, ready to walk in Connemara National. The plan was to walk up Diamond Hill to a perch of 1300 feet above sea level. We were rewarded with views of the Atlantic and our Heather Hill cottage in a neat row of white squares in a quaint borough. The sun was out, paired with a light breeze, but conditions change quickly on the coast. We continued to walk up the path and spotted our first Irish ass in the corral. A cloud bank gusted in, and we endured five minutes of rain on an otherwise bright, sunny morn. Theresa and I pulled up our hoods and kept walking, watching amused while Karla and Jen produced bright pink umbrellas. We were hiking with Mary Poppins divas! I watched in anticipation of one wind gust that would rip the flimsy umbrellas out of their hands then down the trail.

The rain tapered, and sun returned within minutes. The incline steepened while views improved. The trail went from pebbles to rocks, and the summit was littered with large rocks and stacked cairns. We added a rock to the pile to mark our successful hike. Karla made the hour trek easily, so I was hopeful my tall, skinny volleyball friend would survive the upcoming Turf Guy. The panoramic Atlantic coast lay to our west, while a lough flanked Kylemore Abbey tucked in a wood far below to the north. The restored stone castle amid the deep blues and greens of lake and woods showed off its historic grandeur with little effort. Kylemore Abbey was our next stop after lunch in the park cafeteria. Our lunches of Irish staples included hot tea and puréed vegetable soup served with a dense and flavorful slice of brown bread.

Next up, just a short drive away, we notched our first castle tour. Kylemore means "bigwood" and is now a functioning Benedictine Abbey. Just over 100 nuns keep a careful watch over this magnificent facility. The gothic stone castle,

chapel, and mausoleum were built by the Henrys, Margaret and Mitchell, from 1867–1871. Mr. Henry was from Manchester, England, where he was a business tycoon, a surgeon, and a politician. Records show that King Edward VII, accompanied by Queen Alexandra and Princess Victoria, visited Kylemore Abbey, while touring Connemara back in 1903. At the time of the royal visit, the castle was still in ownership of its original owner Mitchell Henry.

The tour includes a spacious manicured garden and greenhouse. Kylemore Abbey is second only to the Cliffs of Mohr for western Ireland's coveted top tourist trap. I was happy to be a tourist that afternoon, no crowd-battling required. The four of us strolled along the lake, followed trails, and eventually made it to the main gardens. To support the nuns and Ireland tourism, I paid the fee and saved my ticket for my journal. We were once again graced with another vibrant rainbow, the fourth of the day, perched over the gardens this time.

Looking back, we crammed a lot in for one day. The hike and castle tour led to a brief stop at our cottage to change for a birthday dinner at the Renvyle Hotel and Inn, in honor of Jimmy's thirtieth. We coordinated all nine for the meal. Dinner featured festive toasts to Jimmy, the lone male on the trip. The celebration continued on a loosely organized pub crawl that produced a motorboat treatment for the birthday boy performed by a buoyant and busty local. Funnier yet, she followed us (It's hard to miss nine people traveling in a pack.) to Molly's Pub where live acoustic reggae pumped from the speakers. Our group attempted to blend with the locals while making space on a cramped dance floor. Guinness consumption continued as we danced and sang along.

However, Jen and Karla were becoming antsy, worrying about the adventure race the next morning. Before they snuck back to the cottage, Jen discovered one of the musicians outside trying to fix his broken guitar. She struck up a conversation and offered her roll of duct tape to secure his string saddle and strum plate to the base. He was amused by Jen's accessories and inquired, "Why ar ye travelin' with a roll of duct tape?" He beamed proudly once his instrument was back in strumming condition. After the fix, we waved goodbye to Karla and Jen. Seven of nine enjoyed the last set of tunes and a version of "Brown Eyed Girl." Later, we cheered as the musician dedicated a song to the American girls who had saved the night of music with a roll of tape. Jen missed the dedication with the self-imposed curfew. Looking at my watch, I made out a blurry, pixelated 1:00 a.m.

Pot Bunkers, the Turf Guy Challenge, and the Sharpest Rock in Ireland

During the pre-trip planning researching the Connemara area, Theresa stumbled upon a YouTube video of the Turf Guy Challenge, the Irish equivalent to a Tough Mudder with a few fjords and bogs thrown in. She emailed it around to Jen and Karla, joking about adding it to our itinerary. After watching the muddy Irish challenge, Jen actually decided to sign up and talked Karla into doing it as well. Theresa and I tried to explain, "We were kidding!" but it only spurred her on. She was smitten with the idea of telling the story of her adventure well before the race began. During a pre-trip planning session, she suggested we do it together. Theresa and I each responded with a vehement, "Hell, no." The bog plunge and 40-degree temperatures provided plenty of reasons to decline and opt for a day at the golf course instead. Besides, I felt compelled to play a round of golf in the country that had been hitting little white balls since 1858. It was neighboring Scotland that began the tradition at Prestwick Golf Club in 1851.

In Ireland, the Royal Curragh Golf Club was founded at Kildare in 1858, the oldest course on the Emerald Isle.

We split up into three distinct groups on Saturday. Jen and Karla became known as the mud hens once they set off to Killary Adventure Center for the Turf Guy. The golfers included Jimmy, Julie, Theresa, and me for a round at Connemara National Links overlooking the ocean near Clifden. Another mellow group stayed back for some cruising and shopping: Andrea, Shelly, and MaryBeth. We gathered later in front of the cottage fireplace to swap stories.

The Atlantic had taken a Valium: its rigid winds slowed to a mellow breeze, making it a balmy 50-degree hot spot. Jimmy had piloted us that morning through Bally Connelly, past Clifden, and to Connemara National Links. The 45 minutes by car went swiftly while I fixed my gaze on the coastline marked with black seaweed coating all the rocks in the bays. My gaze eventually shifted to expanses of green for golfing. Thankfully, our battered rental clubs were not an indication of how much we enjoyed the links on a sunny coastal day. None of us minded the sub-par equipment with the ever-present views of ocean blue over top of swaying grasses.

I still sported a ski cap with my khakis and sweater as we navigated our way around the links and strategically placed pot bunkers. Julie, Theresa, and I stretched on hole 1, swinging our clubs back and forth to loosen our lower backs. Jimmy declared his driver a super-rope, the flex equivalent to a piece of licorice. The Twizzler did not serve his swing speed well, which resulted in some erratic drives. My opening drive was acceptable in the short grass. It was good *craic* to hit a golf ball down the fairways, with lots of roll on hard-pack links grass. I hit a five iron 175 yards on several holes. Julie and Theresa smacked wormers as well; we cackled while the ball scooted quickly up and over small knolls in and out of sight. We rationed our balls; we each brought only three, so I took great care of them based on a limited supply. The front nine paced well, and I notched half of a hundred on the card.

Our ravenous group of golfers pounded sandwiches before teeing off on 10. I found my way into pot-bunkers on 10 and 11. On the front nine, there was minimal success in getting out of the signature

bunkers. On 10, I took a different approach, hooded my club, and swung directly down with full velocity. In a poof of sand, the ball lifted over the wooden bunker wall and landed on the fringe. I celebrated with a fist pump and raised my club over my head in a surprised, triumphant stance. Scores suffered on the back nine – the bunkers were abundant. The difficulty level went up, the greens narrowed, and the bunkers multiplied. We were distracted by the idyllic green fairway views, prompting more attention to photographs. I have some delightful photographs to go with my 56 on the

back nine. Theresa led the way with a 46, for a 96 total. Jimmy had smartly switched drivers, hitting a 270-yard drive to end his round. We celebrated back in Clifden at Guys Pub first with Irish coffees. We dined on calamari, crab/potato cakes, and plates of fish and chips before checking in with the rest of the gang.

Later, back in Letterfreck in the warm confines of our living room, the golfers huddled with the mud hens for a spirited exchange. Karla displayed her abraded elbows and knees. They had completed the challenge, except for an optional plunge into the hypothermic fjord waters. Jen explained how the organizers seemed befuddled that two American girls wanted to get dirty, cold, and wet on their holiday. She laughed heartily, recalling their advice about the fjord plunge. One guy offered, "Oh, yah, ya cud totally get hypo-termia, but te good kind." Jen and Karla continued, taking turns describing running through the bog, throwing chunks of peat, army-climbing over obstacles, and leg-fighting with an Irishman on a rope crossing. Ten kilometers later they emerged with duct-taped shoes still intact and bog caked in their hair and in their teeth. For the remainder of the trip, Jen couldn't rid herself of a bog scent that wafted after her for days.

The stories eventually died down with pots of tea, taking turns in the shower, then on to dinner plans at Angler's Rest Pub in Tully Cross. A local duo was performing some traditional music and later tunes by Johnny Cash and Merle Haggard. Irish musicians love American country music, so you'll hear it mixed in with "Whiskey in the Jar" or "Galway Girl." The mud hens bowed out early, no doubt tired or needing time to pick the bog out of their ears, noses, and teeth. Most of us stayed and pulled up short stools near the peat fire, anxiously awaiting the next set. I sipped a frothy Guinness with the remaining gang. We reminisced about our day of golf and swapped more stories.

Andrea took the prize for the most noteworthy happening. While I sipped my Guinness, my eyes widened to a story of her truncated drive into town. While we were golfing, Andrea announced she was taking the car to do some shopping, and off she went from Tully Cross toward Letterfreck. Finally behind the wheel, she slid on her sunglasses and smiled in anticipation of doing some exploring on her own. Within the first kilometer, Andrea found (in her words) the sharpest rock in Ireland, which sprung out from the shoulder of the windy road. That rock punctured two tires and left her stranded temporarily until the Ford could be towed to a local mechanic. He delivered the news that he would need two days to fix it and it would add €300 to her trip budget. Our car fleet went from three to two. For nine people this was more than a minor inconvenience. Andrea finally got her chance to drive, but her drive time lasted less than five minutes. Exasperated, her blue eyes bulged, and her eyelashes fluttered. She declared, "I don't know what happened—the rock just came out of nowhere."

Mass and Famine Fjord Walk

Sunday morning dawned with a haze behind my eyes, assuredly from the peat fumes and one too many Guinnesses. To atone for my transgressions, I joined the clan at an Irish Catholic mass at Tully Cross. The locals welcomed us while we filled a complete pew near the front. Mass featured music from local students, and then the priest delivered a homily about making good choices in our lives. I was reminded of a lyric in a Gaelic Storm song, "I go to mass on Sunday and back to the pub on Monday." Mass concluded with a choir version of "Let It Be." The entire congregation sang along for the recessional hymn. Filing out of church, we nodded at our Tully Cross friends, some of whom we had met at the pub the night before. After a brief organizational huddle, we decided to take a proper Irish walk in the countryside. A couple of locals volunteered directions to the Bunowen trailhead just a few miles up the road.

We gathered all nine after an abbreviated lunch. Crammed in two cars instead of three, we struggled to find our turn but eventually spotted a Bunowen sign on a rock mostly covered by tall grasses. We parked the cars on the side of the narrow road at a fence gate, where we began our walk. MaryBeth waved us on and opted to stay back with a book.

The Bunowen Trail followed a historic famine walk from Ireland's troubled and meager past. The guidebook suggested that we imagine some starving Irish walking along the path in hopes of a morsel and brighter future. I distinctly remember Shelly remarking as we walked, "Why did the Irish starve when they were surrounded by lakes and an ocean full of fish?" I pondered and looked directly over the deep and chilly Killary Fjord. The fjord was lined with nets and a buoy system for mussel farming. The potato famine is certainly nothing to joke about, but Shelly was right: why not switch to seafood when there are no potatoes? I stared out at the fjord, where the cold blue met misty green banks leading to mountainous tops. A muddy two-track led us all on a picturesque ridgeline that eventually led to a small fishing village.

Jen and Karla led the way back along the muddy path and were startled by a fast-approaching sheep herd. The small stampede of about 50 picked up speed while Jen started to panic. They ran directly down the road toward us. Two herding dogs suddenly appeared, and a shepherd, who barked a few commands, altered their path toward a small barn. We watched the spectacle, amused by Ireland's most prevalent wildlife. The sheep's gray matted coats were always blotted with a spot of spray

paint, usually pink or purple. After the sheep stampede turned docile, we returned to our leisurely seaside hike. The walk was a warm-up for tomorrow's hike up Mweelrea Mountain.

MaryBeth was still engrossed in her book as we approached the car with steamy windows. Cramming back into the cars, we headed just north to Lenaan. It was my turn at the wheel, and I focused mightily on keeping the edge of the car near the middle yellow line, properly avoiding sharp rocks along the edge. Andrea, to my surprise, commented on my driving!

I pulled in street-side unharmed near Hamilton's Pub, and we happily filed in for refreshments. A peat fire warmed the pub while our group of nine kept the barkeep hopping. They were featuring vegetable soup with a slice of brown bread. The soup, the bread, and the Guinness seemed to improve at each pub. Bartenders and servers alike always seemed amused when our group piled through the door. The time spent in the pubs will always be my quintessential memory of rural western Ireland.

Mweelrea Mountain (Mill-Ra):
A Hike without Ropes

The word "bog" was spoken no fewer than a hundred times within a two-day time span after the Turf Guy by the mud hens. Still vacillating over their wet challenge, they were unnerved when our hike started across a wetland area before marching up a steep incline. Our foursome squished from one grass tuft to the next searching for dry footfalls and the elusive trail.

Before leaving for Ireland, Jen, Karla, Theresa, and I agreed we would do a big hike during our stay. The trail guide listed Mweelrea Horseshoe as strenuous, describing a five- to seven-hour timeframe to complete the out and back. It was categorized as one of the hardest hikes in Ireland. Elevation gain was about 1,600 feet from bog to peak. When Theresa bought the trail book at the café, the owner handed it to her, "Thank ye. Slog-on, girls." Slog-on was exactly what we did that day.

By 9:00, we were out of the cottage and pointed north on N59 again past Lanaan, around a big lough toward Ben Burry and Mwellrea Peaks to the west. The sun shone brightly, but a brisk breeze called for layers and a jacket. My eyes watered from the bursts of ocean-fed breezes, prompting sunglasses. We parked near a famine monument and scouted around for the trailhead. Without the guidebook and a detailed trail description, we'd never have found the trail. After walking north and south 100 yards with no visible point of entry, we split the middle and headed in between the lough and the lake.

Our shoes were partially submerged after only a few feet of lowlands. I looked back and watched Jen and Karla search for dry footfalls; the grim set to their teeth highlighting their level of discomfort. Theresa gave up on dry grass and just splashed forward. After 10 minutes, we found the makeshift bridge that confirmed our route. We started up. After that, the terrain went from soggy to damp, creating suction-like noises as we walked. Mysteriously, the Ireland bog ascended above sea level. I slogged on behind Theresa, unphased by the conditions.

We paused to look up at the ascent the book described as the summit. The col was just above a horseshoe-shaped ramp. The peak was at 1,700 feet (900 meters), with some ominous sheer rock sections we would not attempt. The pitch steepened, and I unzipped my first layer. I felt like the monkey in the middle that day; Theresa plowed forward, not minding to wait much for our two slower companions. I kept an eye on Karla, who nervously peered at the approaching steep. We followed a grassy ridgeline over a combination of rocks and more bog. I carefully selected my route for fear of sinking in muck up to my knee. The terrain and the pitch had us gasping and glowing. We aired out our jackets and passed around granola bars.

The difficulty ramped up, and the tall girls (Karla and me) were relegated to all fours at points to prevent slipping backward. The moist green hillside gave way to steely rock and scree. Hiking transitioned to a scramble, and I caught myself reaching out with one arm, feeling less steady. There was still no visible trail except for rock troughs that led us up and across small waterfalls. I kept peering back and caught a flash of Jen's green jacket behind a huge boulder. I may have witnessed the last moment of a barrel roll, over her shoulder and on to her side after losing her footing. After many long moments waiting, she appeared around the boulder, upright but looking

exasperated. Almost 50 yards ahead, I waited to be sure she was okay. Karla was watching intently, and after a significant pause, she too kept going. I called to Theresa and hand-signaled her to find a flat spot to rest and eat our packed lunch. It seemed like the appropriate time to do an attitude check before the last section.

Switching my camera to video mode, I panned the scene as Jen and Karla approached. Narrating what I saw, I kept up a stream of commentary.

"We've made it about halfway, and it's been a challenge. The views are impeccable." I shifted the camera toward Jen. "This hike is labeled difficult. How are you feeling about the climb so far?" Jen's eyes narrowed as she came toward me, stopping just short of my lens. "I would rate this hike as STUPID," she spat back at me, clearly exasperated. I clicked the video button off and glanced at Theresa, who pretended not to notice while eating her snack.

Jen informed us about her slip and fall incident while munching on bread, cheese, and salami. In a serious tone she asked, "Shouldn't we have ropes for this section?" Inquisitive looks passed between Theresa and me, not knowing how to answer. Instead, we passed fruit and granola bars. The only conversationalist was Theresa, who seemed quite pleased with the goat-like trail. Even though I adore snack time, the wind chill prompted a visual review of our goal and a quick restart. There was one long, steep section to the ramp that led to the summit. I encouraged Karla and Jen to continue only if they felt comfortable. They both concurred the wet ground was making them feel tentative. For the moment, the four of us began again the process of climbing, squishing, and reaching up the hill. Route finding became even more treacherous. I leaned into the hill and surveyed below me. Karla seemed perplexed about where

to step next, and I sensed her raging internal debate. Jen, just ahead of her, watched, worried, and then looked up at me. She stopped abruptly and ran her fingers and hand across her neck in symbolic fashion. The motion clearly indicated they were done. I yelled to Theresa to hold up and confirmed with Jen that she would hike down with Karla. Four hikers became two.

I caught up with Theresa. Side by side, we pressed thighs and calves to burning sensations, but within 20 minutes we made the ramp to the top. A shock of cold wind greeted us as we topped out and walked near the edge, spotting Croagh Patrick. An expansive view ranged west to the sea and north to Westport and Clew Bay. The emerald green of the island is deepest when flanked by the ocean. The height made me gasp, both for air and for the beauty. A mountaintop view never fails to inspire, so we both naturally lifted our arms wide in a tribute to Mwellrea Mountain.

From the peak, we actually spotted the trail for the descent, following closer to the river. I peered down and saw two tiny specks moving slowly below. Our companions were safe and making progress back. The way down was more difficult. We slipped, slid, and sank into muck several times as we navigated down the steep pitches. I slipped sideways twice, sending my hand and wrist into the wet ground. My shoes and pants, from ankle to hip, were smeared with Ireland's bountiful bog. Theresa stepped in a bog hole up to her knee, causing one abrupt stop. Through the bog obstacle course, we zigzagged down discussing how irritated Karla and Jen were at us for pushing them too far. Theresa continued on confidently about how good balance was imperative for such excursions. Simultaneous to the comment, her foot caught a loose rock, sending her swiftly earthward on

her forearm and stomach with a thump. I gasped at her wipeout and reached down to help her up. "Take a minute, okay," I said as she pried herself up. She wrung out her wrist, "I'm okay. That's what I deserve for being boastful. God clearly gave me a sign to be more humble."

We picked up the pace as the trail began to level closer to the river and we caught the mud hens halfway back. We'd been at it for five hours. On the hike back, I thanked the

mushy bog beneath my feet, saving our knee and hip joints from further trauma. Another sheep herd crossed our trail, and instead of the bridge, we followed a two-track and crossed the river by stepping on black stones embedded in the flowing water. The silver Ford glinted at us in the sun as we approached, signaling our successful return. Later that afternoon and into the evening, we continued around N59 to Westport then back to Heather Hill Cottages.

I became a whiskey drinker that night to celebrate completing the hardest hike in Ireland. After dinner at the Dew in Letterfreck with the whole gang, a smaller contingent split off to Paddy Coyne's for music and Jameson on the rocks. We bantered with the locals singing along to Parach Jack's acoustic version of "Bad Romance" by Lady Gaga. Our bartender, Lucy, gaily fetched whiskey and beers while we sang along and encouraged Parach on a musical fusion of top 40, country, and traditional Irish tunes. My cheeks glowed pink, and my eyes sparkled as hours turned to moments under the influence of mountain air and whiskey. At closing time Lucy had slipped away, and the tab was nowhere on the bar. We searched around and found her in the front bar with friends sipping a Budweiser. "Oh dear," she said, "I completely forgot abot ya girls. I'm sure I'd av' found ya tomorra." We paid our tab and left Lucy a huge tip!

Island of the White Cow

With a full week in the Connemara region, we had time to take a ferry from the island to another island. We bounced off ocean swells for a half hour to Inishbofin, an island loaded with history. Cleggen was the port town where the aging ferry docked. We made the voyage on a rusty, grease-stained, rickety boat manned by a sparse crew of five. Standing on the top level of the ferry required hats and gloves to ward off the brisk winds. Thankfully, our boat did not have the gumption to go any faster than 20 knots. We passed menacing rock outcroppings as our pilot navigated into the harbor. Ruins of Cromwell's barracks still stood in disarray, built in 1656 atop the shiny, wet, blackened, jagged rocks. The English Puritan Cromwell, known for his brutality, had imprisoned many Catholic priests at that spot. Cromwell hanged priests from the rocks as the tide came in, letting them dangle in the swells until they drowned. More history that demonstrates a deep religious philosophical clash where neither side was willing to bend or compromise.

Inishbofin looked isolated and cold; the chill from the ocean waves crept into my fingers and toes as we disembarked. Only 350 Irish called the island home. A witty Irishman led us on a bus (passenger van) tour around the island's perimeter, continuing with more stories of England's brutal ruling years. He detailed the salt tax that affected the fishing industry in the midst of the potato famine. Our guide chatted, and we answered questions about our holiday highlights so far. Theresa and Jen chimed in about our hike to Mweelrea. By his reaction he was familiar with the mountain's reputation. He asked, "Did you approach from the east or the west?" followed by, "Did you all have ropes?" Clearly vindicated, Jen piped in while pointing vehemently at Theresa and me. "I told you we needed ropes!" Firing back, "What— tied together you would have pulled us all down the mountain." I suppressed a snort and am still confused about the role of the ropes and how they would have improved our trek. Plus, I recalled making it to the summit of Kilimanjaro without a rope.

Our van tour ended after a short walk around the harbor area at Day's Pub. Dramatic waves crashed on the sheer cliffs along the perimeter road. With a shiver, we watched hefty waves hit the rocks and send water crashing 20 feet in the air. We walked by a guesthouse where Nicolas Cage had once holed up for a long holiday. Day's Pub was the only establishment open, so our crew piled in and cupped our chilled hands around bowls warmed on the outside from streaming soup. Julie had found a nice perch near the lone fire for some sketching, while some of us walked. Julie's sketches reminded me that I was sorely behind in my journaling (maybe spending too much time each evening at the pubs).

Galway Girls Go to Dublin

I am not known for my shopping stamina, but a quest for a pair of new boots dominated my time in Galway. On a previous visit, with little time to look around, I was drawn to the boot shops.

We left the friendly confines of our Irish borough for Galway then on to Dublin for the rest of the trip. A mist settled in while Jen piloted the car east, this time past Kylemore, looking stately and mysterious. I bounced around in the back seat and helped navigate to the rental car office. Jen, Karla, and I high-fived about not getting lost and proudly handed back our keys after announcing we had not added any dings or scratches.

The other clan was still en route, so the three of us set about walking and shopping in Galway. I made a beeline back to Logues Shoe Shop and smiled at the displays that held stylish tall boots in every color. Just a year ago, under a severe time crunch, I had found a pair only to be denied because my size was out of stock. My luck changed on this occasion. A cheerful shop attendant, Pearl, brought out several pairs for me to try. I waved Karla and Jen on, agreeing to meet up for lunch. I tried a to-the-knee black leather boot adorned with a buckle at the ankle. I spotted another similar black riding boot then slid on a mid-calf distressed gray suede pair. It was the latter that won my heart. Comfortable, stylish, and unique—no one back home would have anything quite like this. Pearl rang me up, and thankfully I didn't check (at the time) the Euro-to-dollar conversion. Grinning, box in tow, I joined my two companions for lunch

at the Cellar. We power-shopped for another half hour after a plate of fish and chips. Three scarves were added to my bag before I checked my watch. Lingering too long, I had five minutes to get to the train bound for Dublin.

I was the last of nine to board the train. Theresa looked relieved when I sat down next to her. I showed off my prized purchase to a unanimous thumbs-up from the gang. The three hours clipped by, which gave me time to catch up on writing. Green fields flew by my window, and they eventually faded for city brick and buildings. Karla and Jen were in front of me, seated facing an Irish couple traveling back to Dublin. Karla leaned forward on her tray to steal a nap en route. Her seatmates commented quietly to Jen, "Well, wit all yer adventures, I bet every one of ya ar banjaxed." *Banjaxed* was the Irish word for "thoroughly worn out." Thankfully, our B&B was just two blocks from the train station. Our host, Grainne, greeted us at her family-owned Gatehouse Bed & Breakfast. She had six rooms, of which we needed four. We all split off to find rooms and roommates and discuss a plan for dinner. Ryan's was the dinner choice, a short walk from the Gatehouse. Fish and seafood were the specialties, so Jimmy ordered a vat of steamed mussels that arrived in a heavy-duty black crock pot, placed in the middle of our table.

The process I had grown ever patient with began again: picking drinks, ordering food, and who was sharing with whom. The busy restaurant was a perfect place for our boisterous group of nine to blend in. Stuffed on mussels, we decided to walk it off and find the Brazen Head, the oldest pub in Ireland. The six-block walk helped make room for the Guinness blitz we encountered at yet another lively pub. Established in 1198, the Brazen Head was a maze of small rooms and bar areas obviously converted from a once inhabited residence. Every inch of wall space in the pub was adorned with artifacts, posters, photos, patches, and Irish tidbits of all sorts. It was like looking at plaid and stripes on hangers, a labyrinth of wallpaper with no place to focus. Someone from every country in the world had made a mark on this famous pub. The first round of Irish nectar arrived, and more patrons began to file in when the music was slated to start.

A four-piece named McIntyre began a lively session a solid half hour late. Their instruments included a mandolin, bodhran, guitar, and harmonica for good measure. The all-guy band become immediately friendly with our group of eight women, engaging us with questions and lively stories. Off securing another Guinness, I returned to my seat to find Jen perched up front next to the jovial bodhran player clearly enjoying the female attention. The tunes began to flow, and we impressed the other patrons with our knowledge of the traditional pub songs and the clapping rules to "Finnegan's Wake" and "Whiskey in the Jar." We clapped on and made room for six guys visiting from Norway in similar festive spirits, imploring the bartender to stir up baby Guinness shots. The room was jammed, the temperature rose, and another round of songs spurted through the makeshift speakers. Next to our table, two couples from Rhode Island leaned in and asked if we could teach them the clapping, wondering how we acquired this important skill. We had Michigan Irish Music Festival to thank for our prolific knowledge of Irish tunes and antics.

We had to shush the Norwegians for being too loud during the slow songs, but the session continued with 40 clapping people crammed in a cozy space. The mix was traditional pub songs with some classics mixed in, like John Denver's

"Country Roads." The pints kept arriving one after another like planes coming in on a metro airport runway. I have no recollection of how many I consumed or if it was just one pint that never went empty. We told the band we had an Irish dancer in our group and goaded Shelly into doing a jig. She obliged to the loud cheers of the entire room. I love Irish musicians, who seem to be just as good at storytelling as making music. They engage with their audience and seem compelled to strike up conversations with strangers. A collective sigh escaped the small crowd as the last song was introduced just before midnight. We clapped, stood, and thanked the band, all firefighters moonlighting as musicians. They had not heard of Michigan Irish Music Festival, but of course of the Milwaukee festival, the largest in the US. Jimmy passed along my MIMF business card to the band, telling them to look us up. The card earned us a free CD while we settled up our large bar tab.

Everyone was banjaxed, so we walked the six blocks back and made a quick stop at a Topas petro station for a late snack. I went to the window and asked the clerk for Crunchie candy bars. The chocolate fusion with a seafoam center was a delicious nightcap.

The Perfect Pour in Dublin

Throughout my journey on the island, a drinking theme prevailed. The chapter is aptly named "The Liver Dance." The trip was about learning to dance with a partner who was smooth and creamy, a tall Irish stout that flitted about the room making circles and flourishes while commanding the bar. The Irish are damn proud of their drinking (and dancing) prowess. At most pubs, they had a habit of stacking up empty kegs outside the side or front entrance, as if they were showing off and bragging about how much was drunk in their establishment. The Irish don't hide their barrels behind a fence or fenced barricade; they flaunt their successes for all to see.

An ambitious city tour of Dublin included the MOMA (Museum of Modern Art), Kilmainham Gaol (Dublin's jail), and the Guinness Storehouse tour, followed by tastings at the Jameson distillery. Disappointed, we learned MOMA was closed for exhibition updates, so we strolled the gardens before heading to a well-told history lesson at the gaol. I listened, engaged, as our guide described the gaol's most famous prisoners and Ireland's troubled past en route to independence. It was 1916 when the rebellion kicked off years of violence, leading to the eventual independence from England. Children as young as five had been imprisoned for stealing food to survive.

I thought about my nephews (Asa and Jude back home, a similar age). The majority of the Irish leaders in the rebellions of 1798, 1803, 1848, 1867, and 1916 were imprisoned there.

We moved on from a sobering history to brewing. A long walk left us hungry as we entered the St. James gate entrance at Guinness World Headquarters. We shelled out €20

for the privilege of supporting Ireland's most profitable export. We sipped our first sample on the Tasting Experience level. The experience culminated in a lesson on how to pour the perfect Guinness – The long pour. If poured correctly, you need two minutes and a special pint glass adorned with the harp in the logo. The harp serves as a marker for the first part of the pour. The glass needs to be held at 45° without allowing the nozzle to touch the glass. Push the tap handle away during this part of the pour. Once the beer is filled ¾ full, it must rest for 60 seconds before the second part of the pour. To tap the glass off, pull the tap toward you. No nitrogen is released, producing the perfect caramel-colored head. I have a certificate on my office wall certifying I have achieved the perfect pour according to Guinness standards.

The Gravity Bar at the top of the Storehouse completed our tour with panoramic views of the city and the Wicklow Mountains to the south. It was three hours well spent adding knowledge and numbers to our pint totals. During our pub tour around Ireland, we were shocked to learn that the no.1 selling beer in Ireland is Budweiser, then Heineken and Carlsburg. Apparently, Guinness is more popular outside of Ireland.

Seven floors of exploration left our feet tired, so many of us crammed into a cab for the cross-town ride to the Jameson distillery. Being a whiskey newbie, I took notes on all four varieties during our tasting. Andrea also gave it a go, but she made her famous cat hairball face, the flavors not agreeing with her tastebuds. We sniffed, swirled, and sipped Jameson original, 12-year, Jameson Reserve, and the 18-year. In between sips, Jimmy treated us to squares of dark chocolate, a surprisingly delightful pairing. I selected the 12-year as my favorite and informed Theresa and Julie that a lovely warm feeling had started to spread in my throat that migrated right to my heart. The remaining tastes were added to steaming coffees brought over by our attentive bartender. The caffeine was perfectly timed so we could push into the evening for more Dublin exploration.

Dublin Final Friday

I bookended my tour with one of Ireland's finest exports: prolific authors. On a rainy Friday, I toured the Dublin Writers' Museum. For the city visit, try the hop-on, hop-off green bus line that makes stops at all the typical tourist places including Trinity College, museums, Grafton Street, and Christ Church Cathedral. That morning, we split into two manageable groups. The family crew headed by bus to New Grange for a tour of a prehistoric site, while Karla, Jen, and I stayed in the city. Also on the same day in 2011, Michael D. Higgins, Ireland's new president, was sworn in.

The newspapers detailed his plan to restore the Celtic Tiger during his seven-year term. Dublin Castle was the site of his swearing-in, but I missed the pomp and circumstance in the midst of an audio tour about Yeats, Joyce, and Swift.

It was a typical Irish day punctuated with raindrops and a chilly breeze. The three of us stepped out into the rain to catch the bus outside of Ryan's Pub. The weather dictated layers and our best slickers. I pulled my hood up and watched the hens battle with their umbrellas once again in the wind. Frequent gusts of wind sent the umbrellas' spines flipping

backward, threatening to randomly gash a commuter's eyes. I kept a wide berth on the short wait for the bus.

The first stop was Jameson's distillery since the hens had missed the chance yesterday. We walked up Bow Street to the entrance, where I split from the girls during their tour. I found a café across the way for a solid hour of quiet writing time. I ordered tea with a scone and set my damp jacket on a chair to dry as I scratched out notes from the past two days. I was lost in words and occasionally noticed as hungry Irish walked by me with plates of breakfast. The teacup warmed my clammy hands, and I looked out, watching the rain grow steady and fast. The raindrops flowed into torrents off the roofs and patio umbrellas just outside my window. An hour passed in just moments, and the girls came to collect me after their tour.

I asked the girls how the whiskey tasted at that hour as we hopped back on the bus for the Writers' Museum. The rain ramped up, but my spirits were not dampened—about to be inspired by literary giants. Once inside, I popped on my earpiece and began a self-guided tour, devoted to the likes of Jonathan Swift, James Joyce, WB Yeats, Bram Stoker, Oliver St. John Gogarty, Oscar Wilde, and so many more. The display cases held antique manuscripts, black and white photos, journals, typesetting tools, and fountain pens that made the craft seem even more romantic. I was genuinely surprised by the sheer numbers of writers Dublin and Ireland had produced. One could surmise, from great strife and turmoil (famines and oppression), art/writing and expression blossomed. Surrounded by volumes of history, I smiled and thought about my budding writing hobby. (My first book was published in early 2012.) I meandered into the bookshop and library to scout the journals and souvenirs. The hens found me and hoped I was ready to hop on the bus again for more touring.

Next hop-off was Trinity College, the famous university established by Queen Elizabeth in 1592. It housed the original library and long hall that held the exhibit displaying the Book of Kells. The Book of Kells is Ireland's most treasured historical artifact dating back to the ninth century. The four gospels of the Bible are preserved in this lavishly decorated manuscript translated by monks around the year 800, complete with a Celtic flare for design. Each day, a new page is turned, so on a tour you'll only see one open spread, not the whole book. Jen paid the fee to walk the long hall and wait in line to see the Book of Kells while I milled in the bookstore with Karla. I peered outside hoping for a break in the rain to capture a photo of the famous tower in the midst of pedestrian and student traffic near the entrance. We walked down an open outside hall while the rain peppered down. Thankfully, there are pubs on every corner. We needed to dry out again and find some sustenance. O'Donahugh's beckoned us inside with a sign on the door reading "Food and specials daily." We shook out soggy coats and ordered soup, brown bread, and a Guinness. Happy and warmed, we spooned in potato and leek soup and sipped our frothy beverages. We conferred in between bites and decided on Grafton Street for our last stop. I peeked outside while grabbing our bill and reported back that the sky had brightened and the rain had stopped.

We just missed a glimpse of the new Celtic Tiger. Plumes from the following buses and a quieting street sent everyone back to cheering on Ireland, who thumped Estonia 4-nil.

Our group piled back to our table and took turns pouring beers from our very own table-tap system in the middle of the high-top. Only in Ireland can you pour your own pint with a running digital counter. I practiced a long pour or two and watched amused as the digital monitor clicked upward with each milliliter. Collecting the tab and paying our final bar bill was the endnote—my liver dance was over, and it was time to return home to find another partner.

Nancy Hands Pub hosted our party of nine for a final round of craic on the island. Ireland football (soccer) was on the television, and we crowded around a large round high-top. Baskets arrived with copious amounts of chips and other fare like burgers and fish. In the middle of dinner, a local at the bar yelled, "Guys, the new president is coming through!" Everyone bounced off chairs and crowded out the front door in time to catch a glimpse of the motorcade and police escort disappearing down the street.

To continue to follow Laura and her travels, visit her website and subscribe to her blog at www.TravelLightBook.com

Sample from Laura's blog. January 2017.

276

Destination Wedding (With No Guests)

I've been single since 1999, 17 years have passed since my divorce and the end of my marriage. I'd been in/out of relationships, navigating borders to stay safe from being disappointed and betrayed again but mostly just living life, not fixated on finding a soulmate. I just let my independent nature guide me. So why after all that time did it make sense to reenter foreign territory and embark on a scary border-crossing full of questions. Josh is what happened…. lightning does strike and blind squirrels do find nuts! Surprises, human connections, divine interventions are all around us. It's just a matter of being open and receptive to the meteors that enter your life and crash into our quirky little spaces.

This December 29th I found myself standing on a slab of rock beneath Looking Glass Falls in the Pisgah National Forest staring into hazel/brown eyes, my hands engulfed by my soon-to-be husband. Reverend Susie began addressing Josh and me.

Welcome! We are gathered here in the presence of God to celebrate the joining of this man and this woman in the unity of marriage. Laura and Josh, today you form a partnership. May the promises you make this day lead to a lifetime of love and happiness.

The falls cascaded down as words and vows encapsulated in a moment in which I found myself not just smiling but grinning. Josh grinned back. Susie continued and tourists skirted us to gawk at the falls, the photographer moved stealthily, soft clicks recording our ceremony. It was just the two of us, Reverend Susie, Amanda the photographer and a few strangers who tried not to interrupt a wedding ceremony. It was perfect.

Our goal: to focus on the relationship, not a big fat wedding that costs a bazillion dollars that we could otherwise spend on several vacations. We'd rather celebrate booking a companion flight into the future. There was no white dress, no tuxedo, no cake, no flowers, no congregation, no reception, no DJ and no chicken dance. There was simplicity, a commitment to each other for adventures or misadventures and to love and grow with one another. It felt right to be outside, to be with nature and God's universe surrounding us. We toasted the union after with craft beers at Sanctuary Brewing (a symbolic name for the day) in nearby Hendersonville, followed by an intimate Italian dinner at Marco's Trattoria in Brevard.

Bonus, the honeymoon was built in. We bookended the wedding week in North Carolina mountain biking Blue Ridge single-track and exploring the Asheville area, chocked full of amazing culinary and craft beer choices. Asheville is officially another Beer City, like Grand Rapids, Michigan just a little more eclectic and edgy. Consider the names of the breweries we visited: Wicked Weed Funkatorium (a specialist in sours), Burial Brewing, Hi-Wire, Boojum Brewing, and Greenman Brewing. And, we stumbled onto Beer Vegas at Oskar Blues and Sierra Nevada's east coast locations. Both are huge brewing facilities and taprooms, the opposite of micro. Love was in the air. I fell in love with the Barrel-Aged Big Foot at Sierra Nevada and then fell hard again with Old Chub Scotch Ale and the Ten-Fidy Imperial Stout at Oskar Blues. We returned again to Oskar Blues for a New Years Eve Hootenanny with three local bands, the opener called The Pretty Little Goats.

Yup, bluegrass and they all wore gray and red flannel pajamas on stage. With plenty of New Year's Eve fuel in our bellies, we took advantage of the free shuttle to and from Brevard and snuck a NYE kiss on the way back to our Airbnb apartment.

Now, it's January 2017, I'm learning to say husband, not boyfriend and I am wearing a ring that I constantly fiddle with. That particular finger has been naked for an exceptionally long time. It's a good daily reminder that change presents itself usually when you're not paying attention. I've discovered, people surprise you, and you find new space in your own soul for love, fun, truth and peace.

The adventures of Holmes & Watson have officially begun!

Author's Note

Regular people go on adventures too and regular people can make a difference in the lives of those less fortunate around the world. When you buy this book you'll be supporting my efforts to give back to sustainable and responsible tourism. A portion of proceeds from this book proudly supports the work of the Planeterra Foundation. Planeterra is a non-profit organization committed to turning travel into impact by helping local communities earn an income from tourism. Help us change lives through travel. To learn more, visit www.planeterra.org

Planeterra
Planeterra.org

Thank you

Thank you most of all to the companions who took part in the adventures in *Travel Light*, they understand the fundamental importance of seeing and understanding the world, its people, places and cultures. Theresa, Steve, Kim, Jen, Andrea, Ginger, Deb, Randee, Jim and Maureen, thank you for understanding and supporting my habit. Thank you to those who helped me in the adventurous Year of 40: Laura, Diane and my Michigan Irish Festival colleagues, Dar, Sarah, Ben and Scott. A special thank you is due to Sue for her Alaska guiding skills and Enrique for his knowledge of Madrid. And to others who joined for an adventure: Karla, Rosie, Jimmy, MaryBeth, Shelly and Julie.

I am grateful to my family for instilling a sense of adventure and awe in me at a young age. Special thanks to my parents Marshall and Becky Holmes and to my siblings Ben Holmes, and Charla-Holmes Proctor.

And though much of this book was written before I met my husband Josh, he has an important place in my story and in my heart. We'll continue to share the adventures of Holmes & Watson in the next chapters of life. Check them out in the blog.

Also, a very special thank you to my writing group and friends who provided valuable and critical feedback along the book journey: Jean Seward, Lisa Kraus, Angela Sweet-Christian, Linda Bengston, and Trish Lopucki. I am indebted to the entire team at Jenkins Group that guided me through the process of editing and publishing a book. Special thanks to Devon Ritter and Linda Bengston for their patient editing and proofreading.

People do judge a book by its cover so I am grateful to Michelle Dewey for her design and formatting skills on the cover and throughout the book.

To all of you, companions and readers, I hope your path leads to many more adventures.

Reference List

Good Morning America

Expedia

The Atlantic

The Journal of Applied Research in Quality of Life

www.projecttimeoff.com

www.statista.com

Time magazine, "Save Our Vacation" by Jack Dickey

World Travel Statistics

NOAA (National Oceanic and Atmospheric Association)

www.NorthCountryTrail.org